Human Resource Management in China

D1525841

The approach to managing human resources has changed significantly in China over the last twenty-five years as its transformation from a state-planned economy to a market-oriented economy continues. By adopting a broad notion of HRM, while remaining sympathetic to the strong emphasis on relationship management in Chinese culture, Fang Lee Cooke builds on the foundations of traditional Chinese HRM practice and brings it right up to date, including analysis of currently under-explored issues such as diversity management, talent management, new pay schemes and performance management.

Including extensive first-hand empirical data and pedagogical features such as vignettes and case studies, and written by a leading scholar of HRM in China, this book will be of great use on upper level undergraduate, postgraduate and MBA courses covering international/Chinese management and HRM as well as appealing to practitioners and scholars interested in Chinese Business, Asian Business and Human Resource Management.

Fang Lee Cooke is Professor of HRM and Chinese Studies at Monash University, Australia. Her research interests include employment relations, gender studies, strategic HRM, knowledge management and innovation, outsourcing, Chinese outward FDI and employment of Chinese migrants. She is the author of *HRM, Work and Employment in China* (2005), and *Competition, Strategy and Management in China* (2008).

Human Resource Management in China

New trends and practices

Fang Lee Cooke

McConnell Library Radford University

WITHDRAWN

Routledge
Taylor & Francis Group

LONDON AND NEW YORK

First published 2012
by Routledge
2 Park Square, Milton Park, Abingdon, Oxon OX14 4RN

Simultaneously published in the USA and Canada
by Routledge
711 Third Avenue, New York, NY10017

Routledge is an imprint of the Taylor & Francis Group, an informa business

© 2012 Fang Lee Cooke

The right of Fang Lee Cooke to be identified as author of this work has been asserted by her in accordance with the Copyright, Designs and Patents Act 1988.

All rights reserved. No part of this book may be reprinted or reproduced or utilized in any form or by any electronic, mechanical, or other means, now known or hereafter invented, including photocopying and recording, or in any information storage or retrieval system, without permission in writing from the publishers.

Trademark notice: *Product or corporate names may be trademarks or registered trademarks, and are used only for identification and explanation without intent to infringe.*

British Library Cataloguing in Publication Data
A catalogue record for this book is available from the British Library

Library of Congress Cataloging in Publication Data
Cooke, Fang Lee.
Human resource management in China : new trends and practices / Fang Lee Cooke.
   p. cm.
Includes bibliographical references and index.
1. Personnel management – China. I. Title.
HF5549.2.C6C66 2011
658.300951 – dc22   2011010551

ISBN: 978-0-415-55379-7 (hbk)
ISBN: 978-0-415-55380-3 (pbk)
ISBN: 978-0-203-80397-4 (ebk)

Typeset in Times New Roman
By Glyph International Ltd.

MIX
Paper from
responsible sources
FSC
www.fsc.org   FSC® C004839

Printed and bound in Great Britain by
TJ International Ltd, Padstow, Cornwall

To my son Jack

Contents

List of figures   viii
List of tables   ix
Acknowledgements   x
List of abbreviations   xii

1   Managing human resources in China: evolving institutional environment and key issues   1

2   Recruitment, retention and staffing strategy   20

3   Human capital, training and development   44

4   Performance management   67

5   Pay systems, pay gaps and employers' reward strategies   87

6   Equal opportunity and diversity management   112

7   Workers' representation and voice   133

8   Employment laws and regulations   156

9   Leadership and management development   180

10   Strategic human resource management – progress and prospects   199

Notes   215
References   216
Index   242

Figures

1.1   Relationships between the state and other institutional actors
      in shaping HRM practices   7
2.1   Informal employment in China   34
2.2   Forms of informal labour organizations   35
3.1   The Chinese approach to employee participation
      and innovation   54
7.1   Administrative structure of the All-China Federation
      of Trade Unions   137
8.1   Major employment-related laws and their interconnections
      and impacts   158
8.2   Interrelations between institutional actors   168
9.1   An overview of the Chinese management development system
      in the post-Mao era   187

Tables

1.1 Employment statistics by ownership in urban and rural areas in China   3

1.2 Number of employed persons at the year-end by sector   5

1.3 Number of employed persons in urban units at year-end by sector   6

4.1 Key characteristics in performance assessment/appraisal practices in China   73

4.2 Difficulties encountered in performance management – survey findings   82

5.1 Composition of a total pay package   88

5.2 Proportion (%) of female employees by selected ownership and sector and annual average wages for all employees in urban units (end of 1995 and 2008)   97

6.1 Diversity management issues in the USA/UK and China   115

6.2 Forms of inequality and types of workers affected   117

7.1 Union membership level in unionized organizations   138

7.2 Characteristics of two models of unionizing migrant workers   144

7.3 (Emerging) forms of organization, representation and protection of workers   147

8.1 Trends of labour disputes in China (1994–2009)   162

8.2 Labour disputes appealed and settled by arbitration committees in China (1995–2009)   163

8.3 Impacts of the Labour Contract Law and the Labour Disputes Mediation and Arbitration Law on institutional actors and their responses   167

9.1 Desired and actual competence gaps in global business leadership   191

10.1 New developments in HRM and the role of actors   202

10.2 Major similarities and differences in HRM practices and employment outcomes on different groups of workers   203

Acknowledgements

I would like to thank my family, colleagues and friends in China, Britain and Australia for their unfailing support and encouragement in my quest for knowledge and interest in research and writing. Particular thanks go to David Cooke for proofreading chapters 1, 9 and 10, Malcolm MacIntosh for proof-reading chapters 2, 7 and 8 and Alan Nankervis for proof reading chapters 5 and 6. All errors remain solely my responsibility.

I would also like to acknowledge the following journals and publishers for allowing me to reuse part of the materials in this book. In particular,

Part of Chapter 1 comes from Cooke, F. L. (2011e) 'The role of the state and human resource management in China', *International Journal of Human Resource Management*, London: Routledge.

Part of Chapter 2 comes from Cooke, F. L. (2011c) 'Talent management in China', in Scullion, H. and Collings, D. (eds) *Global Talent Management*, a volume in the Global Human Resource Management series edited by Randall Schuler, Susan Jackson, Paul Sparrow and Michael Poole, London: Routledge.

Part of Chapter 3 comes from Cooke, F. L. (2005b) 'Employee participation and innovations: the interpretation of "learning organisation" in China', *The Human Factor*, November 2005–January 2006, 26–30, New Delhi: IIPM.

Chapter 4 is an updated and extended version of Cooke, F. L. (2008e) 'Performance management systems in China', in Varma, A. and Budhwar, P. (eds) *Performance Management Systems around the Globe*, London: Routledge, pp. 193–209.

Part of Chapter 5 comes from Cooke, F. L. (2011d) 'Labour market disparities and inequalities', in Sheldon, P., Kim, S., Li, Y. and Warner, M. (eds) *China's Changing Workplace*, London: Routledge.

Part of Chapter 7 comes from Cooke, F. L. (2007) 'Migrant labour and trade union's response and strategy in China', *Indian Journal of Industrial Relations*, 42, 4: 558–84, New Delhi.

Chapter 8 is an extended and revised version of Cooke, F. L. (2012) 'The enactment of three new labour laws in China: unintended consequences and the emergence of "new" actors in employment relations', in Lee, S. and McCann, D. (eds) *Regulating for Decent Work: New Directions in Labour Market Regulation*, Basingstoke: Palgrave Macmillan. Reproduced with permission of Palgrave Macmillan.

Abbreviations

ACFTU	All-China Federation of Trade Unions
ACWF	All-China Women's Federation
BHMC	Beijing Hyundai Motor Company
CCP	Chinese Communist Party
CEC	China Enterprise Confederation
CEIBS	China Europe International Business School
CEO	chief executive officer
CIPD	Chartered Institute of Personnel and Development (UK)
COE	collectively owned enterprise
CSR	corporate social responsibility
DM	diversity management
EMBA	Executive Master of Business Administration
EO	equal opportunity
ESO	employee share ownership schemes
FDI	foreign direct investment
FIE	foreign-invested enterprise
HCN	host-country nationals
HR	human resources
HRD	human resource development
HRM	human resource management
HPWS	high-performance work system
ILO	International Labour Organization
IR	industrial relations
JV	joint ventures
MBA	Master of Business Administration
MNC	multinational corporation
NGO	non-governmental organization
PA	performance appraisal
R&D	research and development
SOE	state-owned enterprise
SME	small and medium-sized enterprise
TVE	township and village enterprise
WLC	work–life conflict
WTO	World Trade Organization

1 Managing human resources in China

Evolving institutional environment and key issues

Overview

The human resource management (HRM) and employment relations environment in China has witnessed profound changes since the mid-1990s. These changes are associated with the downsizing and privatization of state-owned enterprises (SOEs), the introduction of performance management systems in the public sector and government organizations, the growing strength of the private sector in the economy, the continuing growth of foreign direct investment (FDI) in China, the participation of rural migrant workers in urban economic activities and the continuing pressure of unemployment, with a growing proportion of highly educated unemployed. These developments have led to a process of informalization of employment on the one hand, and the introduction of a series of labour regulations to control the labour market and employment relations on the other. Here, the Chinese government faces the dual pressure of having to attract foreign investment and the need to ensure that foreign multinational corporations (MNCs) conform to China's labour regulations.

Meanwhile, caught between formidable resistance from private sector employers to union recognition and the growing need to defend workers' rights and interests against a context of declining labour market security, the adequacy of the Chinese trade unions in representing workers has been widely questioned. For state sector workers, although 'the profound structural transformation from state socialism' towards a marketized economy has eroded much of their established workplace welfare benefits and job security, the majority have accepted this life-time change without radical forms of protests (Blecher 2010: 94). For rural migrant workers, marketization has brought them new opportunities for improved living standards and social uplifting, albeit not without the heavy price of family separation and health and safety risks.

The dynamic context of HRM and employment relations in China raises a number of questions. What is the role of the state in shaping HRM policies and human capital development? What are the likely impacts of new labour laws on employers and what are their responding strategy and tactics? What innovative practices have emerged as part of the trade unions' strategy to organize and represent workers outside the state sector? Are these practices a more permanent feature in employment relations of a socialist market economy or are they merely transitional models in response to the growing discontent of the Chinese workers in the global production chain? What HRM practices/labour strategies are firms adopting to gain competitive advantages or at least to overcome some of the constraints they face? Have these strategies and practices led to the deterioration of job quality for some and new opportunities for others? How may labour market opportunities and employment outcomes be varied amongst workers of different age, gender and residential status? And what is the likelihood of alternative forms of organizing or workers' self-organizing in light of the absence of effective union representation? This book aims to address these issues through the examination of changes in the environment and the interactive dynamics of institutional actors.

From state socialism towards a market-driven HRM model

Founded in 1949, socialist China has over 60 years of history. For the first three decades until the end of the Cultural Revolution in 1976, the personnel management system in China was highly centralized under the state planned economy regime. Personnel management during this period exhibited two major features in terms of its governance structure and the substance of the personnel policy. First, personnel policies and practices at the organizational level were under the strict control of the state through regional and local personnel and labour departments. Centralization, formalization, standardization and monitoring of personnel policies and practices were the primary functions of the then Ministry of Labour (for ordinary workers) and the Ministry of Personnel (for professional and managerial staff). It was these ministries' responsibility to determine the number of people to be employed, sources of recruitment and the pay scales for different categories of workers. State intervention was also extended to the structure and responsibility of the personnel functions, including performance management, at the organizational level. Managers of all levels were only involved in the administrative function and policy implementation under rigid policy guidelines (Child 1994; Cooke 2005a). Second, job-for-life was the norm for the majority of employees in urban areas (Warner 1996), irrespective of the work attitude and performance outcomes of the individuals. Wages were typically low with only a small gap between each grade as a result of the egalitarian approach to redistribution. Monetary incentives and personal advancement were regarded as incompatible with socialist ideology.

These characteristics were dominant in the personnel management system of the country because, until the 1980s, over three-quarters of urban employees worked in state-owned units (see Table 1.1). The situation of state dominance started to change in the late 1970s, following the country's adoption of an 'open door' policy to attract foreign investment and domestic private funds in order to revitalize the nation's economy. In parallel to this economic policy, the state sector has witnessed radical changes in its personnel policy and practice, as part

Table 1.1 Employment statistics by ownership in urban and rural areas in China* (Figures in million persons)

Ownership	1978	1980	1985	1990	1995	1998	2000	2002	2005	2009
Total	**401.52**	**423.61**	**498.73**	**647.49**	**680.65**	**706.37**	**720.85**	**737.40**	**758.25**	**779.95**
Number of urban employed persons	95.14	105.25	128.08	166.16	190.93	206.78	231.51	247.80	273.31	311.20
State-owned units	74.51	80.19	89.90	103.46	112.61	90.58	81.02	71.63	64.88	64.20
Collectively owned units	20.48	24.25	33.24	35.49	31.47	19.63	14.99	11.22	8.10	6.18
Cooperative units	—	—	—	—	—	1.36	1.55	1.61	1.88	1.60
Joint ownership units	—	—	0.38	0.96	0.53	0.48	0.42	0.45	0.45	0.37
Limited liability corporations	—	—	—	—	—	4.84	6.87	10.83	17.50	24.33
Share-holding corporations ltd.	—	—	—	—	3.17	4.10	4.57	5.38	6.99	9.56
Private enterprises	—	—	—	0.57	4.85	9.73	12.68	19.99	34.58	55.44
Units with funds from Hong Kong, Macao & Taiwan	—	—	—	0.04	2.72	2.94	3.10	3.67	5.57	7.21
Foreign-funded units	—	—	0.06	0.62	2.41	2.93	3.32	3.91	6.88	9.78
Self-employed individuals	0.15	0.81	4.50	6.14	15.60	22.59	21.36	22.69	27.78	42.45
Number of rural employed persons	306.38	318.36	370.65	472.93	488.54	492.79	489.34	489.60	484.94	468.75
Township & village enterprises	28.27	30.00	69.79	92.65	128.62	125.37	128.20	132.88	142.72	155.88
Private enterprises	—	—	—	1.13	4.71	7.37	11.39	14.11	23.66	30.63
Self-employed individuals	—	—	—	14.91	30.54	38.55	29.34	24.74	21.23	23.41

Source: adapted from *China Statistical Yearbook 2003*: 126–7; *China Statistical Yearbook 2010*: 117.

Note
* Since 1990, data on economically active population, the total employed persons and the sub-total of employed persons in urban and rural areas have been adjusted in accordance with the data obtained from the 5th National Population Census. As a result, the sum of the data by region, by ownership or by sector is not equal to the total (original note from *China Statistical Yearbook 2003*: 123).

of the Economic and Enterprise Reforms begun in the early 1980s (Child 1994). One of the major changes has been the retreat of direct state control and the consequent increase of autonomy and responsibility at the enterprise level in major aspects of their personnel management practices, including the widespread adoption of performance-related bonus schemes to supplement low wages. These changes were followed by several rounds of radical downsizing in the SOEs and, to a lesser extent, in the public sector and government organizations throughout the 1990s. This has led to a significant reduction of the state sector and the rapid growth of businesses in a variety of business ownership forms (see Table 1.1).

In particular, the number of private enterprises as a business ownership category has soared since the mid-1990s. In 1995, the number of people employed in private enterprises in urban areas was 4.85 million compared with 112.61 million in the state-owned sector. By the end of 2009, private enterprises were employing 55.44 million people whereas the employment figure in the state-owned sector was 64.20 million (see Table 1.1). Unconstrained by the historical heritage and government control encountered by their state-owned counterparts, or by corporate influence and limited local understanding experienced by their foreign-invested counterparts, private firms in China are regarded as being more flexible, innovative and risk taking (e.g. Wang et al. 2007).

At the same time, China's economic structure has undergone significant changes. While some industrial sectors have experienced slow growth or even contraction, other sectors have seen rapid expansion at different periods since the 1980s (see Tables 1.2 and 1.3). In general, the country's economic structure has been shifting from the agricultural and heavy industrial sectors towards the light manufacturing and service sectors. In particular, employment in the mining and quarrying industry has seen major decline, whereas health, education, finance and insurance, real estate, and telecom and IT industries have experienced significant growth. The growing diversity of ownership forms and business nature has different implications for HRM practices in different firms in China. The business strategy pursued by firms and their product and labour market positions further influence the nature of employment relations between the employer and the workers.

The role of institutional actors

According to Bosch et al. (2009: 1), institutions 'are the building blocks of social order; they shape, govern and legitimize behaviour. Not only do they embody social values but they also reflect historical compromises between social groups negotiated by key actors'. This book adopts an institutional approach to analysing HRM practices in China within the broader context of the changing labour market and regulatory environment in order to understand how institutional actors overlap and interact with each other and shape the HRM practices with different employment outcomes for individual workers. Here, we adopt Bellemare's (2000: 386) definition of an actor in an industrial relations (IR) environment as

Table 1.2 Number of employed persons at year-end by sector* (Figures in 1,000 persons)

Industry	1985	1990	1995	1998	2000	2002**
Farming, forestry, animal husbandry & fishery	311,300	341,170	330,180	332,320	333,550	324,870
Mining & quarrying	7,950	8,820	9,320	7,210	5,970	5,580
Manufacturing	74,120	86,240	98,030	83,190	80,430	83,070
Electricity, gas & water production & supply	1,420	1,920	2,580	2,830	2,840	2,900
Construction	20,350	24,240	33,220	33,270	35,520	38,930
Geological prospecting & water conservancy	1,970	1,970	1,350	1,160	1,100	980
Transport, storage, post & telecommunication services	12,790	15,660	19,420	20,000	20,290	20,840
Wholesale, retail trade & catering services	23,060	28,390	42,920	46,450	46,860	49,690
Finance & insurance	1,380	2,180	2,760	3,140	3,270	3,400
Real estate	360	440	800	940	1,000	1,180
Social services	4,010	5,940	7,030	8,680	9,210	10,940
Health care, sports & social welfare	4,670	5,360	4,440	4,780	4,880	4,930
Education, culture & art, radio, film & television	12,730	14,570	14,760	15,730	15,650	15,650
Scientific research & polytechnic service	1,440	1,730	1,820	1,780	1,740	1,630
Governmental organizations, party agencies and social organizations	7,990	10,790	10,420	10,970	11,040	10,750
Others	13,190	17,980	44,840	51,180	56,430	62,450
Total	**498,730**	**647,490**	**680,650**	**706,370**	**760,850**	**737,400**

Source: adapted from *China Statistical Yearbook 2005*: 125.

Notes

*Employed persons refer to the persons aged 16 and over who are engaged in social working and receive remuneration payment or earn business income. This indicator reflects the actual utilization of total labour force during a certain period of time and is often used for the research on China's economic situation and national power (original note from *China Statistical Yearbook 2005*: 181).

**In 2004, the *China Statistical Yearbook* changed its presentation of the number of employed persons at the year-end by sector to include workers in urban units only. The classification of industrial sectors was also adjusted. Statistics of selected years are presented in Table 1.3.

Table 1.3 Number of employed persons in urban units at year-end by sector (Figures in 1,000 persons)

Industry	2003	2006	2009
Farming, forestry, animal husbandry & fishery	4,845	4,352	3,737
Mining & quarrying	4,883	5,297	5,537
Manufacturing	29,805	33,516	34,919
Electricity, gas & water production & supply	2,976	3,025	3,077
Construction	8,337	9,887	11,775
Transport, storage & postal services	6,365	6,127	6,344
Telecommunication and IT	1,168	1,382	1,738
Wholesale & retail trade	6,281	5,157	5,208
Hotel & catering services	1,721	1,839	2,021
Finance & insurance	3,533	3,674	4,490
Real estate	1,202	1,539	1,909
Leasing & business services	1,835	2,367	2,905
Scientific research, technical services & geological prospecting	2,219	2,355	2,726
Management of water, conservancy, environment & public facilities	1,725	1,870	2,057
Services to households & other services	528	566	588
Education	14,428	15,044	15,504
Health care, social securities & social welfare	4,858	5,254	5,958
Culture, sports & entertainment	1,278	1,224	1,295
Governmental organizations, party agencies and social organizations	11,710	12,656	13,943
Total	**109,697**	**117,132**	**125,730**

Source: adapted from *China Statistical Yearbook 2010*: 123–5.

'an individual, a group or an institution that has the capability, through its action, to directly influence the industrial relations process, including the capability to influence the causal powers deployed by other actors in the IR environment'. We also support Michelson's (2008: 27) argument that these actors do not necessarily have to be influential at all three levels, i.e. the workplace, organization and institutional level, at all times.

We focus on the role of the state (both central and local), trade unions, employers and their associations, employment agencies, non-profit organizations, and vocational and higher education institutions (e.g. business schools) as actors in employment relations and labour market development (see Figure 1.1). We include these actors, some of them extended agencies of the state, for two related reasons. One is that 'the body of literature concerning new actors and processes in employment relations remains small' (Michelson 2008: 21). As Heery and Frege (2006) pointed out, there is an increasing range of actors whose role in shaping industrial relations has largely escaped the attention of IR researchers. These include the state institutions as well as private agencies such as management consultants and employment agencies. According to Heery and Frege (2006: 602), these institutions 'promote isomorphism in

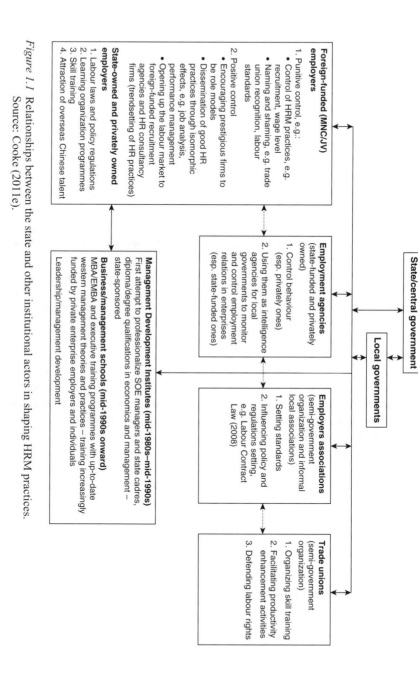

Foreign-funded (MNC/JV) employers

1. Punitive control, e.g.:
   - Control of HRM practices, e.g. recruitment, wage level
   - Naming and shaming, e.g. trade union recognition, labour standards
2. Positive control
   - Encouraging prestigious firms to be role models
   - Dissemination of good HR practices through isomorphic effects, e.g. job analysis, performance management
   - Opening up the labour market to foreign-funded recruitment agencies and HR consultancy firms (trendsetting of HR practices)

State-owned and privately owned employers

1. Labour laws and policy regulations
2. Learning organization programmes
3. Skill training
4. Attraction of overseas Chinese talent

Employment agencies (state-funded and privately owned)

1. Control behaviour (esp. privately ones)
2. Using them as intelligence agencies for local governments to monitor and control employment relations in enterprises (esp. state-funded ones)

State/central government

Local governments

Employers associations (semi-government organization and informal local associations)

1. Setting standards
2. Influencing policy and regulations setting, e.g. Labour Contract Law (2008)

Management Development Institutes (mid-1980s–mid-1990s)
First attempt to professionalize SOE managers and state cadres, diploma/degree qualifications in economics and management – state-sponsored

Business/management schools (mid-1990s onward)
MBA/EMBA and executive training programmes with up-to-date western management theories and practices – training increasingly funded by private enterprise employers and individuals
Leadership/management development

Trade unions (semi-government organization)

1. Organizing skill training
2. Facilitating productivity enhancement activities
3. Defending labour rights

Figure 1.1 Relationships between the state and other institutional actors in shaping HRM practices.
Source: Cooke (2011e).

employer practice, even in societies with flexible, lightly regulated labour markets, and weak employers' associations'. The arguments of Michelson (2008) and Heery and Frege (2006) are highly applicable in the Chinese context.

The other reason is that the role of the state and its agencies in shaping the HRM and human resource development (HRD) agenda in China has received little research attention so far. The shift from direct state control to state directive guidance, the deepening of the marketization process and the resultant growing autonomy of state-owned enterprises and the rising economic power of the private sector mean that the state has to increasingly rely on other actors to enforce its strategy. Interactive dynamics amongst actors have been noted in other societal contexts (e.g. Martinez Lucio and MacKenzie 2004; Osterman 2006; Michelson 2008), but have been much less understood or even expected in the Chinese context where obedience to authoritarian instructions has been a more familiar story. The absence of this kind of investigation in state-led HRM/HRD initiatives and organizational responses to these interventions creates a significant gap in our understanding of how the state propagates ideas of HRM and develops training and learning programmes on new forms of management via various actors. As we can see from Figure 1.1 and Table 10.1, the Chinese state has been mobilizing other institutional actors in more subtle and strategic ways to promote, with a level of success, certain HRM practices and management behaviour.

The role of the state

Economic globalization and changing ideologies on the role of the state have led to different responses from governments regarding their regulatory role in employment relations in the last two decades (e.g. Martinez Lucio and Stuart 2004; Bamber et al. 2010). In western economies, this has often taken the form of de-regulation or 're-regulation', as MacKenzie and Martinez Lucio (2005: 500) argued. There is also an inclination to move away from a hard, i.e. regulatory, approach towards a softer, i.e. voluntary, approach to managing employment relations through the adoption of innovative schemes such as social partnership (e.g. Martinez Lucio and Stuart 2004).

In China, the change of government leadership to Premier Wen Jiabao and Chairman Hu Jintao in 2003 marked the beginning of the pursuit of an economic development policy that emphasizes social justice, social harmony and environmental protection. This is a significant departure from an efficiency-driven economic development policy pursued by their predecessors typically influenced by the economic thinking of Deng Xiaoping – the architect of modern Chinese economic development. As part of the reform, visible changes can be seen in the role of the Chinese state in the employment sphere, for example, from a dominant employer to a regulator (Cooke 2010c). Its intervention approach is also becoming more sophisticated, from the heavy dependence on administrative regulations towards a regulator with combined mechanisms of legislation, standard setting, best practice sharing and the promotion of 'progressive' HRM practices and corporate social responsibility (CSR).

State intervention in shaping HRM policies and practices is universal to all countries, albeit the level and forms of intervention may differ across states and over time. Such intervention often takes two forms: direct intervention through HRM laws and regulations, and soft or normative intervention through government-led initiatives and campaigns aimed to promote certain desirable HRM practices and management behaviour (e.g. Kuruvilla 1996; Godard 2002; Martinez Lucio and Stuart 2004; Mellahi 2007). The effectiveness of both forms of intervention varies but should never be overestimated. This is particularly the case in the latter due to 'the lack of enforcement powers' of the state (Mellahi 2007: 87).

In emerging economies, state intervention remains a vital and an increasingly common feature in shaping HRM and HRD (e.g. Budhwar and Debrah 2001; Wang and Wang 2006; Mellahi 2007; Rees et al. 2007). In China, the vast skill gaps and deficiency in management competence necessitates strong government intervention to meet the demand of economic growth. The fact that China is a one-party state and has a relatively stable, albeit for some autocratic, government means that the state and its extended agencies may have more scope than democratic regimes to intervene at various levels. This is in spite of the fact that the level of state intervention and participation in HRM is not homogenous across other actors. Nor is the state's influence a 'continuous' presence (Bellemare 2000) in the operation of these actors. The ways through which and the types of HR issues on which the state seeks to influence the employers, particularly between foreign-funded/joint venture firms and Chinese-owned enterprises also differ (see Figure 1.1).

There are two main objectives in the state intervention in employment relations and HRM practices in China. One is to facilitate enterprises to establish harmonious employment relations as part of its agenda to build a harmonious society (see Li and Xiang 2007; Warner and Zhu 2010). The other is to combat the severe skill shortage problem and raise the skills level of the workforce in order to enhance the competitiveness of the nation through innovation and high value-added production. This includes raising the level of management competence, professional standards and craft skills. In order to fulfil these objectives, a number of labour regulations and state-led HRM and HRD initiatives have been launched. These regulations and initiatives are implemented via other institutional actors in coercive, directive, cooperative and voluntary manners (see Figure 1.1 and Table 10.1).

For example, an interesting development of state initiative in HRM is the superannuation scheme (see Table 10.1). The government issued the 'Trial Regulation on Enterprise Superannuation' in 2004 and the 'Provisional Regulation on Enterprise Superannuation Fund Management Agency Qualification Accreditation' in 2005. These regulations require firms to set up superannuation schemes (pension funds) to combat the worsening social security provision problem in China. This, the state argues, is part of the CSR that business organizations need to embrace. Individual firms are given the autonomy to design their own plan based on the characteristics of the workforce, and the needs and financial situation of the business. It was reported that leading firms are adopting this scheme to help attract talent (Yang and Wu 2006; Zheng 2007).

Trade unions

Trade unions are an important institutional actor in employment relations. Only one trade union is recognized by the Chinese government – All-China Federation of Trade Unions (ACFTU). The ACFTU is one of the eight 'mass organizations' (non-government organizations) in China that operate under the leadership of the Chinese Communist Party (CCP). Existing studies on the Chinese trade unions have mostly been critical of their institutionally incapacitated position and operational inefficacy (e.g. O'Leary 1998; Taylor et al. 2003; Clarke 2005; Hishida et al. 2010). In principle, funding for the ACFTU comes from a number of sources, including:

1. Membership dues of 0.5 per cent of union members' monthly salaries.
2. Trade union funds of 2 per cent of payroll from enterprises, institutions and government departments.
3. Contributions from enterprises and undertakings run by the trade unions.
4. Other sources, such as donations.

At the ACFTU municipal branch level, sources of funding typically come from: 1) fiscal funding from the municipal government for union officials' wage costs; 2) ad hoc funding from various sources for activities and fairs; 3) 2 per cent of the total wage bill of civil servants in governmental organizations; 4) levy of 40 per cent of the trade union membership fees from enterprises; and 5) charity donations from enterprises and individuals as a form of publicity for the trade union in society. The level of resource tends to drop significantly below the municipal level. In addition, union officials encounter difficulties in collecting the levy from their subordinate branches and enterprises in part because they are in financial constraints. Officials need to chase them for it repeatedly because they too will need to hand in their levy to the higher authority (Cooke 2008c). Union activities are mainly held at the provincial and municipal branch levels, often in the form of disseminating CCP messages and implementing state-led initiatives. As we shall see in chapters 7 and 8, CCP-dependence and resource constraints limit the ability of grassroots unions to carry out their functions properly and develop capacity. Nevertheless, union activities, where carried out effectively, are beneficial to the workers, who do not object to the existence of the ACFTU per se but are frustrated by its incompetence. Union functions include, for example, facilitating production activities and skill training (see Chapter 3), representing workers' rights and participating in the drafting of labour legislation (see chapters 7 and 8).

The institutional position of the trade unions and its functioning raises two important questions. First, is the structure of the ACFTU detrimental to its survival, embeddedness in the political system, its function, and the prospect of improving workers' quality of employment? This is an important question in view of the declining strength of independent trade unions in many developed countries in part as a result of the globalization of production and sourcing. A second related question is: what is the nature of China's labour movement in its contemporary economy, and is the ACFTU's function detrimental to China's labour movement? It is true that the way the ACFTU is set up and operated has led to the questioning by international trade union organizations, labour movement activists and scholars of the legitimacy of the ACFTU as a trade union (e.g. Taylor and Li 2007). But given the fact that a considerable number of independent unions around the world have been finding it difficult to survive or exert influence at the policy level without political alliances, the ACFTU's dependence on the CCP-government is arguably crucial for its survival and embeddedness in the political system. Without this political patronage as licence to operate, the prospect of having any organizing body to represent the workers effectively will become even more opaque. As Clarke (2005: 16) observed, 'if the trade unions are not able first of all to secure their institutional survival, they cannot be in a position to develop their representative capacity, as is clearly shown by those [in] Eastern and Central European countries'.

Employers' associations

Unlike developed economies where employers' associations are developed, provide a range of services to their member employers and form pressure groups to influence government policy and legislation, employer associations in China are generally much less well-established and independent. Similar to the ACFTU, the China Enterprise Confederation (CEC) is the only official employers' association that the state recognizes at the national level as the sole representative of employers' interests. The state forms some kind of unequal partnerships with these organizations, which often act on behalf of the state and help implement government policies (see Unger and Chan 1995; Unger 2008). Facilitating the development of a harmonious relationship between the stakeholders and providing training and HRD are amongst the listed responsibilities of the CEC. The subordination to state control means that the CEC has limited autonomy beyond state-sanctioned activities. Nevertheless, it is important to note that the lobbying power of Chinese employers is rising outside the CEC. They are able to form pressure groups rapidly to exert pressure on the government at the national level if forthcoming regulations and policies are perceived to have a significant negative impact on their business environment, such as was the case in the promulgation of the Labour Contract Law in 2007 (see Chapter 8). At the grassroots level, even small employers are developing the awareness of the need and ability to organize to represent their interests (see Chapter 2 on the local shipbuilding industry for example).

Employment agencies

Despite being in existence for over two decades (see F. Xu 2009 for an overview), employment agencies represent a relatively new institutional actor in employment relations in China. The majority of employment agencies and job centres have been set up by, or under the auspices of, the local governments since the mid-/late 1990s to provide services at the lower end of the labour market. In 2001, there were a total of 26,793 employment agencies, 70 per cent of them funded by the local governments at various levels as part of the multi-level employment services network. By 2009, the number of employment agencies had grown to 37,123. The number of employees working in the employment agencies had increased from 84,440 in 2001 to 126,000 in 2009 (*China Labour Statistical Yearbook 2002* and *2010*). This significant growth was a response to the large-scale downsizing in the state sector, the continuous inflow of rural migrant workers to urban areas to seek employment and the growing number of unemployed school leavers and college graduates (Li et al. 2006; Cooke 2011d).

There are a number of characteristics of employment agencies in China. First, they emerged and grew with the advantage of government support, as the vast majority of them were, and many still are, state-owned/controlled. They are supposed to play a transitional role that facilitates the government in changing its function through the marketization of employment services (Li et al. 2006). In reality, the relationships between the employment agencies, local governments and employers are intricate (see Figure 1.1). Second, the majority of employment agency firms provide services for the lower end of the labour market (even though some of them label themselves as 'talent agencies'). They mainly cater for disadvantaged groups of workers such as laid-off workers, rural migrant workers and unemployed college graduates (Li et al. 2006). Third, agency workers normally register with the employment agency for work. They only enter an employment relationship with the agency firm when they are sent to work in client firms (Li et al. 2006). Fourth, the employment agency industry is highly unregulated (Li et al. 2006). They are governed mainly by administrative regulations issued at the local level and implemented with considerable discretion.

In spite of a number of limitations, employment agencies play an increasingly important role in the labour market and the use of agency employment forms a strategic part of employers' staffing strategy to gain competitive advantage (see chapters 2 and 8).

HR consultancy firms and outsourcing providers

Not all employment agencies are controlled by the state or private firms; nor are they confined to the lower end of the labour market. The opening up of the labour market to foreign-owned HR businesses has led to the growth of foreign-owned recruitment/headhunting agencies and HR consultancy firms in China.

In 2002, the Chinese government issued the 'Regulation on Talent Market Management' which allows foreign-owned employment agency firms to enter the Chinese market and provide services, initially through the joint venture of Sino-foreign employment agencies (Zhou 2002). The entrance of well-established foreign-owned HR operators facilitated the creation of an HR outsourcing/consulting market. Together with MNCs in other industries, they play an important role in trendsetting and raising the HR standard and competence level of the country in a short period of time, given the low starting point of the profession. Western-originated HRM practices, such as assessment centres for recruitment and promotion, 360-degree appraisal and performance management systems, coaching and mentoring, work–life balance initiatives and HR outsourcing, are now becoming popular amongst Chinese firms. However, transferability remains the key challenge, as shown in the chapters that follow. The enactment of the Labour Contract Law and the Labour Disputes Mediation and Arbitration Law in 2008 also created opportunities for HR consultancy firms to provide administrative and legal services for firms which are keen to avoid operational hassles and which lack the legal knowledge required (see Chapter 8). In short, HR consultancy firms and outsourcing providers can be seen as an emerging actor, despite being in an embryonic form, and as private agencies with limited influence. As the HR consultancy and outsourcing industry becomes more developed, these firms are likely to help create some form of isomorphism in the development and implementation of HRM techniques in China.

In short, this book adopts an institutional approach to explore the relationship between the state and other actors in the discussion of the promulgation of employment regulations and some of the HRM practices that the state intends to propagate through other actors. Whilst the institutional context and functions of these actors are illustrated in more detail in the chapters that follow, their dynamic interactions and respective influences in shaping the regulatory environment and labour market outcomes are perhaps best exemplified in Chapter 8 and Figure 8.2. As far as possible, we also present the workers' views regarding their role in shaping employment relations and HRM practices and their perceptions of these issues. These perceptions are influenced by the changes in the workers' demographic profile and the associated preferences and values.

Structure of the book

This book consists of ten chapters. Together, they outline the broad trends in HRM and employment relations in China and the role of institutional actors associated with the major changes at both national and local level. This macro picture is substantiated through the evaluation of organizational practices informed by empirical studies conducted by the author and others. Each chapter deals with one or more related themes in the HRM/employment relations field. These thematic foci reflect not only traditional concerns in the Chinese context, but also some of the latest developments that have caught the attention of international scholars and global operations, such as CSR, work–life balance and diversity management. We examine various HRM practices, such as recruitment, staffing, training and development, pay and performance management, against a broader context to assess the extent to which firms are able to develop and deploy their human capital and transform it into their organizational capabilities and competitive advantage through various control and motivational mechanisms.

When illustrating organizational practices, the chapters draw examples from different groups of employees/workers, where appropriate, in order to contrast their labour market positions and employment outcomes. Given the extensive number of studies already available on HRM and employment relations in China, this book makes an attempt to focus on important topics that have been relatively less well covered in existing literature and to tackle the topic from a perspective that has been less applied. For example, in Chapter 5 on pay practices, gender pay gaps and private sector pay practices are the two key issues for discussion since they have been less well covered in the study of HRM in China. This is especially the case for gender pay gaps, which have been studied mainly from the labour economics perspective. The appreciation of the political, economic and social factors in pay determination is important in informing our understanding of the likely causes of gender pay gaps and the extent to which gender discrimination may have contributed to pay inequity.

An important objective of the book is to provide an up-to-date and comprehensive account of changes and new developments in various aspects of HRM and employment relations in China. To achieve this aim, the book draws together studies that focus on HRM at the organizational level, HRD at the macro level and studies on industrial relations, labour politics and employment regulations at various levels to understand how human resources (broadly defined) are developed and deployed and what opportunities and constraints employers may face in making their choices. As such, the book takes a broader approach than is often the case in mainstream HRM textbooks.

This introductory chapter (Chapter 1) presents an overview of the major changes in the labour market, employment regulations and HRM practices and how these changes may impact on employment relations and employment outcomes for workers in China. More importantly, it outlines the role of institutional actors in influencing these changes, and how their roles are shaped by the competitive and institutional environments and through the interactions between the actors and the environments. This chapter provides an analytical framework which guides the discussions and analyses of key issues in HRM and employment relations in the remaining chapters of the book.

Chapter 2 examines firms' recruitment and staffing strategy at both ends of the labour market and the role of the state in the creation of these labour market conditions. At the upper end of the labour market, it analyses the tensions in, and challenges to, talent recruitment and retention in China in a period of economic and social transformation. As we can see in this chapter, the main challenge is the shortage of managerial and professional talent. Given the deficiency in the educational institutions and the reluctance of firms to invest in training and development, poaching is a widely adopted method for firms to acquire talent. In addition, performance-related reward is commonly used as a motivational mechanism to stimulate high performance. In other words, firms are focusing on employees' current performance rather than their future productivity. With the exception of a few prestigious MNCs, HRM practices in the majority of firms in China are neither systematic nor human-goals-oriented as prescribed in western strategic HRM literature.

At the lower end of the labour market, the growth of the informal employment sector since the 1980s was a result of government policies. Creating opportunities for informal employment was a necessary step to address the Chinese government's employment priority during its labour market transition period. Informal employment also supports the efficiency argument in that both individuals and employers benefit from this employment. For the former, it is a vital source of income to support their livelihood. For the latter, it helps the survival and increases the competitiveness of many businesses. Within a decade, informal employment has become a major form of employment in China. However, workers in informal employment are by no means a homogenous group. Even at the lower end of the labour market, laid-off ex-SOE workers and (rural) migrant workers fare very differently in terms of the policy support they receive, the types of jobs they crowd in and the treatment they receive from their employers and other stakeholders.

Chapter 3 focuses on issues related to skill training and learning. We explore the role of the stakeholders in addressing the skill shortage problem. For example, what has been the role of the state in human capital development? What kind of training policy and learning initiatives have the state been propagating in light of the increasing role of the governments of other countries in raising their human capital to gain national competitive advantage? What has been the strategy of employers in the provision of training and development for their employees against a tight labour market in which poaching and reduced employee loyalty have become common experience?

Performance appraisal practices have long existed in China, albeit with strong Chinese characteristics. In Chapter 4, we review the development of performance management systems in China, including characteristics in each stage of the performance management process and unique features in firms of different ownership forms. We also examine some of the new developments in this HR function and assess the extent to which firms in China are beginning to adopt western performance management practices as part of the import of western techniques that are promoted as more effective HRM mechanisms than existing Chinese practices. The chapter highlights a number of challenges in performance management. Some of them may be universal in different societal contexts, others prove to be specific to China. In particular, performance management in Chinese firms tend to be closely related to financial reward rather than development oriented. Performance management is arguably one of the HRM areas in which the influence of Chinese cultural values is not only most profound but also enduring.

Pay is one of the most important aspects of HRM and employment relations. Pay equity is essential to any pay system not only as the most basic foundation for social justice, but also as the minimum incentive to secure cooperation and commitment from the workforce. However, pay determination criteria are largely marked by the characteristics of economies, industrial sectors and ownership forms. Chapter 5 first examines the unique features in the pay system in China. It then focuses on one aspect of the pay system which has attracted little attention in the study of HRM in China – gender pay gaps. Gender pay gaps are caused by a range of societal, organizational and personal factors, including gender norms and employers' discrimination. This chapter shows that whilst gender pay gaps in China are arguably relatively small compared with those found in other economies, there is evidence that conventional gender norms and employers' discrimination contribute to this gap at the macro level. At the firm level, the chapter reveals some of the emerging trends of pay practices in the private sector. In particular, performance-related pay and stock options are found to be popular reward schemes used by many firms studied to incentivize performance and retain talent. Finally, the chapter outlines the scope and level of social security provisions nationally and local configurations. As Dickens and Hall (2003) argued, the level of provision of social securities by the state has a profound impact on the decisions and behaviour of both employers and employees in employment relations. This is particularly the case in developing economies such as China where the provision of social security is often limited both in the level of funding and in those who are able to benefit from it. The tensions in employment relations created by compulsory social security provision are played out in full force in the enactment of the Labour Contract Law, a topic which will be more fully discussed in Chapter 8.

Chapter 6 investigates issues related to workforce diversity in China, where both the legal position for diversity management and the demographic characteristics of the workforce differ significantly from those found in western societies. The chapter takes the western-originated concept of diversity management in the strategic HRM context as a starting point and uses it as a guide to investigate how the concept is understood and operationalized in China. Issues explored include formal diversity management policies adopted by companies and informal practices deployed by managers. The chapter critically assesses the extent to which the western notion of and approach to managing diversity is appropriate in the Chinese context. It explores how local line managers and HR managers make sense of equal opportunity and diversity issues and manage them in a pragmatic way. It argues that the starting point and process of managing diversity in the Chinese context are different from the US/UK approach as a result of institutional and cultural differences. The chapter highlights a number of sources of inequality in employment practices and labour market outcomes for groups of workers who are disadvantaged because of their age, gender and residential status. It also examines the nature of work–life conflicts, forms of organizational interventions and coping strategies from individuals. The chapter has implications for western MNCs that intend to adopt a global HR strategy and promote their diversity management initiatives to their operations in different parts of the world in order to enhance organizational performance.

Workers' collective representation plays a crucial role in the negotiation and fulfilment of employment terms and conditions. However, such a role is often difficult to secure in developing economies due to the absence of effective representing bodies or the inability to enforce the legal rights of representation. Chapter 7 deals with issues related to workers' representation and voice, beginning with an overview of the labour rights of Chinese workers. It then reviews the functioning of the ACFTU organizations within the structural and resource constraints they face as well as the wider economic, political and cultural environment within which they operate. It critically analyses a number of key aspects related to unionism in China against the context of radical state sector reform and the emergence of the market economy. These include: the governance structure, power base, resources and roles of the ACFTU, and the changing profile of union constituency and their perception of the efficacy of the ACFTU (also see earlier section on the trade union in this chapter on the funding of ACFTU). In particular, we examine the regulatory role of the ACFTU, including its input in the design and enforcement of labour regulations as well as its legal position as the legitimate representational body of workers. We also investigate new initiatives and strategy from the ACFTU in organizing the millions of rural migrant workers toiling in the export-oriented manufacturing zones, on construction sites and in informal employment. Tensions inherent in the ACFTU's multiple functions are highlighted, particularly its subordination to the Chinese Communist Party on the one hand, and its official role in defending workers' rights on the other. In view of the growing number of labour dispute incidents in the last two decades and in 2010 in particular, the chapter contemplates the prospect of Chinese workers' democracy in the country's transition from state socialism towards a marketized economy with socialist characteristics. It points to a need to understand the dynamics of political ideology and strategy in informing decision making in order for us to make sense of the potential for not only new forms of labour representation, but also freedom of expression.

Chapter 8 continues with the discussion of workers' labour rights and enforcement through a critical review of the making and working of the three employment and labour laws promulgated in 2007 – the Employment Promotion Law, the Labour Contract Law and the Labour Disputes Mediation and Arbitration Laws. As we can see from previous chapters, institutional actors may be confronted with diverse priorities and pressures and respond in pragmatic ways to maximize their interests and/or to minimize disadvantages. Some scholars (e.g. Buchanan and Callus 1993; Fudge and Vosko 2001; Bosch et al. 2009) have therefore argued strongly for the need for labour market regulations in order to regulate actors' behaviour. In the Chinese context, the tightening provision of labour legislation is both a necessity and a challenge. This chapter shows that the enactment of the above three new laws has triggered different responses from the actors. It brings to the fore the actors' dynamic interactions which, despite demonstrating a high level of complexity, have remained largely unnoticed in the studies of employment relations in China. In revealing the dynamics of state policy, regulation and interaction amongst institutional actors at the organizational and institutional level, the chapter shows that the slack enforcement of central laws, often through the localized version of the laws, allows the Chinese reformist state to have both protection and flexibility. A direct consequence of this is the dilution of protection to the workers at best and the deterioration of their existing job security and employment prospects at worst.

In Chapter 9, we turn our attention back to human resource management by focusing on an important yet relatively under-studied topic in existing literature outside China – leadership and management development in the Chinese context. The chapter begins with a brief review of the characteristics of leadership and the nature of management in China. Here, Chinese values are found to be influential in the management outlook of the younger generation of Chinese managers but are nonetheless being diluted by western values. A second key task of the chapter is to assess the scope and impact of management development. In particular, the role of the state and education institutions proves crucial in developing management competence, including the development of MBA/EMBA courses. Has the massive investment and growing provisions in management education helped create a sufficient pool of managers who are competent and capable of managing global operations? Findings from snap-shot surveys conducted by international management consultancy firms seem to have painted a rather pessimistic picture. Equally, studies on fast-growing private firms reveal some major tensions between the demands for training and development from managers and managerial candidates on the one hand, and the reluctance of firms to invest in such activities for fear of retention problems on the other. This finding echoes that in the training and development of employees as discussed in Chapter 3. Finally, the chapter reveals the immense challenges some private firms are facing in succession planning and the effective management of managers, especially at the senior level. Opportunistic and unethical behaviours are reported to be an endemic and thorny issue that constrains the healthy growth of private businesses.

Finally, Chapter 10 concludes the book by first recapping the regulatory, economic, social and demographic changes in the labour market and employment environment in China. It then summarizes some of the new developments in HRM and the role of institutional actors in their propagation. Against this context, the chapter addresses a number of important issues: have Chinese firms become more strategic in their approach to managing their human resources? If so, what types of HRM practices have firms adopted to enhance their performance? Do the high-performance/commitment-oriented HRM practices promoted in the United States and Britain which have been found effective in other societies have the same positive impact in the Chinese context? If not, what may be the variations and why? Perhaps not surprisingly, the chapter found that societal culture remains a highly valid factor in explaining the enduring differences in Chinese HRM practices and those adopted in western countries. Whilst Chinese firms are beginning to embrace HRM practices originated in the West, these practices need to be adapted in order to be accepted by Chinese employees. Further, the demographic nature of the employees, such as age and gender, are likely to influence the impact of HRM practices, leading to different psychological and organizational outcomes. The chapter concludes with a set of research questions which researchers may find useful for future investigations.

2 Recruitment, retention and staffing strategy

Introduction

Recruitment and staffing is an area that is under-studied in HRM in China (Han and Han 2009). Meanwhile, skill shortage and workforce retention have been a growing challenge to many employers. Existing studies on labour turnover in western literature have come from a number of distinct but related perspectives, such as the labour market, the psychological and the human resources perspectives. The labour market perspective contemplates the external environment of the organization, such as unemployment rate, skill shortages and job opportunities (e.g. Carsten and Spector 1987; Gerhart 1990; Smith et al. 2004). It is argued that the availability of alternative job opportunities can raise comparative dissatisfaction with a current employer and lead to turnover decisions (Smith et al. 2004). Labour turnover per se is not necessarily a bad thing for business. Indeed, turnover may be desirable by employers when recruitment cost is low, labour is highly substitutable and turnover can break union solidarity (Smith et al. 2004). By contrast, the psychological perspective focuses on individuals within the organizational context and investigates their turnover intent and decision. Individuals' traits and behavioural characteristics are seen as important in turnover decisions (e.g. Griffeth et al. 2000; Morrell et al. 2001). Within this perspective, organizations are seen to have more control in the management of turnover by designing a range of HR practices that can attract, incentivize and retain the right types of employees (e.g. Coff 1997; Shaw et al. 1998).

Literature on strategic HRM and talent management draws on both perspectives and elaborates on how leading businesses that wish to maintain a competitive advantage should develop a holistic set of HR policies to attract, develop, motivate and retain the best and the brightest against a context of the intensifying global 'war for talent' (e.g. Pfeffer 1998b; Cappelli 2000; Williams 2000; Scullion and Collings 2011). In their literature review of research on global talent management, Tarique and Schuler (2010) identified three main external drivers of global talent management challenge: globalization, demographics, and the demand and supply gap.

In the Chinese context, globalization has led to the brain drain of home-grown talent through international migration and from Chinese-owned firms to foreign-owned multinational corporations (MNCs) operating in China. A striking feature of China's economic and social change following its 'open door' policy enacted in 1978 has been the growing number of young people participating in higher education. This vast investment in education, however, has not provided the necessary talent pool for the country's rapid development. What may be the institutional failure? In the meantime, globalization and marketization are having an evident impact on the traditional cultural values and socialist ideology that were once held by the nation. What may be the expectations and aspirations of the younger generation of the Chinese workforce in a period of transition?

This chapter addresses these issues, drawing on the perspectives of the labour market, organizational psychology and human resource management. It highlights the tensions in the Chinese labour market. On the one hand, an increasing number of firms are experiencing worsening skill shortage and retention problems and consequently engaging in the 'war for talent'. On the other hand, a large number of semi-skilled or unskilled workers are having difficulty in gaining employment or are saturated in low-paid and insecure jobs. The chapter examines what types of HRM practices are being used by firms to attract talent and tackle the retention problem. Particular attention is paid to the recruitment and retention of managerial and professional employees in well-performing private firms. It also looks at informal employment and the deployment of flexible labour strategy by employers at the lower end of the labour market for more reasons than cost reduction. The role of the state in addressing the talent shortage issue and the role of the employment agencies as a labour market actor for un-semi-skilled labour are also reviewed. Some of the issues and initiatives identified in this chapter will be discussed in more detail in the following chapters. Other issues related to recruitment, such as gender, age, residential status and discrimination, will be covered in Chapter 6. We conclude with a number of implications for HRM theory and organizational practices.

Talent shortage and challenges to retention

Employee turnover has been one of the most important topics in management research (Gardner 2002; Lee et al. 2006; Niederman et al. 2007). Failure to retain talent is considered one of the most expensive HR problems (Holtom et al. 2005). This is not only because of the loss of the human and social capital of the individual concerned, but also the negative impact (e.g. morale of the remaining employees and the image of the company) such turnover may have on the firm (Lee et al. 2006). HR theorists and gurus have called for a strategic approach to talent management (e.g. Boudreau and Ramstad 2005; Scullion and Collings 2011).

Similarly, proponents of a high-performance/commitment model of HRM practices argue that hiring competent employees, providing effective training, incentive compensation, decentralized decision making, and developing and promoting people within the organization will lead to a highly qualified and productive workforce (e.g. Huselid 1995; Huselid et al. 1997; Pfeffer 1998b).

Empirical research studies have also found a significant relationship between HRM practices and organizational outcomes such as employee turnover (Arthur 1994; Huselid 1995; Paul and Anantharaman 2003; Haesli and Boxall 2005). Whilst a bundled approach is advocated (e.g. Huselid et al. 1997; Macky and Boxall 2007) to maximize the effect of HR practices, emphasis is placed on the use of non-financial incentives as effective methods of talent retention. These include, for example, providing written performance plans, providing good support in coaching and career development and providing a supportive work environment (Lepak and Snell 1999; Deckop et al. 2006). Companies are urged to adopt a total rewards strategy which includes financial benefits, training and career development opportunities and other incentives to retain talent (Malila 2007). Recent studies in China have highlighted the positive effect of good HRM practices in talent retention (e.g. Zimmerman et al. 2009; Cooke 2011c). Research evidence also suggests that leading companies are now paying more attention than before to employee growth and welfare (i.e. humanistic goals orientation) in order to retain talent (Chen 1995; Levering and Moskowitz 2004; Wang et al. 2007).

The challenge to recruiting, developing and retaining managerial and professional talent in China has been widely noted (e.g. Björkman and Lu 1999; Goodall and Warner 1999; Zhu et al. 2005; Malila 2007; Tung 2007; Wang et al. 2007; Dickel and Watkins 2008). Multinational corporations and privately owned Chinese firms alike are facing difficulties in attracting and retaining managerial and professional talent due to the shortage of their supply at national level. Talent[1] shortage has become the bottleneck for business growth for many firms. In the state-owned sector, the consequence of deficit in competent business leaders proves catastrophic. According to a survey of 2,000 loss-making state-owned enterprises, 82 per cent of them were loss making as a result of poor management (Lu 2008).

This talent shortage is a direct consequence of the tight labour market and the accelerating demand for well-trained and experienced professionals and managers. A study conducted by Manpower in China found that 40 per cent of employers have difficulty in filling senior management positions. Whilst skill shortage for middle managers is slightly less, this has triggered a wage war (Arkless 2007). McKinsey & Company's study in 2005 predicted that Chinese firms seeking global expansion would need 75,000 leaders who can work effectively in the global environment in the next ten to fifteen years (Farrell and Grant 2005). However, the current stock was only 3,000 to 5,000 (Grant and Desvaux 2005, cited in Farrell and Grant 2005). Similarly, Mercer's survey in the mid-2000s on attraction and retention revealed that 72 per cent of MNC respondents believed that the biggest challenge in recruitment was a lack of qualified candidates in the Chinese market (Wilson 2008).

The rapid expansion of higher education has created a paradoxical situation in the labour market in China. On the one hand, there is mounting pressure for graduate employment. In 2009, some 6.1 million university graduates entered the labour market (*China Statistical Yearbook 2010*). Only about 70 per cent of those graduated in 2008 found employment within a year (*The Economist* 2009). On the other hand, there is an increasingly severe shortage of skilled workers and managerial talent. Worse still, the most highly qualified graduates are lost due to a brain drain to overseas, adding further to the talent shortage problem. It was reported that 80 per cent of the graduates in high-tech-related subjects from Tsinghua University have gone to the USA since 1985. A similar proportion (76 per cent) have done the same from Beijing University (Pan and Lou 2004). Tsinghua and Beijing universities are the two top universities in China. Other premium universities encounter similar trends, albeit to a lesser extent.

The repatriation of thousands of graduates trained abroad has not alleviated the shortage of management talent. A study of Chinese graduates returning from their overseas education revealed that half of them have no formal work experience – a major constraint on their employment opportunities. Only half of the companies are satisfied with the performance of their overseas returnee employees. Employers from industries that require China-specific knowledge, such as real estate, construction, consultancy, legal, finance and banking, and manufacturing are far less satisfied with their returnee employees than employers of other industries. In addition, foreign-invested companies show a lower level of satisfaction (less than 30 per cent were satisfied) of their returnee employees compared with state-invested firms (over 60 per cent were satisfied) (cited in *Development and Management of Human Resources* 2008). Interviews by the author with over 40 MNC employers participating in two job fairs in 2008 and 2009 in the UK also confirmed that employers felt a significant gap between what they seek and what Chinese graduates trained overseas and in China possess.

A key problem is that the Chinese educational system emphasizes theoretical knowledge and abstract problem solutions instead of the development of practical skills and independent and critical thinking. Reproduction of existing knowledge tends to be the mode of study instead of cultivating creative learning. Students who are brought up with this mode of passive learning often find it hard to adapt to the western style of learning and consequently few are able to rise to the challenging opportunities presented by western MNCs. In addition, it is believed that the one-child policy enacted in the early 1980s by the Chinese government to control the explosive growth of population has produced a generation of young people (known as the post-80 generation) who are spoilt by their family, dependent, unwilling to endure hardship but eager to have early success (Cooke 2011c). Given the constraints in recruiting, developing and retaining managerial and professional talent, many firms have turned to poaching as a quick fix. Indulged by a tight labour market, individuals are encouraged to look outside their company for better opportunities. They also become less tolerant with their employer when their demands are not met.

Existing studies showed that career advancement is a major reason for the turnover of talented employees, lured by the inflated job titles and salary packages offered by firms desperate to attract talent. For example, the study conducted by Manpower in China, mentioned above, revealed that two-thirds of respondents made their job move for better career development opportunities. Only 15 per cent of respondents indicated that their main reason for leaving is the prospect of better pay and benefits (Arkless 2007). However, other research studies revealed that pay is actually far more important in people's job choices and behaviours than we are led to believe and that financial reward is one of the most important factors in retention and motivation in China (e.g. Chiu et al. 2002; Rynes et al. 2004). For example, the Watson Wyatt study 'Work China Employee Attitude Survey' that polled employees from 100 companies in China showed that compensation is by far the most important factor influencing job quit intent. In addition, 'better benefits' is the third most cited reason for turnover (cited in Leininger 2007). This is because earning power is a strong indicator of not only the individuals' ability to work, but also their economic and social status in the newly found materialistic culture in the country in the process of marketization. Nevertheless, it is important to note that career development opportunities, training programmes, mentoring and a positive working environment remain crucial to attract and retain talent.

A study by X. L. Xu (2009) on the job quit intent of 197 technicians in 40 foreign-funded and privately owned manufacturing plants in Shenzhen City revealed that two-thirds of the informants intended to leave their employer as soon as they found a better job elsewhere. Dissatisfaction with their salary level, lack of training and promotion opportunities and lack of space for personal growth were the three main reasons for the technicians to leave their previous employer. Informants also reported that the biggest benefit of training was to increase their competence and knowledge, which did not contribute directly to promotion or enhanced job prospects elsewhere (see Chapter 3 for more discussion on training and development).

The above findings are supported by those of a study jointly conducted by Development Dimensions International (DDI) and the Society for Human Resource Management (SHRM) in 2007 on employee retention in China (Howard et al. 2007). According to this survey of 215 HR professionals and 862 employees (over 80 per cent of them work in foreign-owned MNCs), 38 per cent of the HR professionals reported that turnover in their organization had increased in the past 12 to 18 months. Over 70 per cent of employees had resigned from previous jobs, and nearly one-quarter had already held three or more jobs, despite their relative youth. Moreover, 22 per cent said they were likely to leave their positions in the next year. Lack of growth and development opportunities with the current employer and the availability of better career opportunities elsewhere were by far the two top turnover reasons. Better financial return was the third highest ranked reason for turnover. However, Howard et al. (2007) noted that official turnover reasons failed to convey the whole story in the light of the discrepancy between the HR professionals' and the employees' responses. This is in part because employees are unlikely to disclose sensitive reasons such as a poor relationship with managers. The same study further revealed that three of the top four employee retention drivers are directly related to leadership. They are: having a good manager, being recognized for good work and having great company leadership (Howard et al. 2007).

Howard et al.'s (2007) findings echo those by Hui et al. (2004) and Chan and Wyatt (2007). Hui et al.'s (2004) study observed that Chinese workers value highly a good interpersonal relationship with their supervisors and tend to reciprocate with affective commitment and citizenship behaviour to their supervisor rather than their organization. This reflects the traditional Chinese culture that values interpersonal relationships within a social hierarchical order and suggests that a poor relationship with superiors may be a key factor for turnover. Similarly, Chan and Wyatt's (2007: 512) study on the quality of work life of 319 employees in the Shanghai area found that esteem need is the most important factor for life satisfaction and turnover intention, and that managers are more likely to stay with the organization in which 'they feel a greater sense of recognition and appreciation of one's work inside and outside the organization'.

In this section, we have examined the skill shortage problem and the major reasons for the turnover of talented employees. In the next section, we will investigate further the career aspirations of young graduates and their preferences in selecting employers.

Young graduates' career aspirations and choice of employer

What are the career aspirations of Chinese young graduates? How are they socialized in forming their career expectations? And what types of employers do they desire to work for? A comparative study by Cooke et al. (2007) of 85 British and 125 Chinese postgraduate students in the business and management discipline in a top university in the UK in 2005–6 shows clear differences as well as similarities between Chinese and British students in the sample in their career aspiration, and ability to plan and influence their career choices. More specifically, the majority of students interviewed could not really separate their career aspirations from their career plans. It seems that students did not make this distinction not because their career aspirations had already matched their career plan, but because they have never explored in-depth what their career aspirations would be in life. Rather, what students may call 'career aspiration' is a career plan formulated during the last years of their secondary education. This experience was greatly influenced by their national educational system, national economic and social realities and, for many overseas students, by their parents. The issue of insufficient career guidance in secondary educational institutions, as well as sources of student support for developing career skills prior to undergraduate and postgraduate education also emerged. Even though most students have received some form of support in developing their career skills (e.g. careers service, interviewing skills, curriculum vitae (CV) writing, etc.), it is unclear the extent to which these students have received organized support in identifying their career aspirations and formulating plans prior to developing their career skills. In comparison with their British counterparts, Chinese students in the study were far less well prepared with their career skills. They also reported having received much less institutional support in developing these skills. This finding highlights a significant gap in the Chinese university education system – the failure to incorporate employment skills in their mainstream teaching.

Over 80 per cent of Chinese (as well as British) students were aiming at professional or managerial jobs. Students also responded that, in five years time, they would like to have secured a senior management post in a company or a well-paid job. Most British students have developed their career aspiration out of personal interest, whereas career aspirations of the Chinese student informants emerged out of a need to use their degree qualification. Family and friends do have some influence in both British and Chinese students' career aspirations, but for more Chinese than British students, family and friends have a strong influence. However, when asked to state the level of pressure received from their parents for their careers, the majority of students, both British and Chinese, responded that they receive no pressure from their parents, while a small number stated some pressure. Other sources of influence, such as school teachers and university lecturers and friends and peers, have some influence on the students' career aspirations, while the media seem to have a much stronger influence on the aspirations of Chinese students than those of the British students. The findings of this study indicate that overseas Chinese postgraduate students in the UK are more influenced by their parents' expectation in their career aspiration than their British counterparts in part because of the pressure they feel for spending so much money to go to the UK to study and in part because family ties are stronger in the Chinese paternalistic culture. In addition, overseas Chinese postgraduate students in the UK differ in their career aspirations from their British counterparts in that the majority of Chinese informants revealed that working abroad for multinational firms was their top choice. Good opportunities for career progression and development of skills are the two main criteria that Chinese students use when selecting employers. On the other hand, British students are more interested in the extent to which the job is interesting, thus emphasizing the intrinsic value of the job. Overall, the Chinese students tend to have a clearer career focus than the British students in the sample. They also tend to look for employment in large international or multi-national firms.

A nationwide annual survey of university students' choice of employers revealed further information on what they want from the employers. According to *HR Manager* (2009), a study of 188,937 Chinese university students from 629 universities on their opinion of best employers showed that telecom, finance, Internet, energy/electric/chemical, computing and durable goods are amongst the most popular industries for graduates as employment destinations. It is important to note that foreign-owned MNCs are no longer the top employer of choice for university students. Instead, for the first time since the annual university students' survey began in 2002, state-owned enterprises became the top employer of choice in 2009, overtaking wholly foreign-owned firms. Twenty-nine of the top 50 best employers in 2009 were Chinese-owned firms. This is partly to do with the fact that SOEs, in response to the government's request, did not carry out any redundancies during the 2008 global financial crisis, and they are providing improved benefits and more stable employment relations than before. Their management competence is also improving. By contrast, a large number of foreign-funded and joint-venture enterprises in China had reduced the level of compensation and contracted employment by laying off employees and reducing the level of graduate recruitment. The same survey also showed that Chinese firms are progressing rapidly in a number of HR-related aspects including: pay and benefits level, training and development, enterprise culture building and corporate branding. In some aspects, they have surpassed their foreign-owned competitors. According to the survey, the top criteria used by university students to assess 'best employers' include, in order of importance, development, compensation, brand and culture. More specifically, having a high level of income, scope and opportunity for development, good reputation of the firm, and fair and transparent deployment of staffing are the most important elements in each of the four categories respectively (*HR Manager* 2009).

Facing strong competition in the labour market for good quality jobs and facilitated by the relatively easy access to higher education both abroad and at home, young people are seeking to advance their education further and further. According to *Human Resources* (2009), higher education does bring return to human capital investment. For example, in 2009, the ratios of the average starting salary for diploma, bachelor, Masters and PhD graduates were: 1:1.33:2.06:3.44, with the actual average monthly salary of 1,725 yuan, 2,294 yuan, 3,550 yuan and 5,937 yuan respectively. In particular, IT and real estate industries were the highest paying sectors, with Masters graduates specialized in the IT discipline topping the salary league table at 8,000 yuan (monthly average). Amongst firms of different ownership forms, Sino-foreign joint-venture firms were the highest paying employers. Pay level in state-owned enterprises is very close to that of wholly foreign-owned firms. In general, the larger the firm size, the higher the salary level. It is therefore not surprising that most graduates desire to work for large and joint-venture/foreign-funded firms in the high-paying industries.

Zimmerman et al. (2009) observed that younger Chinese employees may value career opportunities, housing benefits and sponsorship of education more whereas older employees may appreciate social security provision and longer-term benefits. Si (2009) also noted that compared with experienced workers, university graduate job seekers are more idealistic and attracted to the corporate branding and prestige. Therefore, corporate brand value, corporate culture and total reward are some of the elements that can be advertised readily to attract graduates. Meanwhile, individuals are well aware of their skill gaps and are eager to enhance their CV for better career prospects. According to a study (cited in Lu 2008) conducted in the three largest cities in China – Beijing, Shanghai and Tianjin – 70 per cent of respondents currently in employment wish to carry out further education or training to enhance their knowledge and skill base for better career prospects. In particular, there is a quest for professional qualification related type of learning.

In the light of the problems associated with the skill shortage and talent retention, what is the Chinese government doing to address the issue? What recruitment and retention strategies do firms use to attract, motivate and retain talent? And to what extent do employers' talent retention practices match the individuals' expectation? We examine these issues in the next two sections.

The role of the government in developing and attracting talent

The role of the state in addressing the skill shortage problem is two-fold: through education and development (see chapters 3 and 9 for further discussion) and through the repatriation of overseas talent. In particular, expanding the higher education sector is seen to play two functions. One is to delay employment needs to ease unemployment pressure; the other is to develop human capital. As such, China's higher education sector has expanded dramatically since the mid-1990s, especially since the early 2000s. In 2001, there were a total of 1,225 state-funded regular higher education institutions. By 2007, the number had risen to 1,908. In 2000, over one million full-time students (950,000 graduates and 58,767 postgraduates) graduated from universities; in 2007, 4.79 million (4.48 million graduates and 311,839 postgraduates) graduated (*China Statistical Yearbook 2008*). In 2009, more than 6 million graduates (*People's Daily Online* 2010) were to enter the labour market for the first time in search of quality employment. As noted earlier, this rapidly increasing number of university graduates may be a human capital asset as well as a source of mounting pressure for employment due to the mismatch of skill portfolio of the graduates and employers' needs.

In terms of talent attraction, the intervention of the state has been primarily focused on supporting the state sector and to a lesser extent the private sector. This often takes the form of policy guidelines and state-led initiatives. For example, in December 2008, the Chinese government launched the 'Thousand Talents Plan' that is aimed to attract up to 2,000 (Chinese) talents from overseas. Eligible candidates should be below 55 years old and are top-level academics or experts in the areas of science and engineering, finance and banking, operations management and risk management. They should be able to contribute to innovation and product development or assume senior management roles with entrepreneurship. Successful candidates will be allocated to national key innovation projects, university laboratories, high-tech science parks or state-owned commercial banking institutions. They are to be offered handsome relocation and salary packages and research funding (*People's Daily Overseas Edition* 2009; Wheeler 2009).

In fact, encouraging overseas Chinese talent to repatriate has been a top priority of the government. Local governments often participate directly as organizers in annual international recruitment fairs to attract Chinese scholars and students overseas to return to China to take up key managerial and professional positions. The extent to which these overseas recruitment fairs are effective is not known, but they provide sought-after opportunities of overseas trips for government officials. In addition, favourable policies, science parks and entrepreneurship incubation centres are developed by provincial and municipal governments to accommodate overseas returnees (known as *haigui* 海归 in Chinese). SOEs are also starting to cast their recruitment net in the international market for senior management and key technical posts. By the end of 2008, 0.39 million of the 1.39 million Chinese who went abroad for higher education studies since 1978 (the year when China adopted its 'open door' policy) had returned to China (Cai 2009), though not all of whom are sought-after talent. Whilst these policy interventions and initiatives have attracted an increasing number of experienced expatriate scholars and professionals to return to China, interviews by the authors with professors and SOE managers as well as conversations with Chinese scholars overseas who had explored the option of returning to China revealed that returnees sometimes experience setbacks after returning to China. Promised resources are not always in place in time and Chinese colleagues may not be fully cooperative as they feel uneasy about the returnees receiving preferential treatment. Reversed cultural shock presents further barriers to repatriation settlement.

Strategy for talent attraction and retention in private firms

Empirical studies on talent management and retention have revealed a number of key practices adopted by employers in China to motivate and retain talent. These include: financial reward, promotion, creating a happier work environment and talent management programme, as shown in the author's (Cooke 2009c) study of 65 private firms of small-and-medium and large size in a wide range of industries in 2007–8. Interestingly, in spite of and because of the skill shortage, training and development are less likely to be adopted by employers in Chinese private firms to retain talent for fear of turnover (see Chapter 4 for more discussion). Instead, they recruit ready-trained employees. In this section, we look at the findings of Cooke's (2009c) study in more detail.

Recruitment of ready-trained candidates

According to the senior managers interviewed, at least half of the 65 firms studied do not recruit university graduates who have no work experience, with occasional exceptions. One manager from an engineering design company disclosed:

> We only recruit no more than 1 per cent of fresh university graduates each year. Due to the expansion of university education in recent years, the quality of the graduates has declined. Each year, our Beijing Headquarters will accept some 30 students for internship, but we don't necessarily retain them for employment. In fact, only a couple may be kept on.

Another manager from an IT firm revealed additional restrictions his firm imposed in recruiting graduate candidates – some of these are of a discriminative nature:

> First, we don't recruit top students from top universities because they tend to spend too much time studying and ignore social skills development. They are also more likely to compare income with their fellow classmates in premium cities and become dissatisfied with what they have got here.
>
> Second, we don't recruit students who came from poor rural family background because they tend to have inferior primary and secondary education, less general knowledge and may display rural people's narrow mindedness. Financial pressures also make them more money-minded and short-term oriented.
>
> Third, we don't recruit candidates who have worked in foreign-owned firms for many years because they tend to have expectation of clear lines of responsibilities and stick to a rigid business process. They are not flexible and proactive. As a private firm, our business systems and processes are not as well established as that of foreign firms. We need people to be flexible and are willing to go extra mile for the firm as and when they are needed.

Other firms also reported firm-specific rules in their recruitment. For example, one law firm makes it clear that it does not accept self-recommended applications. Several firms have a financial reward scheme to encourage their employees to headhunt candidates for the firm. They believe that this employee referral method can reduce recruitment cost and bring in more reliable candidates who are already familiar with the company's culture and will be able to fit in easily due to their prior relationship with employees of the firm. This finding supports that of Han and Han's (2009) study, which suggests that network-based recruitment practices appear to be more effective in attracting high-quality candidates in part because of the strong social ties that can be generated between the company and the candidates and the quality of information received by the candidates through this approach.

Financial rewards and recognition

The 65 managers interviewed by the author commonly reported that financial reward remains the major motivational and retention incentive. In particular, stock options and profit-related bonus schemes were reported as the most effective means of retaining key staff. As a couple of the managers revealed:

> Offering good salary is the main point of attracting good candidates, never mind enterprise culture or other HR techniques.
>
> (A manager of a hotel)

> Performance-related pay is an excellent idea. There is no ceiling to an employee's pay. This encourages employees and managers to over achieve.
>
> (A manager of a bank)

When asked if the motivational mechanisms offered by their firm are in line with what their key employees want, managers believed that there is a good match in general. They pointed out that employees are less keen on spiritual reward but prefer to have more training and, even more so, stock options. Short- and medium-term stock options are the most preferred financial reward sought by key employees in firms that are experiencing rapid expansion, particularly those in the finance and real estate sector. However, the motivational effect of financial reward should not be overestimated (see Chapter 5 for discussion). In addition to financial rewards, most firms have some schemes of spiritual recognition as rituals which conform to Chinese culture. For example, a manager of a law firm revealed that the firm recognizes employees' achievements outside the firm, such as winning competitions or professional awards. Additional prizes will be awarded by the firm to those who have 'gained honour for the firm'. Managers all agreed that recognition alone has no impact on retention.

Creating a happy and harmonious work environment

Some managers interviewed were aware of the danger that their firms have been concentrated too much on targets and bonuses, and not enough on long-term planning and other aspects of HR that focus on employees' well-being. A number of firms, particularly those in the IT, consultancy, finance and real estate industries, have reported work intensification for their professional and managerial employees due to heightened competition and/or rapid business growth. This has led to health problems and retention issues. As some managers observed:

> Some of the employees left because the firm was growing too fast. They said, 'The firm is growing too fast, I cannot keep up with it even though I am running all the time. Why should I work so hard? Why should I give myself so much pressure?'
>
> (A manager of a finance company)

> People don't like to work long hours any more. They want some relaxation and enjoy life.
>
> (Director of a media company)

Work–life balance is a problem commonly reported by the managers in these fast-growing private businesses. For example, one manager revealed that he received over 300 work-related emails a day on average. So he had to deal with them everyday in order to avoid a backlog. To address these problems, some firms have started to introduce employee welfare initiatives, social activities and mutual support schemes to create a happy and supportive environment in the workplace. Four companies have hired professionals to provide counselling services. Other employee assistance programmes are being introduced to help employees cope with their stress. In some firms, social activities are organized to allow employees to demonstrate their skills (e.g. composing poems, drawing and painting) and enable managers to get to know the employees better. Funds are reserved for employee welfare activities. For example, in a law firm, there will be at least one collective event each week for bonding and relaxation. Employees provide emotional support as well as donations of money to colleagues who encounter sudden and major family problems, such as the serious illness of a child or parent. Efforts are made to nurture a joyful organizational culture to make employees happier and the workplace more harmonious.

Whilst managers interviewed all emphasized the importance of establishing a good working environment as a good way to motivate employees and retain talent, they did recognize that it would take a long time to develop such an organizational culture.

Talent management programme

According to the senior managers interviewed, only a small number of the 65 firms studied have a formal talent management programme in place. Some of them reported that the schemes have had good effect in retaining and deploying talent. Most firms have no talent evaluation scheme in place to assess the value of talent. Fewer than ten managers reported that they do not have retention problems. Although nearly half of all managers interviewed believed that their firm has an action plan in place to combat the retention problem, most of them agreed that the plan is far from being comprehensive. Most retention plans only contain two or three of these aspects: career planning, company benefits and welfare, profit sharing, stock options, training and career development opportunities and a performance management system. The majority of managers believed that these schemes were only partially effective in retaining talent. A small number of managers also revealed that the firm was not doing enough to build an emotional bond with their key staff to enhance their engagement. No formal exit interview/management process is in place in any of the 65 firms. One firm reported having more than one person on the same post to avoid the loss of knowledge when an individual leaves.

Nevertheless, managers have generally reported that their firms are beginning to pay attention to talent management and to set up motivational mechanisms for talent management. More emphasis is placed on qualification and performance in promotion. They are also paying more attention to training and career development. Whilst only a small number of firms have formal succession planning schemes, as noted above, more reported some informal mentoring system to identify and cultivate talent. For many firms, the ability to provide growth opportunities, i.e. early and rapid promotion, to ambitious managerial employees proves crucial in retaining talent (see Chapter 9 for more detailed discussion on promotion and the management of managers).

In the sections above, we have examined the skill shortage problem, career aspirations of talented individuals, the role of the state in addressing the skill shortage problems, and the HRM practices adopted by employers to attract, motivate and retain talent. In the next section, we will turn to the other end of the labour market where individual workers possess little human capital and bargaining power in the labour market.

Informal employment in China

Patterns of growth

Informal employment is a common feature of all labour markets, although the size of the sector, the demographic characteristics of its labour force and the societal context against which the sector emerges and develops vary across economies. In informal employment, market forces play an important role in shaping the employment relations between workers and their employer(s). With the exception of a small minority in the skilled and professional occupations, informal employment is an unprotected form of employment, 'which survived within the award system and indeed flourished in the gaps created by officially sanctioned exemptions from protection and limits in the enforcement and reach of award regulation' (Campbell 1996: 571). As such, the informal sector remains poorly regulated or unregulated in many countries. The notion of 'decent work' advocated by the International Labour Organization (ILO) is closely related to the job quality of informal employment (ILO 2002). This consists of seven basic forms of security: labour market security, employment security, job security, work security, skill reproduction security, income security and representation security (see Standing 1997: 8–9).

The use of informal employment in the form of temporary, seasonal, casual, part-time or hourly paid work has long existed in China, albeit on a much smaller scale than recent years (Cooke 2006). These forms of employment have been found on farms, in manufacturing plants, in government and public sector organizations for ancillary work, but primarily in the expanding private sector. The term 'informal employment', however, is a relatively new concept in China that was first introduced by the labour authority of Shanghai in 1996. Informal employment (also known as 'non-standard employment' or 'flexible employment') as a flexible labour strategy has been gaining rapid attention in China since the late 1990s as a result of the massive downsizing in the state sector, the rapid expansion of the private economy and the migration of surplus rural labour en masse to urban areas.

Workers engaging in informal employment can be found in three types of organizations: 1) organizations operating in the formal sector; 2) organizations operating in the informal sector; and 3) loosely formed informal employment organizations (Hu and Yang 2001; He 2003; Gao et al. 2007; also see figures 2.1 and 2.2). Generally speaking, informal employment incorporates non full-time, temporary, seasonal and casual work in the informal sector. It also includes full-time temporary work in formal organizations, self-employment and those employed by the self-employed (Wang and Tan 2003). It is 'informal' in a sense that the workers often do not have a formal employment contract and have little, if any, social security provision in reality, disregarding what the

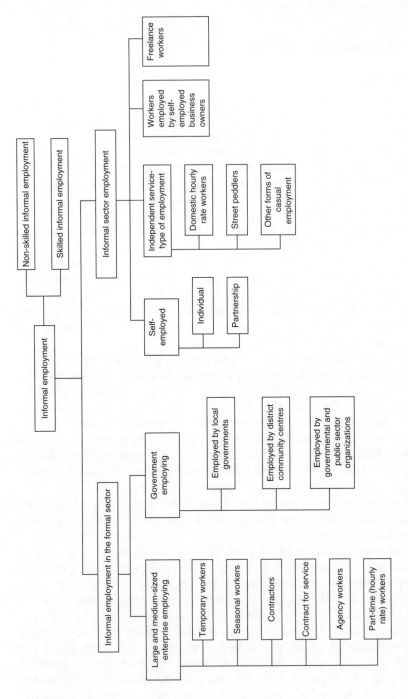

Figure 2.1 Informal employment in China.

Source: adapted from He (2003: 498) and Hu and Yang (2001: 70).

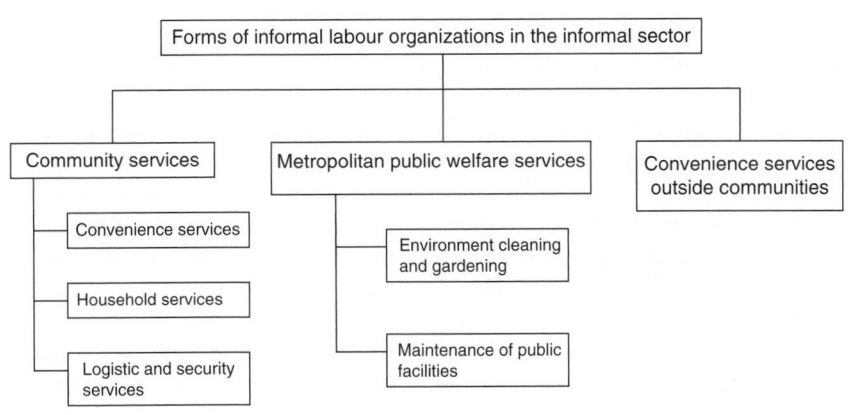

Figure 2.2 Forms of informal labour organizations.
Source: adapted from Gao et al. (2007: 119).

labour laws specify. According to Hu and Yang (2001), the proportion of workers in informal employment is relatively low in the state-monopolized industries and monopoly service industries such as telecommunication and finance, but is much higher in competitive industries that are labour intensive such as retail, catering and community services.

Researchers (e.g. Peng and Yao 2004; Zhang 2004; Shi and Wang 2007; Wu 2008) on informal employment have noted the lack of consensus in China on the precise definition and classification of informal employment. They have also pointed out the absence of official information on the total number of workers employed in this mode and what forms of employment they take. Nevertheless, it is estimated that some 150 million workers are engaged in informal employment in the urban area, representing over 20 per cent of the total employment in the urban area. They made up 58 per cent of the workers in the industry sector and 52 per cent in the service sector (The State Council 2006). The informal employment category comprises two categories of workers: 1) laid-off workers, unemployed persons and retirees from the urban area; and 2) rural migrant workers employed in the urban areas. There is also a group of entrepreneurs and professionals engaging in self-employed businesses who are relatively well-educated and skilled. But this only consists of a very small proportion of those in informal employment. A survey carried out by ACFTU on re-employment of laid-off workers in selected cities found that 80–90 per cent of the laid-off workers who regained employment in 1999 were engaged in informal employment (Jiang 2003).

There have been controversies about the term 'informal employment' ever since its introduction in China in the mid-1990s (*Yangzi Evening News* 2001). Scholars (e.g. Chen 2000; Zhu 2001) believe that it is a term that degrades the social status of the job and therefore has a negative impact on those who are engaged in the sector. Many enter this type of employment from an already low social status (e.g. rural migrants and laid-off workers). It is worth noting that the Chinese government and official bodies tend to use the term 'flexible employment' to neutralize its negative image (Cooke 2008d). However, the Chinese 'government's choice of words is not entirely a matter of optics' (F. Xu 2009: 439). Instead, the Chinese model of flexible (informal) employment bears two unique features that differentiate it from those found in other countries, particularly in the developing world. One is that flexible employment is promoted 'by the Chinese government as a specific response to the problem of re-employing the masses of former workers laid off from the state sectors' (F. Xu 2009: 439). Another related feature is that 'flexible employment in China is much more organized and less "informal," with more government intervention than equivalent employment in many other developing countries' (F. Xu 2009: 439).

Encouraged by the government's drive of creating employment through various flexible employment schemes, employers, particularly those in the labour-intensive private sector, then actively take advantage of this employment strategy to maximize their staffing flexibility, to save labour cost and so forth (see below for examples). Consequently, since the mid-1990s, employees in China have been experiencing a sharp swing from a once rigid internal labour market dominated by the state sector to a collection of external local labour markets that are increasingly informal and unprotected. One outcome of this process of labour market transformation and dynamism is rising inequality that is manifested as disparities in earnings, employment security and working conditions (Cooke 2011d, also see Chapter 6).

Employment terms and conditions

Existing studies on terms and conditions of workers in informal employment have revealed a similar picture: low level of job security, extremely low wage (often with delay of wage payment), poor working conditions, long working hours with few or no rest days, and the absence of training opportunities, labour rights and social security protection (e.g. Chan 1998; Cooke 2006; Lee 2007; Shao et al. 2007). This is particularly the case for rural migrant workers, as evidenced in the statistical information revealed by the labour authorities and trade unions as part of their high-profile campaigns to improve the workers' employment and living conditions (Cooke 2007, also see Chapter 6).

The majority of workers in informal employment do not have an employment contract with their employer. According to the statistics from labour inspections, less than 20 per cent of the small and medium-sized private firms had signed contracts with their workers. This figure was much lower in the self-employed business sector (cited in Chang 2008). Since the Labour Law of China (enacted in 1995) only covers those in formal employment, this leaves the majority of workers in a de facto employment relationship unprotected (see below for discussion of new labour laws). For those who have signed employment contracts, the majority of contracts were for a one-year duration. The short-term nature of the contractual relationship renders employment relations unstable at the macro level. Some contracts include unlawful clauses that allow the employers to evade responsibilities on sickness and work-related injuries (Qiao 2008). About 70 per cent of migrant workers have experienced wage arrears (Dong 2008). According to a survey conducted by the labour authority in April 2005, nearly 13 per cent of the workers were paid below the local minimum wage level. Some firms reduced the real wage by unilaterally reducing the unit price of production or raising the production targets which forced workers to work unpaid overtime to complete their tasks. Wage arrears and unlawful deduction of wages were the most common violations revealed in the labour inspections (cited in Chang 2008).

Whilst the enactment of the Labour Contract Law and the Labour Disputes Mediation and Arbitration Law in 2008 has provided a tightened regulatory environment and enhanced protection to the workers in informal employment, the enforcement of these laws proved to be problematic and has yielded only limited positive effect so far (see Chapter 8 for more detailed discussion). It is clear that workers' labour rights are easily breached because of the informality of the employment relationship, the weak bargaining power of the workers who lack labour market advantage and the priority of employment creation over labour rights. In addition, since the majority of workers found their jobs through personal networks, workers are more likely to tolerate mistreatments by the employer due to personal ties (Zhang 2008).

Employers' flexible labour strategy

Accompanying the growth of informal employment is the rising number of employment agencies as an emerging labour market broker and institutional actor. Like western economies, insourcing (Purcell and Purcell 1999) as a form of labour flexibility has been adopted by firms in China since the mid- to late 1990s. Labour dispatch (i.e. sending workers employed by an employment agency to work in client firms) is a major source of business for employment agencies in China. As noted in Chapter 1, employment agencies emerged in China in the 1980s as a semi-state and semi-market institution to provide employment support to laid-off workers and rural migrant workers with an aim to regulate the labour flow in the labour market. They also played the surrogate employer role for foreign-owned firms in the 1980s when the latter were not allowed to hire labour directly (F. Xu 2009). In the 1990s and 2000s, despite being freed from the restriction of employing workers directly, foreign-invested firms use dispatch labour as a way to contain labour cost but at the same time being able to distance themselves from poor labour standards and non-compliance of employment laws, including not signing employment contracts and not contributing to workers' social security premiums (F. Xu 2009, also see Chapter 8 for more discussion).

The employment brokering role may also be played by manufacturers or suppliers of products in the value chain. For example, Gamble and Huang's

(2009) study of the staffing policy in a British-owned decorative material retail warehouse store showed that the store deployed 250 employees and 450 'vendor representatives' (self-employed sales representatives sent from the product manufacturers to the store to promote sales). Vendor representatives, most of whom are in precarious employment without an employment contract, are more diligent, more knowledgeable of the products they promote and more customer-friendly. By contrast, store employees are less interested in their job, in learning about the products they sell or in serving the customers. Yet, they enjoy more employment security and better terms and conditions than their vendor representative colleagues who work alongside them. Vendor representatives are mostly female and non-local residents whereas employees are male and local residents (Beijing) (see Chapter 6 for further discussion on discrimination against gender and residential status). They receive low basic wages and rely on commission to top up their wage. Not only are the employment terms and conditions for the vendor representatives inferior to those of the employees, but they are also subject to discriminative treatments by the managers and employees of the store. Gamble and Huang (2009: 14) found that vendor representatives 'have low commitment to their host employer'. The complex employment relationship between the vendor representatives and their host employer and 'the structurally unequal nature of their relationship with store employees and the store' are seen as reasons that hinder such a development.

Similarly, employers may deploy trainees, apprentices or probationers to reduce labour cost, and the Labour Contract Law is intended to prevent such exploitation but with limited effect. For example, Zou and Lansbury's (2009: 2363–4) study of Beijing Hyundai Motor Company (BHMC), a Korean subsidiary car manufacturing plant, revealed:

> BHMC has made less use of sub-contracting and dispatch labour on the assembly lines, due to the considerable flexibility already provided by the use of fixed-term contracts for production workers, and the labour cost savings from employing a substantial number of trainees on lower wages.... The lower labour costs associated with the comparatively low-paid and non-militant workforce at BHMC have minimised the need to introduce highly automated and mechanised production systems. This has enabled HMC to contain its production costs and adopt a low-cost, high quality strategy to break into the fiercely competitive Chinese market. To maximise this labour-intensive system at BHMC, production tasks are more simplified and fragmented than those at HMC's Ulsan plant. This enables the prompt replacement and training of unskilled workers on the assembly line.

The substantial body of studies on employment practices and the labour market in China have highlighted the once rigid but now reforming employment practices of the SOEs on the one hand, and the high level of job insecurity in the private sector, notably in the sweatshop plants, on the other (e.g. Solinger 1999;

Chan 2001; Hassard et al. 2007; Lee 2007; Warner 2009). What has been less known is the fact that even within the state sector, a two-tier workforce is often employed in which the core workforce consists of those who have 'local urban resident' status and are in the skilled jobs or administrative roles, whereas the peripheral workforce comprises those who may not possess 'local urban resident' status and are in the unskilled/semi-skilled jobs. Some of them may be laid-off SOE workers. Whilst adopting an (enlarging) peripheral workforce at the lower end of the labour market in the western economies such as the UK is an employer strategy primarily to reduce labour cost (Casey et al. 1997; Felstead and Jewson 1999), the state-owned Chinese employers adopt this flexible employment strategy for political, administrative as well as financial reasons, as the example in Box 2.1 shows (also see Box 4.1 for more detail of the company).

Box 2.1 Flexible labour deployment strategy of a small state-owned enterprise

Company A is a state-owned detergent manufacturing company. It deploys a core and peripheral labour strategy. The former consists of 210 plus office staff and skilled production workers who are employees of the company, whereas the latter comprises over 180 non/semi-skilled agency workers engaging in product packaging, portering and transportation. This dual labour strategy has been adopted since 1998. According to the director, Mr Ye, the main reason for using agency workers is to shift 'all the hassles' of people management from the company to the agency firms. This includes the hassle of monitoring birth control of female workers, as the majority of packaging workers are women.[1] These agency workers receive low wages and limited social security protection. Apparently, the agency firms have some sort of agreements with the local labour authority and insurance company that only a fixed number of agency workers will be provided partially with social security coverage. In other words, it is a partial compliance (or violation) of labour laws. This is how they drive down the employment cost. Ultimately, the burden of lower production cost is born by the agency workers. In the meantime, Company A, a model company in the city, has been sponsoring the annual municipal basketball tournaments and school sports events for the last ten years as part of its corporate social responsibility engagements.

Source: interview data collected by the author in 2009.

1 According to the state regulation, employers are responsible for implementing the one-child policy by monitoring the birth control of employees. Companies are to be fined and publicly named for failing this duty.

Conclusion

This chapter examined the skill shortage and talent retention problems in the Chinese labour market. We looked at the role of the state and the employers in addressing this problem. We also outlined what the career aspirations of university graduates are and the types of employers they wish to work for. From the findings of the HRM practices in the private firms and the preference of employees (see also Chapter 4 on performance management and Chapter 5 on training and development), a number of implications can be drawn as follows.

First, the rapid business expansion experienced by many firms in China as a result of the fast economic growth at the macro level is the main cause of talent shortage and retention problems. Since Chinese private firms are relatively young with little stock in-house, they tend to rely on the external labour market for talent instead of growing their own. At the macro level, the tendency of firms to discriminate against job applicants with little work experience is forcing university students to look for employment experience while still studying. This further reduces the quality of their education and creates more training needs once they are in employment, which their employers are not willing to fund. This finding is in line with that uncovered from the study by Yang and Li (2008), who found that the quality of employment, measured by wage level, working hours, training opportunity and social insurance, of university graduates in the Beijing area has declined since the 2000s. In particular, a significant propor-tion of university graduate employees reported that they had not received any training from their employer due to the latter's concern about employee retention problems. Instead, employers prefer to recruit those who are ready-trained. To avoid the vicious circle that is already forming, the Chinese government, universities and employers should develop and promote more formal internship schemes.

Second, the heavy economic orientation of private firms influences the way they allocate resources to the HR function. The HRM practices they adopt are heavily geared towards maximizing the company's financial return through rent sharing with employees. By tying individuals' financial reward to the firm's profit level, firms are putting individuals on the front line of business competition and transferring the risk to them. This strategy attracts those who are motivated by money and success and hence match the individuals with the firm. Whilst the role of financial reward in retaining and motivating talent remains controversial and proponents of high-commitment HRM argue that money is only a hygiene factor (e.g. Pfeffer 1998a), evidence shown in this chapter suggests that financial reward remains the most used and most effective HR mechanism to attract and retain talent, at least in the private sector, in China. This is also in line with that of Horwitz et al.'s (2006) comparative study, which revealed that financial benefits and empowerment initiatives are the two distinctive HRM methods for firms in Singapore and South Africa to attract and retain knowledge workers. While empowerment does not seem to be a key feature in HRM in Chinese firms, opportunity for promotion to the senior level, and its associated pay rise and organizational power, is the most important reason for turnover of managerial staff.

In addition, research evidence from the private sector showed that employees have a strong preference to the HRM practices that will directly enhance their labour market prospects, for example, human capital development through company-sponsored training, and ultimately financial return. They also prefer short-term financial incentives instead of being tied to the firm for the longer term. By contrast, employers prefer to reward employees for their current performance and are unwilling to invest in training for their future performance for fear that these efforts will be undermined by market processes. Here, the efforts–reward tension between the employer and the employees is clear. The materialistic orientation of individual employees and the economic orientation of the firm suggest that employment relations in private firms are largely of a transactional nature. It indicates a sharp departure from the traditional Chinese values that are characterized by paternalism and reciprocal loyalty. It also calls into question the practical utility of the high-commitment model of HRM in the Chinese context. MNCs that wish to transfer their western HRM practices that are humanistic oriented may not succeed without the support of a strong financial reward policy. Future studies should look into the changing psychological contract in employment relations between Chinese employees and their employers. Particular attention should be paid to the social values and work ethics of the post-80 generation who were brought up as the single child of the family and under the strong influence of the materialistic culture currently prevailing.

However, not all Chinese values and traditions have been thrown out of employment relations. A third point to be raised here is that workplace welfare, employee recognition and social events of Chinese style continue to play an important role in maintaining a harmonious employment relationship. These practices are of a collectivist and paternalistic nature and have been adopted by Chinese firms as part of enterprise culture building (Cooke 2008b). They arguably have a high practical value, as well as a symbolic function, in private firms in order to cushion the negative effects of work-intensification and to build stronger social ties with employees. Here, work–life balance initiatives are designed to combat work-related fatigue and satisfy individuals' needs for social bonding, rather than flexi-working for those who have caring responsibilities, as is often the case in western societies. It should also be noted that these HRM practices are essentially hygiene factors and do not have retention effects on their own.

Fourth, Holtom et al. (2005: 337) observed that traditional approaches to understanding turnover have placed 'accumulated job dissatisfaction as the primary antecedent to voluntary turnover'. However, Holtom et al.'s (2005: 337) study showed that 'precipitating events (e.g. a fight with the boss or an unexpected job offer), or shocks, more often are the immediate cause of turnover'. Therefore, Holtom et al. (2005) argue that the role of shocks should be an important component in leadership training in order to minimize dysfunctional turnover. Given the poor people management skills of line managers, as admitted by senior managers interviewed, and given the fact that a job offer elsewhere is a major reason for key individuals to leave the current employer, Holtom et al.'s argument is of particular relevance to the talent turnover scenario in China. Future studies should explore how Chinese firms manage shock events in order to retain talent and whether leadership training in shock management will have any positive impact on talent retention.

To summarize, if attraction, development, motivation and retention are the four key elements in talent management (Williams 2000), then many Chinese firms, particularly in the private sector, are focusing on two of them mainly: attraction and motivation. More specifically, they adopt a proactive strategy in attracting talent by targeting experienced staff to minimize training and induction costs and to maximize productivity. Instead of deploying sophisticated selection procedures to identify the best talent, personal contact is used to identify candidates who are likely to fit in readily with the firm's culture to create group harmony and facilitate retention. In fact, this is a commonly used method to recruit new staff in China (e.g. Björkman and Lu 1999; Smith 2003; Han and Han 2009). As Han and Han (2009) noted, marketization has led to diversified recruitment practices adopted by employers, with a particular emphasis on the social network approach. The Chinese private firms in Cooke's (2009c) study display a high level of pragmatism in talent retention management, relying largely on responsive rather than preventative HRM practices. These practices are non-systematic and individual oriented. These private firms focus on incentivizing performance in a fast-moving business environment and seem to be less concerned about turnover. They seem to accept that turnover is inevitable and there is a limit to what they can do to retain their key talent. The main concern is therefore to maximize their performance during their employment with the firm.

Finally, this chapter also examined the growth of informal employment at the lower end of the labour market, and relatedly, employers' flexible strategy. Like western economies, contingency employment is found at both the upper and the lower end of the job ladder. However, it is at the lower end of the labour market where a large proportion of the informal employment is found in China. It needs to be noted that this form of employment in China is not as informal as that found in some other developing countries in that the former is far more organized and provides relatively better terms and conditions than the latter. The 'informality' in China is largely marked by the residential status of the workers, hence the inferiority of their job security and employment benefits compared with those in formal employment. It is a deliberate strategy of firms to contain labour cost and to avoid other responsibilities associated as an employer. A significant proportion of those in informal employment are engaged via employment agencies, some of which operate in an illegal manner. Hence their employment relationship is an 'agency-mediated market relation, rather than state- or network-mediated' (F. Xu, 2009: 461), making it even more difficult for regulatory protection to be extended to these workers (see chapters 7 and 8 for further discussion).

In some ways, the HR/labour strategy adopted by employers at both ends of the marketized labour market shares something in common. That is, the primacy of financial cost/profit concerns and the desertion of a long-term employment relationship. If workers at the lower end of the labour market are largely forced into this form of employment relations, then those at the upper end may play an active role in shaping it!

3 Human capital, training and development

Introduction

There is now a widespread consensus that a highly skilled and innovative workforce is the most important competitive advantage of a nation for its sustained economic development. Investing in training and creating a learning environment and an innovative culture are seen as crucial means to enhance this competitive advantage (Argyris and Schon 1978; Hamel and Prahalad 1993). Many governments, from both developed and developing countries, have been enthusiastic in introducing new training initiatives and in promoting the notion of life-long learning that are aimed to raise the skill and knowledge level of the nation. Raising the nation's education and skill level has been increasingly high on the Chinese government's agenda. It is increasingly recognized that the worsening skill shortage is causing a bottleneck in production and innovation and that this problem must be addressed urgently for China to compete at the international level and to become an integral part of the global economy. The government's growing effort in reversing the skill shortage problem is evidenced in the promulgation of a series of training regulations and initiatives in the 2000s and in the fact that human resource development has been enlisted as one of the key components of China's Eleventh Five-Year Plan (2001–5). Phrases such as human capital, human resource development, life-long learning, knowledge worker, learning organization and innovation have entered the government's statements and action plans.

However, the role of the state and its agencies in shaping a HRD agenda in China has received limited research attention. The shift from direct state control to state directive guidance, the deepening of the marketization process, and the resultant growing autonomy of state-owned enterprises and the rising economic power of the private sector have rendered the state increasingly dependent upon other actors to enforce its strategy. Such dependence means that the ability of the developmental state to achieve its goals may be circumvented by its local state agencies and other institutional actors. The absence of this kind of investigation on state-led HRD initiatives and organizational response to these interventions creates a significant gap in our understanding of how the state promotes training and learning programmes via various actors.

It is true that the development of human capital requires the joint efforts of key stakeholders such as the state and its related institutions (e.g. the education and vocational education systems), the employers and the individuals and their family. Cooke (2005a) has provided an overview of the development of the vocational education and enterprise training system in socialist China. In this chapter, we focus on the role of the state, the trade unions and the employers in shaping training polices, initiatives and practices at the national level and practices at the firm level. In particular, we investigate the state-led HRD initiatives and analyse the Chinese interpretation and configuration of 'learning organizations' against some of the criteria prescribed in the western HRM literature. We adopt a broad definition of human capital in this book to include education qualifications, skills, competence and work experience. In the second part of the chapter, we highlight trends of training practices in the private sector, drawing on research evidence from both first-hand and secondary empirical studies. The chapter concludes with implications for research, policy and practice on organizational learning, employee participation and innovation in China.

Training policies and initiatives from the state

As noted in Chapter 2, China's economic growth has been accompanied by worsening skill shortages in many areas. To alleviate the problem, the state has taken a two-prong strategy: funding management training and education through the development of management development institutes and business schools, and initiating nationwide skill training programmes through the enterprises. Issues related to management development will be discussed in Chapter 9. In this chapter, we focus on skill training for employees. First we look at the role of the state. A number of state-sponsored skill development programmes have been launched since the early 2000s that are aimed to raise the skills and competence level of the labour force. Below are a few examples, although the effectiveness and impact of these initiatives are not fully understood. In particular, we examine how the state launched the 'learning organization' initiative through a national campaign, involving (state-owned) enterprises and the trade unions.

The '500,000 Senior Technicians in Three Years' programme and the Eleventh Five-Year Plan

In order to combat the skill shortage problem at the senior level, the Ministry of Labour and Social Security launched an initiative in 2004 – the '500,000 Senior Technicians in Three Years' training plan. The plan aimed to train up 500,000 new technicians at the senior level ('golden blue collar workers') in three years between 2004 and 2006, with a focus on the manufacturing and service industry (*Workers' Daily*, 3 November 2004). During the Eleventh Five-Year Plan period (2006–10), the Chinese government intended to train 1.9 million technicians (*jishi* 技师) and senior technicians as well as 7 million technical workers (*jigong* 技工) at the senior level (*People's Daily Overseas Edition* 13 February 2006).

Professionalization of occupations

A number of initiatives have been launched that are aimed at professionalizing occupations in China. For example, the 'National vocational qualification training system for enterprise trainers' was implemented by the Ministry of Enterprise Training in 2003. It is an initiative to train the trainers in order to raise the quality of vocational training. Over 4,000 people had obtained the enterprise trainer qualification in two years (*Workers' Daily* 27 December 2005). Professional bodies are set up and stipulate professional qualification requirements for practitioners. For example, the first national standard for professional managers – 'Qualification Requirements for Practising Professional Managers in the Hotel Industry' – was promulgated in 2004. Within a year, over 5,000 senior and mid-ranking managers had obtained the qualification, according to the Chinese Hotel Association Professional Management Specialist Committee (reported in *Workers' Daily* 29 October 2005).

Sunshine Project

In 2003, the government issued the '2003–10 National Training Plan for Rural Migrant Workers' that aimed to provide basic skill training to the largely unskilled rural migrant workers (known as the Sunshine Project). According to the national statistics, there were 110 million rural migrant workers in China. Only 28.2 per cent of them had ever received any skill training. The training plan is based on a voluntary and tripartite model, with the training cost to be shared by the individuals, the central and local governments as well as employing organizations (Qian and Zhang 2007). This training plan sets a highly challenging task for local governments and employers, given the large number of people to be trained, the low starting point and the reluctance of employers to invest in training up the unskilled labourers. Whilst unskilled rural migrant workers may be willing to be trained, motivation is not high when they have to share the cost, or will be bound by the training-employment agreement with the employer to recoup its training cost. As a result, employers and migrant workers continue to opt for the low-skill/low-wage model. To combat the problem, the government is deploying stick-and-carrot mechanisms. On the one hand, firms that do not spend the specified 1.5 per cent of their wage bill on their employee training budget will have the money taken away by the local government which will then organize the training. On the other hand, the government actively promotes the vocational qualification certification system and mobilizes its extended agencies, such as the education and training institutions and the local branches of ACFTU, Youth League and All-China Women's Federations, to organize training (Qian and Zhang 2007).

Developing HR competence

In 2005, the Ministry of Labour and Social Security launched an HR professional qualification accreditation system for HR practitioners in order to professionalize the profession. It became the largest occupational assessment event at the time, and a total of 200,000 people had taken the examination by 2006. In 2006, major changes took place to improve the examination system for the HR professional qualifications. The revised system emphasizes knowledge renewal and the development of competence. It marks a departure from the existing emphasis on degree qualifications in the profession. The popularity of the HR professional qualification accreditation system will help develop the HR competence of the country. Though there is still a long way to go, over a period of time, this system will provide employers with a pool of HR talent and raise the standard of the profession (*Development and Management of Human Resources* 2006a).

Developing industrial relations competence

In the light of a rising level of labour disputes, local governments have been instructed to develop industrial relations (IR) competence. In response to this, local governments have taken various measures. For example, in 2006, Nanjing city launched its first batch of 41 'wage negotiators' who were trained, certified and appointed jointly by the municipal labour authority and the ACFTU and CEC branches. These negotiators are mainly industrial relations or trade union officers from enterprises. A small number of them are retirees or laid-off employees who are keen to engage in collective negotiation tasks. In order to perform their task effectively, wage negotiators are required to collect all relevant information about the enterprise before each negotiation (*Development and Management of Human Resources* 2006b: 4). This represents one of the many initiatives local governments are developing to facilitate the development of a harmonious workplace relationship for a harmonious society.

The chuangzheng programme – a new national learning and innovation initiative[1]

Perhaps the most widespread and influential initiative is the *chuangzheng* initiative: to build ('*chuang*') a learning organization (创建学习型组织), to be ('*zheng*') a knowledge worker (争做知识型员工). It is a nationwide and state-led initiative launched in December 2003 to promote learning, skill enhancement and innovation. In February 2004, an administrative policy document, the 'Recommendations on the Nation-Wide Implementation of the Initiative "To Build a Learning Organization, To Be a Knowledge Worker"', was issued jointly by nine ministries of China, including the Ministry of Education and the Ministry of Labour and Social Security. The document provides recommendations that are aimed to promote and implement the initiative rapidly throughout the whole country (*Workers' Daily* 19 October 2004). Further administrative regulations have been promulgated in order to tackle the skill shortage problem. Emergency training plans have been formulated for those industries, such as the manufacturing industry and the modern service industry, which suffer the most severe skill shortages (Cooke 2008a).

The *chuangzheng* initiative has been promoted by provinces, cities, industries and enterprises in various forms. For example, a three-month long national contest under the *chuangzheng* initiative was held in March 2004. The contest was sponsored by the ACFTU (see below on the role of the ACFTU in skill development), the *Worker's Daily* (a national newspaper dedicated to work, employment and business issues) and related ministries. It was reported that some 11 million employees from nearly 10,000 enterprises and public sector organizations had been organized by the trade unions to participate in the contest (*Worker's Daily* 19 October 2004). Prizes were awarded to winners in the *chuangzheng* knowledge contests. In November 2004, a four-day skill competition was held in the silk manufacturing industry with over 40 competitors coming from 13 silk producing provinces (*Worker's Daily* 30 November 2004). Enterprises are encouraged to adopt a wide variety of forms of learning and practising, including self-study, technological innovation, skills and performance contests, on-the-job training and problem-solving teams. It is hoped that these mechanisms will provide a learning environment to motivate employees to acquire new knowledge and skills (*Workers' Daily* 19 October 2004).

These activities share two similar characteristics: to raise employees' skill levels through training and competition and to harness employees' innovative ideas through participation and suggestion schemes. The objective is to increase productivity and organizational competitiveness. This has resulted in a renewed enthusiasm in skill competitions and employee participation schemes in innovations in enterprises in China. New model enterprises were born and new role models were identified. Competition winners were rewarded with prizes and promotion. Their achievements serve as examples to help organizations promote the *chuangzheng* initiative further. The *chuangzheng* initiative is aimed at helping to achieve the 'National Training Programme for Advanced Technical Talents' and the '500,000 Senior Technicians in Three Years' training plan promulgated by the Ministry of Labour and Social Security in 2004. Life-long learning, knowledge management, organizational learning and human resource development are by now some of the topics that feature prominently in management literatures and organizational policy statements in China. So is other western-imported management jargon that is perceived to be modern and innovative in management thinking. Whether life-long learning and creativity is now embedded at workplaces remains debatable (Cooke 2008a).

The initiative was pushed to a new height with the state-organized National Conference of *Chuangzheng* Promotion in October 2004. The conference required organizations to deepen the implementation of the initiative by:

- helping employees to develop a mindset of life-long learning;
- ensuring the widest participation from employees in the *chuangzheng* initiative;

- maximizing innovative outcomes; and
- sharing good practices.

Twenty-three large enterprises were awarded National Model of *Chuangzheng* Enterprises at the Conference (see case study examples below). In addition, 200 production teams were awarded 'National Employee Innovation Model Unit' and 300 individual employees were awarded 'National Employee Innovation Expert' (*Worker's Daily* 18 October 2004). Award-winning enterprises use their role model's name to name their innovation taskforce or problem-solving team. For example, Bao Steel (Shanghai) had 16 innovation teams prior to the implementation of the *chuangzheng* initiative. The number of teams had increased to 200 in 2004. Many of the teams were named after the model worker team leader (*Worker's Daily* 28 October 2004).

More broadly, model employees are also encouraged to take on apprentices to impart technical skills and to influence workplace behaviour. Master–apprentice pairs are encouraged to enter competitions. Winning pairs are awarded with prizes and promotion.

Below are three case studies (with pseudonyms) reported in the *Worker's Daily* as exemplary 'learning organizations'. The first two case study firms have been awarded 'National Model Learning Organizations'. These case studies provide a glimpse of the different interpretations and practices of 'learning organizations' in China.

Case study 3.1 Northern Mining Co.

Northern Mining Co. (NMC) is a large coal-mining company that is part of a large mining corporation group in China. NMC was established in the early 1980s with an annual production capacity of 20 million tons. Since the late 1990s, NMC has been implementing a learning organization initiative. The initiative includes: establishing a number of core values for the organization, developing a learning and training network with multiple learning mechanisms, and heavy investment in training facilities. In the last five years, NMC has invested more than 15 million yuan (US$1 was approximately 8 yuan) to build a modern training centre, over 3 million yuan to equip 16 multi-functional classrooms, and 2 million yuan in simulation training environments such as rock climbing and emergency drills. Employees can receive training in many different ways, including formal lectures, guest speaker presentations, simulation exercises, self-learning and distance learning. In addition, NMC's learning organization policy requires each employee to spend at least one hour each week in the training forum that focuses on health and safety, sharing good practices and innovative ideas, and making suggestions for production/business process improvement. NMC organizes an annual skill contest and vocational skill assessment for its employees to raise their skill level. It also deploys special task forces to solve specific technical problems in the production process. NMC also mobilizes external forces to help encourage learning and innovation activities. For example, it participates in conferences and discussion forums to share good practices with other leading enterprises in China that aspire to be a learning organization. NMC has exported nearly 900 of its key technical workers to other mining companies in the same corporate group to promote the good practices of NMC and to bring back good practices from other companies. All these activities have enhanced the employees' ability to adapt to new technology and innovativeness. NMC was awarded the 'national model learning organization' and has been one of the most profitable mining companies in the industry in China for the last eight years.

Case study 3.2   Oriental Engine Manufacturing Co.

Oriental Engine Manufacturing Co. (OEM) employs over 6,200 employees and is a large engine manufacturing company in China with a 40 per cent market share in hydraulic engines and 33 per cent in thermal engines. Over 60 per cent of its workers are below the age of 35. OEM set itself three propositions in becoming a learning organization.

Propositions

1. *Chuangzheng* as a necessity for enterprise development in order to enhance its technological competitiveness in the global market.
2. *Chuangzheng* as a necessity for employee development in order to raise their skill level and update their knowledge base.
3. *Chuangzheng* as a necessity for the trade union to protect workers' rights to education and development in order to increase the quality, innovativeness and competitiveness of the workforce.

Methods of implementation

1. Building a strong enterprise culture and value branding. A comprehensive set of company documents that contain company history,

company values, production procedures, workplace procedures, etc. is provided to each employee. A company-wide debate was held on the theme: 'OEM needs to develop, what should I do?' The purpose of the debate was to reach a common understanding among the workforce that 'The Enterprise needs me to develop, I need the Enterprise to survive.' These activities were deemed necessary because of the young profile of the workforce.

2. Rewarding role models and promoting good behaviour.
3. Creating a learning environment and reward mechanism in which employees have the 'I want to learn' desire. Each employee must receive 30–50 hours of off-the-job training. Training outcome is assessed and points accumulated for each employee. Skills competitions are held regularly. For example, in 2002 alone, 4,500 employees took part in 134 occupational skill drills and competitions. Junior and middle-ranking managerial positions are appointed by competition. Between 3 and 5 per cent of the poorest performers will be displaced from their posts.
4. Creating a clean and modern factory environment.

Perceived effects

These company-wide learning activities are reported to have tangible effects:

- In 2003, some 530 cases of innovation were reported by employees, with a total cost saving of 8 million yuan. Seventy-eight of the cases won awards at various levels. OEM was the only enterprise in its province that was awarded the National Model Enterprise of Technological Innovation in 2003.
- There has been a significant increase in employees' educational and occupational qualifications and skills levels since 2000. By 2003, over 57 per cent of employees held polytechnic qualifications or above compared with 45 per cent in 2000. Nearly 30 per cent of workers were in the 'senior' skill category compared with less than 20 per cent in 2000. More importantly, there was a saving of 3 million yuan in medical bills.
- There had been a dramatic increase in productivity from 17,410 yuan per employee in 2000 to 60,173 yuan per employee in 2003. The ratio of quality-related productivity loss was reduced from 59 yuan per 10,000 yuan output in 2000 to 14 yuan per 10,000 yuan output in 2003.
- Workplace disputes and grievances among workers were reduced to the minimum.

Case study 3.3 Trade Union Org.

Trade Union Org. (TU Org.) is a municipal trade union organization that is part of the municipal government in northern China. The management of TU Org. felt that the increasingly diverse and complicated nature of labour management relationships has rendered their traditional ways of working inappropriate. This has prompted their desire to become a 'learning organization'. Three aspects of 'learning' were specified:

1. study of political theory to provide ideological guidance for the trade union officials;
2. study of legislation and government policies to enhance the quality of the trade union officials; and
3. study of technical aspects of the job to enhance the competence of the trade union officials.

TU Org. specified that each trade union official (all full-time) must study at least two hours a day. At least 20,000 words of study notes must be taken a year and at least one article written and published as a result of this study. The idea is to make trade union officials more professional and competent.

Interpretation and configuration of a 'learning organization' in China

While learning and employee participation in workplace innovations have long been encouraged in socialist China, particularly in the state-owned enterprises (SOEs) (Cooke 2008b), the notion of a 'learning organization' is undoubtedly one of the new imports of western management philosophies and techniques. These imports are indicative of Chinese management's quest for effective management tools and their desire to be seen as modern and connected with the world. However, several questions arise from the adaptation of this idea. For example, what is the western prescription of a 'learning organization'? Is the western notion of a 'learning organization' compatible with Chinese management culture? Does the notion of a 'learning organization' offer a brand new management approach to workplace learning and innovation in China? What are the major characteristics of 'learning organizations' in China? We address these questions in this section.

Learning organizations – a western prescription

In spite of the critique from western academics of the practice-oriented and prescriptive literature of 'learning organizations' and their preference for 'organizational learning' (Argyris and Schon 1996: 180), there continues to be enthusiasm from employing organizations to pursue this ideal. The notion of 'learning organizations' is persuasive because of its human attractiveness and its claimed potential to facilitate organizational effectiveness and advancement (Senge 1990). According to Pedler et al. (1991), a learning organization is one that is committed to facilitating the learning of all its members and continuously transforms itself. The emphasis is on openness, support and a climate of trust and challenge. Such an emphasis stems from a unitary perspective of the organization (Harrison 2002). Watkins and Marsick (1993: 8–9) similarly define learning organization as one that captures, shares and utilizes knowledge to change the way the organization responds to challenges. They regard the following seven complementary action imperatives as central to learning organizations:

1. Create continuous learning opportunities (Continuous learning);
2. Promote inquiry and dialogue (Dialogue and Inquiry);
3. Encourage collaboration and team learning (Team Learning);
4. Empower people toward a collective vision (Empowerment);
5. Establish systems to capture and share learning (Embedded System);
6. Connect the organization to its environment (System Connection); and
7. Provide strategic leadership for learning (Strategic Leadership).

Birdi et al. (2005) believe that an innovation culture of an organization should include the following elements:

- integration of research and development;
- benchmarking operations internally and externally;
- direct involvement of customers;
- selecting innovative employees;
- acceptance of risk-taking;
- reward of innovation;
- training for creativity and innovation;
- developing a learning culture;
- involving and empowering employees in decision making; and
- developing managers to support the innovation of others.

Storey and Quintas (2001) also argue that similar HR practices need to be in place to support knowledge management, in addition to an appropriate organizational structure. Ortenblad (2002: 216–20) classifies existing perspectives of the 'learning organization' into four typologies. The first type is the earlier perspective of organizational learning which focuses on the storage of knowledge in the organizational mind. The second type views 'learning organization' as 'learning at work' where individuals learn at work on a continuous basis instead of on formalized courses. The third type is the 'learning climate' perspective in which a 'learning organization' is one that facilitates its employees to learn and to develop themselves through a supportive environment. The fourth perspective sees 'learning organization' as a 'learning structure' that is organic and flexible.

Approach to and configuration of learning organizations in China

To some extent, the prescriptive and unitary approach to learning organizations matches the traditional Chinese management style that is paternalistic and unitarist in which employees are expected to treat the company as their family (Cooke 2008b). Practices of 'learning organizations' in China as depicted in the previous section suggest that Chinese organizations tend to adopt the second and third approaches of Ortenblad's (2002) typologies. It is believed that the award-winning 'model learning organizations' share certain common characteristics that have led to their success. These include: treating human resource as the most important strategic resource; maintaining a supportive training and learning environment for employees so that learning becomes a natural part of their organizational activities; establishing a training system that is specific to their organizational needs; and turning learning outcomes and tacit knowledge into innovative ideas to enhance organizational performance (*Workers' Daily* 19 October 2004).

However, the unitarist approach typical of the Chinese management style carries a strong element of coerciveness and simplicity in which commitment, compliance and malleability of employee behaviour are taken for granted (see Figure 3.1).

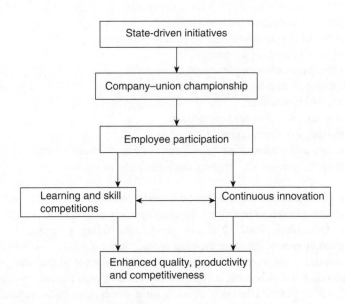

Figure 3.1 The Chinese approach to employee participation and innovation.
       Source: Cooke (2005b: 29).

While participation and empowerment are key elements of a learning organization, the Chinese management style and culture may not be conducive to 'ownership' or 'empowerment' (Elsey and Leung 2004). Despite the fact that task forces and problem-solving teams have long existed in SOEs to tackle specific technological and production problems and to undertake workplace innovations, these are largely elite teams that consist of a small number of highly motivated and skilled persons. There is no evidence that employee involvement en masse is a commonly adopted practice at workplaces. This is notably the case in manufacturing plants where the level of production technology is relatively low and Tayloristic work organization appears to be the predominant mode of production, especially in the foreign-invested plants (Cooke 2005a). In addition, Chinese managers have often been criticized for their deficiency of managerial skills and lack of willingness to learn (Chwee 1999; Zhang et al. 2004). When implementing the *chuangzheng* initiative, Chinese managers may be merely following top-down orders passively instead of genuinely supporting their people to innovate as part of their management competence.

The state-driven learning initiative *chuangzheng* has undoubtedly encouraged an increasing number of organizations to adopt the notion of learning organization. However, there is a danger that companies are following it just as a management fashion without understanding what it really means for them. The term 'learning organization' is taken for granted without necessarily defining what it means and how it is to be configured at the organizational level. For example, who decides that the company will become a learning organization? What criteria are used to measure whether or not an organization has achieved that status? There appears to be no specific criteria in the country or industry, nor is there any professional accreditation body to monitor the consistency of practices and outcomes. No independent measurements are adopted to assess the claimed impact of learning organizations, both financially and socially. The only examples so far have been the reported achievements of award-winning organizations.

While the perceived need to build learning organizations in China is driven down from the top, organizations have autonomy as to how they interpret what constitutes the practice of a learning organization. For example, the three case studies already outlined reveal that while some generic elements of what constitutes a learning organization exist across the three organizations that are in line with what are prescribed in western literature, the organizations appear to be imaginative and elastic in configuring their learning organization practices. It is also evident that none of the 'learning organizations' have incorporated all the elements prescribed in the literature (Watkins and Marsick 1993; Birdi et al. 2005). What is more, it is unclear whether these reported practices are post-rationalization or part of the strategic plan at the outset.

What is clear, however, is that many of the learning organization practices adopted have long existed in state-owned enterprises in China. For example, the promotion of 'role models' has been a favourite approach adopted by the Chinese socialist state to convey its ideology and behavioural norms. Skill and craftsmanship competition has long been a part of enterprise life in SOEs dated back to the early 1950s as an important means to boost workforce morale and to raise the level of skills and productivity during the early period of economic development of socialist China. There has long been a culture of employee involvement (e.g. suggestion schemes and problem-solving teams) in larger and aspiring SOEs in the improvization and innovation of production technology and production process, albeit this culture was not as widespread as it could (Cooke 2008b). In fact, one of the key tasks for trade unions at the workplace level in China has been to help increase productivity through organizing workers to participate in skill training and skill contests, suggestion schemes and innovations (see next section for discussion). Similarly, China has a traditional culture of grassroots-led competition in all sorts of cultural activities. More broadly, continuous learning and self-development has for centuries been regarded as a virtue in Chinese culture which has inspired people to undertake learning activities after they have completed their formal education and beyond their workplace requirements.

The role of the trade unions in skill development

The Chinese trade unions fall within the 'authoritarian' category as one of the 'state instruments', carrying out a 'decisively subordinate role' that is 'concerned with *both* production and protection' (Martin 1989: 78). The welfare role of the Chinese trade unions has been widely noted, as has been their incapacity to defend workers' rights and interests (e.g. Taylor et al. 2003; Clarke 2005; Warner 2008, also see chapters 7 and 8). By contrast, the trade unions' other key role is much less known. That is, as noted above, to help increase productivity through organizing workers to participate in skill training and contests, suggestion schemes and innovation activities. According to the Trade Union Law (2001),

> the trade union shall mobilize and organize the employees to participate in the economic development actively, and to complete the production and work assignments conscientiously, educate the employees to improve their ideological thoughts and ethics, technological and professional, scientific and cultural qualities, and build an employee team with ideals, ethics, education and discipline.
>
> (Article 7)

For example, it was reported that in 2007, nearly 7.3 million valid suggestion schemes for productivity enhancement were put forward by the grassroots trade unions at the workplace level, 3.9 million of which had been adopted. A total of 42.2 million employees participated in work competitions, and another 14 million employees participated in skill contests organized by the workplace unions. In addition, 32.1 million employees had received training organized by the workplace unions (*China Labour Statistical Yearbook 2008*).

Trade union branches above the workplace level are under the dual control (or 'leadership' as it is described) of the local government at their level and their organizational branch at a higher level. A significant proportion of the government-funded/controlled job centres and training centres are operated by the trade unions primarily to help laid-off workers regain employment. According to official statistics, trade unions in 2007 had a total of 2,924 vocational training institutions providing training to 9 million workers nationwide. In addition, there were 2,761 job centres operated by the trade unions in 2007, receiving 3.6 million yuan subsidy from the government. These organizations had reportedly found jobs for over 7 million workers, 4.6 million of whom were laid-off or urban unemployed workers – in the same year, there were a total of 3.5 million laid-off workers and 15.6 million urban unemployed workers nationwide (*China Labour Statistical Yearbook 2008*).

The above statistics, notwithstanding the issue of (in)accuracy of official statistics, only outlines the level of employment, training and productivity enhancement activities that trade union organizations are involved in as part of their official responsibilities. It shows another dimension of how the state mobilizes traditional institutional actors such as the trade unions as its subordinate actor to organize employment and HRM/HRD activities both within and outside the workplace. It does not by any means indicate the level of effectiveness and engagement of workers that these activities have engendered. It is also important to note that the functional priority of the ACFTU branches and consequently resource allocation for their activities may have changed significantly since 2008 in part due to the enactment of the Labour Contract Law and the Labour Disputes Mediation and Arbitration Law (see Chapter 8 for a detailed discussion). Due to resource constraints, ACFTU organizations need to juggle their priority between productivity activities and labour dispute settlements.

Employers' training practices

Level of training provision

Training and development is widely seen as one of the key components of the high-performance/commitment model of HRM practices. Yet, Chinese firms have been criticized for their under-investment in training and development (e.g. Cooke 2005a; T. Li, 2005). Talent shortage and poaching has made many Chinese firms cautious in allocating resources for human resource development for fear of staff turnover. This has resulted in insufficient provision of training and development for employees. For example, Yang and Li's (2008) study found that a significant proportion of university graduate employees in the Beijing area had never received any training from their employer due to the latter's concern about employee retention problems.

In the author's (Cooke 2009c) study of 65 private firms in a wide range of industries in 2007–8, the managers interviewed all bemoaned the shortage of competent professionals and managers with all-round skills and desirable personality, particularly people management skills. As one manager from a finance company remarked:

> All my key staff are hard working, but they are not competent or experienced enough. I find it difficult to devolve responsibility to them in case they make a mess. I have to keep an eye on their work all the time and sometimes ended up doing their job for them. It makes me exhausted and left me with no time to develop the business which is my job.

Paradoxically, the decision as to whether to train staff or not in order to develop their key employees is a major issue facing the vast majority of the firms. Many managers interviewed expressed the dilemma of whether to invest in training their key personnel. This has resulted in insufficient training provided to employees. When asked if their employees were happy with the skill training opportunities provided by the company, 39 managers (60 per cent) believed that their employees were only averagely happy, while 21 (32 per cent) actually believed that their employees were not happy with the training provided by the company. The following comments reveal some of the dilemmas:

> They all want to be trained, preferably by being sent abroad to visit advanced western companies or to go on EMBA courses. If you train them, they leave as soon as they finish the course. If you don't train them, they leave sooner. EMBA course costs a lot of money but we still send them on it in order to retain them. This can only keep them for a bit longer.
>
> (CEO of a software development firm)

> We send them overseas to broaden their experience and to learn from advanced MNCs' practices. They come back and wanting promotion and pay rise.
>
> (HR director of a hotel chain)

Indeed, recent studies showed a negative relationship between career development and organizational performance. For example, Wang and Wang's (2008) study showed that career development actually led to reduced competitiveness of the firm perhaps due to the turnover of high performers. Similarly, Chow and Liu (2009) argued that the relatively high staff turnover rate could significantly undermine the benefits of employee development.

Some firms adopt a less expensive way of training. For example, some companies in Cooke's (2009c) study introduced an employee-led training programme in which individual employees take the lead to provide a training session to colleagues on a certain topic, such as the latest law or regulation, after self-studying the topic first. This method of training was reported by managers to have good effect. Individuals are motivated to prepare for the topic and others are participative in discussions. It not only gives opportunities for employees to develop their presentation skills and logical thinking skills, but also creates a learning and collegial environment in the workplace. One firm felt that the training effect was so good that the initiative was introduced to its subsidiaries. Managers did report that training sessions carried out during working hours are well attended, but enthusiasm dimmed dramatically if the session was organized outside normal working hours.

A number of studies in the 2000s suggest that training investments from employers have shown signs of moderate increase. However, these investments are far from sufficient and are unevenly spread across ownership forms and groups of employees (e.g. T. Li 2005; Au et al. 2008; S. Zhao 2008; Hutchings et al. 2009). For example, S. Zhao's (2008) study revealed that 35 per cent of the sample firms seldom had a training budget and over 28 per cent had only 1 per cent of their wage bill as the training budget. Another 20 per cent had between 1 and 2 per cent of their wage bill as the training budget. Au et al.'s (2008: 19) study of Hong Kong firms operating in the Pearl River Delta area (south-east of China) revealed that sample firms adopted 'a highly differentiated human capital policy' in that training investment in the low-skilled staff is minimal, whereas staff at the intermediate and senior level 'are deemed appropriate for such investment'. In addition, Au et al. (2008) found that firms were more inclined to invest in non-transferable skills than transferable skills, such as degree programmes, for retention purposes.

Similarly, Hutchings et al.'s (2009) survey of 310 semi-skilled and skilled employees in China found that 45 per cent of the employees reported having training in their first week of employment, but less than one-third of respondents reported continuous training on-the-job provided by their organization. On a more positive note, nearly 72 per cent of the employees reported that they had received off-the-job training from their employer during working hours. In addition, some 40 per cent of respondents reported that they had received off-the-job training provided by their organization outside working hours. Training provision was largely initiated by the organization. Individual requests for training that fell outside the scope of this provision were rarely accommodated. Whilst the majority of respondents admitted that the training and development provided by their employer had increased their overall competence and performance level, their engagement in the training activities had not led to a pay rise (over 52 per cent of respondents reported having no pay rise), or to promotion (36 per cent reported having no promotion).

In some organizations, training perks are not fairly allocated even amongst the same group of employees. For example, the author's study of two state-owned municipal hospitals in 2010 revealed that training opportunities for nurses are allocated by managers who may use these opportunities to reward their favourite staff because some training opportunities are off-site at a holiday resort. Going on this kind of training course is like going for a semi-holiday. Staff on training receive the same level of bonuses as those working full-time in the busiest hours.

According to Chen et al. (2009), 41 per cent of the 1,875 firms surveyed across the country used internal training as the main mode of training delivery.

Basic skills (48 per cent) and specialist/technical knowledge (45 per cent) formed the bulk of the training. Only 52 per cent of the firms reported that the training met expectations. These findings indicate that the training provisions in Chinese firms are still narrowly focusing on the technical aspects of the job with little consideration of soft skills that may be important for the job and career development which may help increase staff retention.

Another national survey study of enterprise training (T. Li 2005) also revealed that more than half of the surveyed enterprises do not have a formal written training plan in place that is implemented. More specifically, organizations in the state-owned sector have the highest incidence of training plans and implementation (62 per cent). This is followed by foreign-invested/joint-venture firms (45 per cent). Privately owned firms had the lowest percentage (38 per cent). The same study also showed that the larger the firm size, the more likely the firm would adopt a training plan. However, only less than 35 per cent of the firms would conduct a training needs analysis prior to the training and carry out the training accordingly. Again, private firms scored the lowest in this category (24 per cent). This finding is supported by that of Yang and Wang's (2009) study which showed that entrepreneurs in privately owned small and medium-sized enterprises tend to focus more on capital and markets than human resource development. They typically adopt a transactional cost approach to managing the labour–capital/management relationship.

By contrast, highly educated employees working in large and knowledge-intensive firms receive a much more comprehensive package of training and development support from their employer. For example, Huawei Technologies Ltd (a leading Chinese privately owned IT MNC) established Huawei University in 2005 to provide tailored training courses to its employees and customers. New employees receive one to six months induction training at the university on corporate culture, product knowledge, marketing and sales techniques, and product development standards, etc. The university is responsible for training and developing workers, technicians, managers and future leaders of Huawei. Employees and managers from overseas subsidiaries are selected and sent to Huawei headquarters for training and development in order for them to better understand Huawei's product and marketing strategy. They are expected to internalize Huawei's corporate culture and business process and disseminate it back home. Chinese employees are also sent abroad for assignments to gain wider experience of the product and to understand local customers' needs and technical environment. Cross-functional teamworking between design and application is encouraged to help research and development (R&D) engineers to understand the field situation.

Though less well versed than Huawei in its corporate statements on HRD, Huawei's major competitor ZTE (state-invested), another leading Chinese IT firm founded in 1985, also stresses the importance of employee career development and benefits. A training and development academy is in place in the headquarters to deliver most of the activities. As the majority of its employees are university graduates and are engaged in high-tech production activities, induction training and continuous training are key features, though technical skill acquisition remains the key component of training. Similar to the employee development paths offered by Huawei, ZTE employees are given 'Three Career Development Paths' in which they can choose to follow a technology, service or management career. Like Huawei, Chinese employees may be sent abroad to broaden their knowledge and experience and host-country national employees may be selected for technical training and management development in ZTE (China). It is clear that the ambition to become a major global player in the IT and telecom industry and the nature of the business have encourage both Huawei and ZTE to invest heavily in training and developing their professional and managerial staff. Both firms employ prestigious international consultancy firms to help them design management processes and systems, including some of the HRM programmes. The HRM programmes and policy statements of Huawei and ZTE show a relatively high level of resemblance to those of prestigious foreign MNCs, although the substance still bears many Chinese characteristics, notably corporate culture and work ethics.

Mentoring as a new HR technique

Research evidence suggests that mentoring is being adopted by MNCs and leading Chinese firms as a formal HRM scheme for employee development. The mentoring system is different from the traditional apprentice system adopted in China, particularly in the SOEs during the state planned economy era. The apprentice system focuses on the development of craft/technical skills and behavioural conduct/personality of the protégé within the moral framework defined by the socialist state. By contrast, the mentoring system that is promoted in the western HR literature and adopted by a small albeit increasing number of firms in China has a broader focus. In principle, the mentor is not only responsible for inducting the mentee into the system of the organization, but also instrumental in guiding the career development of the mentee. The emphasis is on both the professional development and personal growth of the mentee and to align their needs with that of the organization. Here, the mentor plays an important role in sharing his/her knowledge about the organization with the mentee, hence re-enforcing the organizational culture. For example, mentoring forms an important part of the training and development system for junior professional employees in Huawei Technologies Ltd. Mentoring is an integral part of the supervisor/mentor's job and their performance in this role forms part of the formal assessment in their performance appraisal (Cooke 2010a).

While mentoring has long existed in China as an informal organizational practice, sometimes without the awareness of either the mentor or the mentee, it is the formal mentoring system developed in the western HRM literature that is being promoted in China. Despite the fact that many foreign MNCs and Chinese MNCs have introduced a mentoring system, a common problem is its patchy implementation contingent upon individual mentors' competence, willingness and preference in their role. For example, an informant from KPMG (China) revealed to the author that some mentors (known as counsellors) meet with their mentee regularly and provide counselling support beyond what the company specifies, whereas some mentees rarely have opportunities to meet with their mentors other than their annual meeting to fill in their annual appraisal form as a formality. More revealingly, the majority of mentors are female senior colleagues as it is believed that women are more suited to the role (Cooke 2011c).

Emerging role of employers' associations and local institutions

In western economies, employers' associations are relatively well developed as a labour market institution. By comparison, this institutional force in the Chinese economy remains relatively weak but is nonetheless growing (see Chapter 8). Although skill training at the enterprise level has so far been largely determined by individual enterprises or left to their own devices, there are emerging signs that employers are beginning to organize themselves to defend their interests, as we can see from Box 3.1.

Box 3.1 The role of employers' association in developing a skilled workforce and regulating the labour market in a local shipbuilding industry

At the grassroots level, an unofficial local shipbuilding firms' association newly emerged to address shipbuilding business needs in an industrial city in Guangdong Province offers a revealing example of how employers are beginning to organize themselves to protect their interests. The shipbuilding industry of the city consists of six small cargo shipbuilding firms located adjacent to each other, each with fewer than 80 workers. They are all privately owned and emerged in the last few years as large and debt-ridden state-owned building firms in nearby cities and provinces have collapsed one after another. According to one of the shipbuilding business owners (Mr Lu, interviewed in April 2009), the association began to form amongst the owners in 2008 to deal with the following issues:

1. To prevent wage wars. Due to the shortage of shipbuilding workers in the local labour market, workers may be lured to other shipbuilding firms by higher wages, a vicious circle would then emerge and by the time a worker returns to the same shipyard, his wage would have gone up by 10 per cent. In addition, some subcontractors may be able to hire more workers and make faster progress with the building work at the expense of other shipbuilding firms, as they all tap into the same pool

of labour. In order to prevent this, all owners of the shipbuilding firms reached an agreement that they will set the same wage level to prevent poaching.

2. To agree on the price for building ships in principle. A firm can reduce the price by no more than 5 per cent when it has no business. This is to maintain the profit level of the industry.

3. To form a pressure group to request the municipal seafaring authority to: 1) speed up the process of approving the new ships so that ship owners can get their ships as early as possible. The unexpected surge of business during the financial/banking crisis[1] means that the authority is understaffed and cannot cope with the volume of business; and 2) organize skill training (via training providers) for welding and shipbuilding basics. Qualified trainees are given a training certificate which allows them to work in the shipbuilding industry. According to the shipbuilding regulation, ship welding requires a specialized welding licence. Each shipbuilding site must have a minimum number of welders with this kind of licence to operate. The shortage of qualified welders is constraining the size of the shipbuilding operation, hence the demand for training from the shipbuilding business owners.

According to Mr Lu, the seafaring authority is more responsive to their requests in a collective manner than when demands are made by firms individually. Each ship approval brings revenue to the authority, so there is a business incentive (officially and unofficially) for the authority to address shipbuilding firms' legitimate demands and complaints. As noted above, the relationship between employers/employers' associations and the local government is economic as well as political, often through the close personal relationship between business owners/senior managers and government officials as their key contacts. In the case here, the shipbuilding firms' association, despite being an informal association loosely formed in order to solve business problems, has been able to mobilize external training resources through the local government to provide skill training for the industry at the municipal level. Such training provision proves vital for the survival and sustainable growth of the shipbuilding business as part of the local economy.

Source: interview data collected by the author in 2009.

1 Ship owners are investing in new ships to take advantage of the lowering prices of shipbuilding materials and bank loan interest during the financial crisis, foreseeing that by the time the ship is ready, the economy will have recovered sufficiently for new businesses.

In well-organized/developed industrial districts, such as industrial parks and export manufacturing zones, where firms may be engaged in similar production and require similar skills, employers may not always respond to skill shortages by poaching and maintaining a wage premium. Instead, they may choose a combination of progressive action to secure their skilled labour supply in collaboration with the local institutions. For example, Li and Sheldon's (2010) study of over 40 electronics plants in Suzhou Industrial Park found that the majority of the employers do provide in-house skill training as well as develop collaborative training programmes with the local vocational education and training schools to meet their skills needs. This is in spite of the fact that most of the employers felt that the latter are deficient in delivering effective training. Only a small proportion of the employers felt that poaching is a threat to their training investment. Here the concentration of plants in one area (i.e. the industrial park), their significance to the local economy and the tight local labour market prove to be important factors in facilitating the development of collaborative action amongst employers and other local institutional actors to safeguard their collective interest. It must be noted that the majority of the firms in Li and Sheldon's (2010) study are wholly foreign-owned plants. It is unclear if domestic firms will adopt similar strategies to combat skill shortage.

Conclusion

This chapter has reviewed the role of the state in HRD in China, with particular reference to a state-led learning and innovation initiative – the '*chuangzheng*' programme. Evidence suggests that the term 'learning organization' has been borrowed from the western management literature as a new platform for organizations in China to relaunch some of their traditional practices to combat skill shortages and to enhance organizational performance. Due to the limitation of space and empirical data, the chapter has taken a broad brush approach. More detailed studies are needed to investigate the extent to which Chinese firms aspire to be learning organizations, the extent to which 'learning organization' offers a genuinely new approach to management and workplace learning, the extent to which a government initiative can be implemented effectively at the operational level, and what support is needed from the government to ensure enduring success.

Equally, a more systematic analysis is also needed to map out the compatibility of the prescribed conditions for a learning organization and the Chinese institutional environment to achieve these conditions. There is currently an absence of debate amongst academics and practitioners in China as to what 'learning organization' means in the Chinese context and in what ways it is similar to and different from the western approaches. Instead, there is a dangerous passion, or rather, fashion, in which 'learning organization' as a western imported concept is embraced uncritically as a progressive given. As we have seen from the case studies, considerable variations exist in the understanding, interpretation and configuration of the concept, a situation which one may justify as 'learning organization with Chinese characteristics'.

Lack of critical awareness notwithstanding, the 'learning organization' initiative is necessarily another step forward for Chinese management towards a more systematic approach to HRD and innovation. It is an example of Chinese management's readiness to adopt western management techniques, at least in name if not in practice. An important management implication is that a more informed and strategic approach is needed when designing and implementing the learning organization initiative. In other words, the initiative has to be part of the business strategy. Adequate support systems, both technical and psychological, have to be in place to facilitate learning and knowledge management. This requires organizational leaders to be more strategic, a requirement that may be challenging to Chinese managers because management competence is considered relatively low in China, especially at strategic level (see Chapter 9 for further discussion).

What is important is that enterprises appear to be paying more attention to training and investing more in it. If employees are receiving more training, having more opportunities to develop and utilize the skills and knowledge that benefit their company and are being rewarded appropriately for those skills, then what a 'learning organization' really means in China is perhaps not a philosophical puzzle that needs to be unravelled urgently. As Deng Xiaoping, the great architect of contemporary Chinese economy, was once famously quoted as saying, 'It does not matter whether it is a white cat or a black cat, as long as it catches the mouse'. However, it is important to note that the state influence in promoting HDR initiatives is mainly within the state sector, where there has always been a relatively high level of state involvement/intervention in training policy and practice (Cooke 2005a). As research evidence shows, training provision in the majority of private sector firms remain largely patchy, unsystematic and under-invested, with the exception of prestigious MNCs particularly in the knowledge-intensive sector.

Due to space constraints, we have not been able to cover more extensively any new developments in vocational education, trends in the external training market, and the role of individuals and their families in skill development and life-long learning. Investing in education and life-long learning is a Confucian virtue that is highly valued in Chinese society (Yang and Wang 2009). It must be stressed here that, as marketization deepens and the Chinese middle class grows, the state and employers are no longer the main investors in HRD. For example, in 1992, government funding made up 84 per cent of the total education funds. By 2006, this was reduced to 64 per cent (*China Statistical Yearbook 2008*). For many families with dependent children, education is often their single largest item of expenditure. Since the 2000s, there has been a dramatic rise in the number of Chinese students going abroad to seek higher education, especially at the postgraduate level. Over 90 per cent of them are family- or self-funded (Yang and Wang 2009; also see *China Statistical Yearbook 2009*).

'This has changed the nature of overseas study from elite education in [the] 1980s and 1990s to mass education in the mid 2000s' (Yang and Wang 2009: 11). And an increasing number of these overseas returnees face difficulties in gaining quality employment, as noted in Chapter 2 (also see Cooke 2008a; Yang and Wang 2009).

4   Performance management[1]

Introduction

Performance management, including appropriate target setting, performance appraisal and reward, is a key element in human resource management. Performance management is currently being promoted as a modern western HRM concept in China. This is in spite of the fact that performance appraisal practices have long existed in China with strong Chinese characteristics. This chapter first provides an overview of the historical development of the performance appraisal system during the state-planned economy period and the ensuing economic reform period. A number of key characteristics and pitfalls in performance appraisal practices are then identified. Some of them are generic in many parts of the world, while others are unique to Chinese cultural values. The chapter also reveals unique challenges to performance management facing organizations in different business sectors. It also examines the types of performance management practices firms adopt. In particular, we analyse for what purposes performance management (e.g. reward, development) is being used by organizations in China and evaluate the extent to which performance management is being deployed strategically by firms to enhance organizational performance.

While a level of simplicity is inevitable in a chapter that is to summarize the performance management practices of a vast country, this chapter avoids a broad brush approach as far as possible by drawing specific examples from primary and secondary empirical data. The primary empirical data came from the semi-structured interviews which the author conducted during 2005 and 2009 with government officials and civil servants as well as managers from state-owned and privately owned companies. The secondary empirical data came from studies published in academic and practitioners' journals as well as scholarly books in both the English and Chinese language. Together, these primary and secondary empirical data sets provide balanced information that covers organizations of different sizes and ownership forms, and different categories of employees and sectors. This spread of coverage is essential because these contingent factors may have significant influence in the way the performance management system is designed, implemented, utilized and perceived by both managers and employees.

For example, performance appraisal may be more widely used in government and civil service organizations in part because it is an established part of their HRM, but performance measurement can be more subjective due to the perceived need to emphasize the ideological dimensions and due to the difficulties of quantifying performance level compared with enterprises. It is these nuances that make the comparisons of performance appraisal/management systems across different organizations and sectors in China more interesting and informative.

Development of performance management system

In line with the development of its personnel management system, the development of the performance management system in China can be divided into two broad periods.[2] The first period was the state-planned economy period during which performance appraisal for ordinary workers mainly focused on attendance monitoring and skill grading tests. The former was used as the basis for wage deduction whereas the latter for pay rises. Since wage increases were frozen during the Cultural Revolution period (1966–76), skill grading tests were in effect not carried out. In addition, personal character traits were used as part of the criteria in evaluating an employee's performance. For the professional and managerial staff (broadly classified as state cadres), performance appraisal was used primarily as a means to select and develop cadres and as evidence for promotion (Zhu and Dowling 1998). In the early years of socialist China, political and technical elites were promoted. However, during the Cultural Revolution period, political performance (e.g. loyalty to the Communist Party) and moral integrity were the key criteria of performance measurement instead of technical competence and productivity. Organizational leaders were not enthusiastic in conducting performance appraisal in part because they lacked informative job specifications and performance indicators and in part because they found the exercise time-consuming (Chou 2005). Another important feature in the performance management system during this period was employee recognition. That is, the recognition of role model employees whose conduct was deemed exemplary of societal values. Its purpose was to embed social moral and ethical values in the workplace.

The second period started from the early 1980s till the present, i.e. the period of market economic development. During this period, and particularly since the 1990s, performance appraisal systems have been more widely and systematically adopted by organizations. For example, Björkman and Lu's (1999) study of 72 foreign-invested enterprises in China found that nearly half of them had adapted their western performance appraisal system to suit Chinese culture. Ding et al.'s (1997: 611) study of 158 foreign-invested enterprises in southern China showed that 'regular evaluation of individual employee performance and setting employee pay levels based on individual performance have become organizational norms'. They also found that workers were receptive of individual-oriented performance measurement and reward in order to maximize their income. However, it must be noted that performance review here is mainly used to determine pay. In fact, performance-related pay is the main method for setting pay rates in the majority of foreign-invested manufacturing plants where workers, many of them rural migrant workers, work extremely long hours in order to increase their wage income.

Performance management practices of firms in different ownership forms and sectors

Research evidence in the 1990s and 2000s revealed some diverse practices in performance management across different sectors and ownership forms, with some being more pro-western practice than others (also see Box 4.1). For example, Lindholm's (1999) survey of 604 Chinese managerial and professional employees from MNCs in China found that they were satisfied with the western-styled performance management system adopted by their company. They particularly liked the developmental approach in the system and were keen to participate in setting their performance objectives and to receive formal performance feedback. It must be noted that prestigious MNCs in China are attractive to those who have strong career aspirations and desire development opportunities (also see chapters 2 and 3).

Bai and Bennington's (2005) study of the Chinese state-owned enterprises in the coal-mining industry revealed that as a result of increasing pressure from intensified market competition, Chinese SOEs were utilizing modern performance appraisal measures as effective tools to enhance their management efficiency and productivity. Their study showed that whilst differences from western performance appraisal practices persist, significant changes are taking place in performance appraisal practices in China that depart from its traditional form. Taormina and Gao's (2009) study similarly revealed that a western approach to performance appraisal can be accepted by Chinese employees, if performance criteria are carefully selected and their suitability established in consultation with employees.

Performance management also became a top priority in the management of government and civil service organizations since the mid-1990s, as part of the state's broader initiative of reforming its civil service function (Cooke 2003). In particular, the 'Provisional Regulations for State Civil Servants' (hereafter 'Regulations') was implemented in 1993. The Regulations placed great emphasis on recruitment, performance appraisal/assessment, promotion, reward and disciplinary procedures in order to improve the transparency and efficiency of the personnel administration. The Regulations were replaced by the first Civil Servant Law of China which took effect on 1 January 2006.[3] The government officials and civil servants whom the author has interviewed commonly reported that their municipal governments have adopted a type of 'management by objective' scheme where performance targets are cascaded down from each level and reviewed on an annual basis.

Cooke's (2009c) study of 65 private firms found that about one-third of the companies reported having introduced a formal performance appraisal scheme that links performance to reward. According to the managers interviewed, this has had a substantial impact on increasing employees' wage income and motivation. Interview data also suggest that the majority of firms focus on quantitative measurement in their performance management which encourages/forces employees to work harder and harder, with financial gain as the main incentive. This performance target is short-term oriented, often on an annual basis. Only a small number of firms are looking for longer-term performance targets. For example, the CEO of a real estate firm reported that his firm was moving towards a longer-range target – from an annual to a three-year target. This, he believed, would save the firm from making targets each year and allow employees more scope to adjust their performance level over a longer period – if they over-perform one year, they can underachieve the following year for whatever reasons without being penalized financially. According to the CEO, this is a good method for a maturing firm when growth is slowing down. It also projects a longer vision to the employees so that they know three years in advance what they need to achieve and what their financial return will be if targets are met. This helps prevent them from leaving the firm.

The same study also found that performance management was used for retention, grading and development purposes by some firms. These have both positive and unintended effects, as observed by some managers:

> Performance appraisal is a two-edge sword. We have a six-monthly appraisal scheme in which poor performers will be made redundant. This has deterred some good candidates from coming to join us. We have problems in attracting talent.
>
> (A manager of a hotel)

> We use performance-related appraisal to determine grades of employees and provide training and career development opportunities for well-performing employees. This has good effect. We have had rapid business growth in recent years.
>
> (A manager of a trading company)

Research evidence from MNCs in China (including Chinese-owned MNCs) points to a diverse range of practices in their performance management. For example, in ZTE and Huawei, the two leading Chinese-owned IT/telecom MNCs in which 50 per cent of the workforce are R&D engineers, performance pressure is internalized and employees are expected to be self-motivated. Long working hours and performance-related pay are the norms. As an established corporate culture, Huawei's employees have a tradition of bringing their sleeping cushions to the office and working there for nearly 18 hours a day, catching only a brief nap underneath the desk when exhausted. The sleeping cushion is seen as a symbol of Huawei's hard-working culture. Aspiring young graduate employees feel the peer pressure to work long hours and achieve results. Huawei's corporate ethos is that those who can endure hardship and are prepared to research hard will get a good return. Each year employees of Huawei go through their performance assessment, the bottom 3–5 per cent of performers will be dismissed, and a similar proportion of managerial staff who are deemed poor performers will also be demoted or dismissed (Cooke 2011c).

Headquartered in Shenzhen, both firms were established in the 1980s when the IT industry in China was in its embryonic form but was ready to take off. Each firm had operations and representative offices in more than 100 countries, employing over 40,000 (ZTE) and 60,000 (Huawei) employees respectively by the mid-2000s. For both firms, working overtime on short notice is a common staffing measure to meet targets and to provide prompt customer service. Managers interviewed by the author admitted that Chinese expatriates in their overseas subsidiaries have been subject to overtime work more than host-country nationals because 'we have more control over our own people and they are more used to the Company's culture [of high performance pressure and excessive overtime]' (manager, Huawei). Chinese expatriates who are deemed unsuitable for their overseas assignments will be repatriated and repositioned. Some of them would be dismissed if they failed to perform adequately in their new posts (Cooke 2011c).

Interestingly, not all western MNCs take a developmental approach to manage their managers in China, as evidenced in ServiceCo (pseudonym), a French-owned subsidiary in Shanghai that provides cleaning, catering, security and facilities maintenance services to industrial parks and commercial centres/ shopping malls. ServiceCo has been encountering serious staff turnover problems amongst its low-grade staff (approximately 1,800 employees). Poor people management skills of the line managers have been identified as the main cause of the company's retention problem. In order to address the problem, ServiceCo introduced employee retention rate as one of the key performance indicators for its line managers. This proved to have some positive effects. In addition, managerial staff are given a selection of company benefits, flexible working time, holidays, pay rises, performance-related pay and company-sponsored training. However, there are limited management development activities in place to help managers improve their people management skills. According to the HR director, the HR department plays mainly an administrative role, with no strategic input in the business. None of the staff, including the HR director, working in the HR department have HR qualifications or come from an HR background. There is no formal HR policy in ServiceCo (Cooke 2011c).

Key factors influencing the performance management system

A number of key factors influence performance management systems in China, mainly in the design of the performance indicators and the process of conducting performance appraisals. While some factors are generic to performance management in many parts of the world, others are specific to the Chinese cultural and institutional context.

Influence of organizational size, ownership and business nature

Variations in HRM practices tend to exist as a result of differences in organizational size, ownership form and business nature of the firm. The same is true in the performance management system in China. For example, M. Z. Chen et al.'s (2004) study of 100 enterprises of various sizes in the IT industry found that, compared with larger firms, smaller enterprises tended to focus on individuals' quality and competence in their appraisal system, including attitude, work intensity, moral integrity and position, and neglected the evaluation of team performance or the quality of customer services. The study also revealed that employees in smaller firms paid more attention to the utilization of their competence, had lower demands for, and expectation from, the performance appraisal system, and were more easily satisfied and motivated than their counterparts in larger firms. In addition, appraisal outcomes in smaller firms were more heavily influenced by the subjective impression of the superior, whereas the intervention of subjectivity was better avoided in larger firms.

Whilst sharing some similarities, the performance management system applied to ordinary employees tends to differ from that for professional/managerial staff. These differences become even more significant between enterprises and government/civil service organizations. Generally speaking, performance appraisal for ordinary workers in China was mainly about linking their productivity and level of responsibility with their wage and bonuses in order to motivate them to work towards the organizational goals (see Table 4.1). This is in spite of the fact that an employee's moral behaviour continues to be part of the appraisal in many state-owned enterprises. By contrast, results of performance appraisals for professional and managerial staff, particularly those in government and civil service organizations, are often linked to annual bonuses and promotion. The state also has a much more hands-on role in designing the performance indicators for government officials and civil servants. In 1998, the Ministry of Personnel introduced a new performance appraisal scheme for evaluating civil servants (Chou 2005). The scheme focused on four main performance indictors as criteria for assessing civil servants' performance: *De* (morality), *neng* (competence/ability), *qin* (diligence/work attitude), *ji* (achievement). Many organizations added another indicator *lian* (honesty/non-corrupted) to the four as corrupted behaviour became relatively widespread amongst government officials and civil servants.

A number of studies have observed the differences in ownership forms in their emphasis of good citizenship behaviour (e.g. Farh et al. 2004). For example, state-owned enterprises stress more on altruism, whereas private firms are more efficiency oriented. Some of these behavioural norms are a Chinese characteristic (Farh et al. 2004).

In principle, performance appraisal for all employees focuses on two aspects: behaviour measurement and outcome measurement. These include the employee's moral and ideological behaviour, competence, skill level and ability to apply skills and knowledge to work, work attitude, work performance and

Table 4.1 Key characteristics in performance assessment/appraisal practices in China

	Main characteristics for enterprise workers	Main characteristics for government officials and civil servants
Purposes of assessment	Financial reward, job grading, job retention	Financial reward, routine appraisal, promotion and grading
Measurements of performance	More quantifiable hard targets Effort (e.g. attendance, work attitude), output (e.g. productivity)	Hard as well as 'soft' criteria Four or five norms *De* (morality), *neng* (competence/ability), *qin* (diligence/work attitude), *ji* (achievement), *lian* (honesty/non-corrupted)
Methods of assessment	Top-down assessment, self-evaluation Tests to compete for posts – 'last one in the assessment out' practices	Self-appraisal, collective/peer appraisal discussion meetings as acts of democracy, top-down assessment, bottom-up appraisal
Frequency of assessment	Monthly, quarterly, six-monthly, and annual (end-of-the-year) appraisals	Six-monthly and annual (end-of-the-year) appraisals
Implementation process	Relatively easier to conduct appraisal/assessment due to more specific purpose and outcome	More problematic to conduct appraisal due to less quantifiable criteria, more complex relationship with peers/superior, and organizational politics Greater level of subjectivity and intervention
Utilization of outcome	Linked to financial reward Little link to training and development Little feedback from superior	Linked to bonus and promotion Little link to training and development Little feedback from superior
Persistent cultural influence v. adaptation of western HR practices	Harmonization, egalitarian norm More widespread adaptation of western-style performance appraisal as part of modernized HR practices to enhance organizational performance	Harmonization, egalitarian norm Less influenced by individualistic performance-related reward pressure More cautious adaptation of western HR practices due to sectoral and ideological differences
Acceptance of performance appraisal practices	More receptive to performance-related reward due to job insecurity and the financial pressure of individuals	More resistant to performance appraisal due to greater level of subjectivity in appraisal criteria and intervention in process

Source: compiled by the author.

achievement, personal attributes, physical health and so forth. It has been noted (e.g. Chou 2005) that the importance of political integrity is now significantly downplayed by leaders in government organizations because of the need to have competent cadres to deliver government functions effectively.

Broadly speaking, performance appraisals for ordinary employees in enterprises tend to be held on a more regular basis than those for government officials and civil servants. This is mainly because the outcome of the former is often directly linked to their financial reward and job security (see Table 4.1). The methods of assessment/appraisal used for ordinary employees in enterprises are also simpler, mainly between the supervisor and the individual being appraised. In some enterprises, the practice of 'competing for the post' is implemented in which the employee who comes last in the test will be removed from the post, receive retraining before returning to the post and made redundant if he/she comes last again (Cooke 2005a). By contrast, annual performance appraisal (end-of-the-year) is the norm in government and civil service organizations. The performance appraisal procedure adopted is more sophisticated. It normally involves the initial self-appraisal, followed by a peer appraisal discussion meeting held collectively in the department as an act of democracy. Finally the department leader will sign the form and submit it to the personnel department for record keeping.

The nature of the business, broadly defined, further influences the performance management system. This is often the case across different departments within the same organization. For example, an observation shared by many government officials whom I have interviewed was that it is easier for heads of revenue-generating departments to get a good rating for their performance than those who are in charge of departments that are prone to public complaints no matter how hard they have worked and how much they have achieved. The police force and the municipal environment cleaning and protection unit are cases in point. However, interviewees also reported that municipal leaders are acutely aware of the need to 'balance the situation' so that staff in the complaint-prone departments are not demotivated because their performance forms a vital part of the overall performance of the municipal government. Municipal leaders may intervene in the performance appraisal outcomes by rotating the top prize between departments (the leaders of which will be rewarded accordingly) or by offering some concessions or other benefits discretely to those departments that are given lower ratings.

Influence of Chinese culture

Despite employees' receptiveness to western-styled performance management, performance appraisal is perhaps one of the HRM practices that displays the most enduring influence of Chinese culture. It has been widely noted that Chinese culture respects seniority and hierarchy, values social harmony and adopts an egalitarian approach to distribution (Hofstede 1991; Takahara 1992; Yu 1998). It is well known that the Chinese respect age and seniority. In an organizational environment, this is often translated into the following assumption: Older age → seniority → higher grade and higher organizational position → higher level of contribution and more value-added to the organization → higher income. Similarly, egalitarianism has long been recognized as a unique Chinese societal culture and continues to be used by some as a yardstick of fairness and equity in rewards, especially in the distribution of bonuses. It has been reported that those who were rated for the top prize had to share their bonuses with their colleagues in order to avoid jealousy and resentment. Employees have also been known to rotate the top award amongst themselves (Cooke 2005a).

Since performance appraisal in China is often narrowly related to financial reward and promotion instead of training and development needs, these Chinese norms play a particularly influential role throughout the appraisal stages. The Chinese cultural norm of modesty and self-discipline (Bailey et al. 1997) is also reflected in the appraisal system because self-evaluation and criticism often form part of the appraisal process and content, particularly in government and civil service organizations. In addition, Chinese employers tend to attach considerable weight to their employees' work attitude and the effort they have made in their work, often disregarding their performance outcome. This norm is typically applied in the selection for promotion and bonus distribution.

The strong influence of Chinese culture in performance appraisal has been confirmed by the findings of a number of empirical studies. For example, comparative studies on the performance appraisal system in Hong Kong, the United States and Britain have highlighted the fact that Chinese culture plays an important part in the design, implementation as well as the utilization of the performance appraisal system in Hong Kong (e.g. Snape et al. 1998; Entrekin and Chung 2001). Hempel's (2001) comparative study of Hong Kong Chinese and western managers also showed the cultural differences between these two groups in their perceptions of performance appraisal and the differing emphasis they held on performance appraisal criteria. Similarly, Easterby-Smith et al.'s (1995) comparative study of eight matched Chinese and UK companies revealed that appraisal criteria in Chinese organizations focus on not only hard tasks but also 'moral' and ideological behaviour. Self-evaluation and a democratic sounding of opinions by peers and subordinates are the commonly used appraisal methods. Studies on performance appraisal practices in MNCs and joint ventures in mainland China further highlighted the tension between what is required to be effective in implementing the western approach to performance appraisal and the Chinese cultural tradition (e.g. Warner 1993; Child 1994; Lindholm et al. 1999). Whilst the former requires individualistic goals setting, face-to-face feedback/criticism, and employee involvement, the latter respects age and hierarchy, values collectivism and emphasizes the importance of maintaining 'face' and harmonious relationships at the workplace (e.g. Lockett 1988; Hofstede 1991).

However, it must be pointed out that changes in cultural mentality are taking place in China, as mentioned earlier. For example, Bailey et al.'s (1997) comparative study of managers in the USA, Japan and mainland China found that whilst the collectivist culture remained pertinent amongst the Chinese managers surveyed, there was a discernible new trend for endorsing individual accountability and initiative in the Chinese enterprises as a result of transformational changes in China's economic policy since the late 1970s. Bai and Bennington's (2005) study also revealed that the Chinese cultural values did not impede the implementation of individual performance-related reward schemes, suggesting that the new materialism has overtaken traditional cultural forces. It can be argued that the Chinese work ethic plays an important role in employees' acceptance of performance criteria set by the firm (Taormina and Gao 2009). It also needs to be noted that the level of employees' bargaining power plays a role in determining the extent to which performance targets and behavioural norms can be imposed on employees by firms, as shown in Box 4.1 and in K. Huang's (2008) study (see discussion on culture as a challenge).

Attitudes of senior management and western influence

We have noted earlier that some elements of western performance management have permeated Chinese performance management practices. The attitude of senior management plays an important role in the transfer of western practices, as Box 4.1 reveals.

Box 4.1 Performance management in a small state-owned enterprise

Company A is a relatively small SOE specializing in the manufacturing and sale of detergent products. It employs over 210 full-time employees as its core workforce (see Box 2.1 for more detail). Located in a medium-sized industrial city that has witnessed a significant level of downsizing and plant closure in the state-owned sector in the late 1990s, Company A has a very stable core workforce which consists primarily of male skilled workers with local residential status. The company was founded in 1989 and became the Chinese partner of a Sino-US joint venture (P&G) in 1994 for a period of five years before the partnership ended. Company A was then bought by a larger SOE and became its subsidiary. It was during its five-year joint-venture period that many of its current management techniques were embedded in the company. These management practices are strongly influenced by western management philosophy, particularly performance management as outlined below. The director of Company A, Mr Ye, was developed from a university graduate employee to be the HR manager by the joint venture. Mr Ye became the deputy director of Company A when the joint venture ended and then the director from 2005. He is highly enthusiastic about the total quality management techniques and other western management techniques.

Performance management of shopfloor workers

An annual employee development plan is implemented on the production employees. The plan emphasizes productivity, safety, quality, cost control and 5S (sort, straighten, sweep, standardize and sustain). This is supported by monthly performance appraisals. Sharing knowledge on problem-solving is emphasized. Workers are required to write up case study reports on the technical problems they have solved which serve as learning material for other workers. Performance points are given for the case study reports by the line manager, which will be accumulated towards the monthly performance review report of the worker. Peer feedback also forms part of the review but it is not done effectively. There is an end-of-year performance review and performance-related reward. Those who have got the highest scores will be rewarded with the highest wages and also promotion when vacancies arise. In other words, the more an employee reports faults and problem solutions, the more he is seen to be a good employee. Each month, all points are publicized. This performance management system is very quantitative-oriented. According to Mr Ye, each year, about 4–5 per cent of employees will complain to the higher-level managers, believing their points had been unfairly allocated by their superior. Complaints are investigated by senior managers and resolved. Usually, only 20 per cent of complaint cases are found to be unfair. Others mainly arise due to personal differences. Performance review is not just individually based and carried out periodically. Rather, it is a collective daily routine. For example, each shift takes responsibility for their production and cleanness of the workshop. Shift team leaders will walk round the workshop together when they exchange shifts.

Performance management of office staff

An annual work plan is communicated to office staff each year. An evaluation team is formed to carry out evaluation of each employee (especially professionals and managers). Horizontal feedback (feedback from line managers and employees from other departments with whom the assessed person/manager has business relations) is sought for each assessed person. This is conducted anonymously. Usually feedback from three or four employees is sought. This is believed to be quite effective. One-to-one feedback is the method used to convey feedback and ask for improvement. Mr Ye believes that this is the most effective mechanism in a small firm.

For all staff in the company, a name and shame mechanism is in place – notice boards have announcements of employees who have committed an offence, which detail what offences have been committed against which rules and what penalties have been given.

According to Mr Ye, ten years after the withdrawal of P&G, the company continues to operate with similar management techniques. He has worked very hard to ensure that the western management practices adopted by the firm when it was part of the joint venture continue to be implemented and improved. As Mr Ye remarked:

> We are very different from other SOEs. We have a much better management system here which has taken us five years to embed as an enterprise culture. We learned this during the partnership with P&G and continue to improve it each year. It is difficult for other SOEs to try to learn western management techniques by paying just a few visits.

He also believes that the relatively small firm size and the fact that many of the employees were trained during the joint-venture period helped sustain these good practices. It should be noted that job insecurity may be an important factor in the workers' acceptance of the western-influenced management practices which may be seen as rather strict and difficult to sustain in other state-owned factories.

Source: interview data collected by the author in 2009.

Major challenges to effective performance management

Performance management in China encounters a number of pitfalls and challenges, as indicated earlier. Some of these are universal and can be found in other societies, others are accentuated by Chinese cultural values, as evidenced above. This section discusses some of these issues further.

Lack of strategic HRM and managerial competence
for performance management

An important element of a performance management system is the alignment of the system with the strategic goals of the organization, because a fundamental task for the former is to ensure the fulfilment of the latter (Williams 2002). However, the vast majority of Chinese organizations do not have any strategic goals, let alone cascading these goals to departmental and individual levels and designing comprehensive performance indictors based on these strategic goals (H. Chen 2003; Yu 2006). Moreover, the information system of many organizations is rudimentary and unable to provide adequate support needed for an effective performance management system.

Since the 2000s, there has been much hype about the notion of human resource management in China. Many HRM concepts and practices were introduced as advanced western management philosophy and techniques, including perform-ance management, performance appraisal, management by objective, balanced scorecard, key performance indicators and so on. Not only have many personnel departments changed their title into HR department, but also HR (personnel) managers started to apply these new HR concepts and tools to their organizations without a real understanding of what they mean and how they can be adapted to suit their organizational environment. As noted earlier, an increasing number of organizations are reported to have adopted performance management schemes and implemented performance appraisal practices. However, the majority of appraisers and appraisees are not aware of what is being assessed and for what purposes. An important part of the performance management system is to utilize the appraisal outcome to inform various aspects of the HRM, including career planning, employee training and development, job allocation and reward. Unfortunately, the majority of Chinese firms still lack a strategic approach to HRM, particularly in employee training and development. As a result, performance appraisal often narrowly focuses on reward instead of utilizing the result to inform career planning and training and development (e.g. Chen et al. 2004).

There is insufficient managerial competence in designing a performance management system and conducting performance appraisals. Discrepancies in performance measure criteria and standards often exist across departments within the same organization, causing grievances from employees when a similar level of performance is given different scores and financial rewards (Liu 2005). A performance management survey conducted by Deloitte Human Capital Consulting (China) in 2003 on 51 Chinese enterprises in a wide range of industrial sectors found that performance indictors were designed by the senior management in 85 per cent of the enterprises (cited in H. Chen 2003: 28). Some 55 per cent of the enterprises did not carry out due diligence in collecting performance data and made little use of performance information systems. Only 4 per cent of the enterprises adopted a 360-degree appraisal system. About 55 per cent of the enterprises gave feedback to appraisees on the areas requiring improvement and only 18 per cent of the enterprises offered training relevant to appraisees in the areas that needed improving. Performance appraisal outcomes were used for bonus distribution (by 88 per cent of the enterprises), promotion, job reallocation or redundancy (77 per cent), wage adjustment (49 per cent), and training and development planning (49 per cent). Nearly 8 per cent of the enterprises did not make use of performance appraisal outcomes at all.

Performance management has not been fully accepted by managers as an effective tool in managing human resources. According to a study conducted by Zhang (2005) who surveyed the managers and workers across the five subsidiaries of a large stock market-listed state-owned enterprise, junior managers appeared to be more conservative and resistant than mid-ranking managers and workers in terms of implementing a new performance management scheme which is intended to relate performance more closely to financial rewards. More specifically, whilst 90 per cent of the mid-ranking managers believed that differential rewards would be more effective than an egalitarian distribution system, over half the junior managers believed that differential rewards should only be implemented when egalitarian elements were also incorporated in the differential scheme. While over 80 per cent of the mid-ranking managers believed that recognition and incentive would have motivational effects, only 12 per cent of junior managers felt this was the case. By contrast, over half the workers surveyed had a positive attitude towards performance-related pay, and only a small minority of 10–15 per cent felt that competition pressure and distributional variations should be minimized. In addition, whilst 64 per cent of the workers believed that their reward was closely related to their group performance, the rest felt that their reward had nothing to do with group performance. This indicates that the alignment of goals and performance level has yet to be made at all levels within the organization.

Performance appraisal seen as a formality

A related problem is that performance appraisal is often seen as a waste of time and not taken seriously by either the appraisers or the appraisees (e.g. Chou 2005). This is particularly the case in the public sector. For example, a manager from a tax bureau whom the author interviewed disclosed that he distributed the annual appraisal forms to his staff for them to fill in rather than conducting the appraisal and writing the comments himself. All he did was to sign his name on the forms without checking them and forward them to the personnel department for record keeping. 'I am too busy to do all that rubbish, especially at the end of the year. I don't want to upset my staff by giving them negative feedback. It is just a formality we have to go through once a year. It is not real work.' A common feature in the performance appraisal is that appraisal outcome is rarely fed back to the appraisee in qualitative comments (Easterby-Smith et al. 1995; Chen et al. 2004). This is in part because line managers are reluctant to provide negative feedback to subordinates in order to avoid causing resentment and resistance from the staff concerned which may impede motivation and performance further.

Avoiding criticizing bad behaviour reflects the Chinese culture of neutrality which leads to the tolerance of poor performers, thus demotivating good performers. The egalitarian and neutral approach to managing workplace relationships further results in the adoption of a broad band approach to performance rating. In most organizations, a quotas system is imposed by the senior authority to classify employees' performance in their annual performance review. For example, according to the state guideline for government and civil service organizations, no more than 10 per cent of civil servant employees should be rated 'excellent' for symbolic purposes, the same is true for the last category 'unacceptable'. This broad band system and the small differentials in prize awards do not provide sufficient motivational or punitive effect to enhance performance level.

For some appraisees whose wage is not related to performance the incentive impact of receiving a good rating is so small that it falls short of being inspirational, to say the least. A mid-ranking civil servant (a department chief of a traffic bureau) whom the author interviewed held the following view, which was shared by several of the civil servants interviewed,

> Our annual performance appraisal is a pointless exercise. It has no value at all. I was rated as the best employee of the year by my colleagues in the bureau last year, but I did not want to take the title, because the reward was so trivial and meaningless. I did what I need to do and what I think I should do, not because I want to get the prize. I feel more comfortable without it.

The lack of utility of performance appraisal as perceived by appraisers and appraisees remains a severe barrier to the effective implementation of performance appraisal, particularly in the public sector.

Subjectivity

It is recognized that subjectivity exists in performance appraisals, especially for jobs in which performance is difficult to quantify and measure. The impartiality and competence of an appraiser in conducting an appraisal also plays an important part in controlling the level of subjectivity. Since the majority of Chinese managers have limited HR training and knowledge, the level of subjectivity may be relatively high when they use their own judgement, experience and preference in conducting the performance appraisal and distributing rewards. On the one hand, certain types of employees may be rated and rewarded favourably; on the other hand, Chinese managers may continue to feel the pressure to adopt a broad band in assessing performance level and an egalitarian approach to the distribution of rewards in order to maintain workplace harmony. As observed by Bozionelos and Wang (2007), the implementation of performance appraisal is much easier and more reliable in departments where performance can be evaluated by objective and quantifiable criteria which limit the influence of managers' subjective judgement.

Cooke's (2009c) study of 65 private firms in China revealed that performance management is a key HR challenge in the view of the interviewees. Many of them were unhappy with the system adopted by their company but were unable to find a good solution. At least 21 managers admitted that their firm did not have a formal performance management system in place. For those that had a system, 32 believed that their employees were only averagely happy with the system. Only five managers believed that their employees were happy with the system. Some managers criticized the firm for embracing 'western

management techniques' that focus on hard performance outcomes and overlook
the softer and more humanistic approach to people management typically found
in oriental cultures. A commonly reported problem in performance management
is the difficulty in setting up a 'scientific', or an objective and fair, performance
management system to strike the right balance (see also Chapter 9 for the mean-
ing of 'scientific'). This frustration actually reveals a lack of understanding by the
managers of performance management in general and what 'western performance
management technique' is more specifically. What they have highlighted is the
problem of subjectivity in performance management and their desire to find the
'holy grail' to manage their employees effectively.

A number of difficulties in performance appraisal were revealed in the survey
mentioned above conducted by Deloitte Human Capital Consulting (China) in
2003 (H. Chen, 2003). Many of the difficulties are related to the subjectivity
in performance measurement (see Table 4.2).

An added dimension of subjectivity in performance appraisal in China is
the way performance measurement criteria are set. As discussed earlier, performance measurement criteria in China tend to be generic, broad and focus on efforts
and behaviours rather than outcomes. There is a lack of individualized
performance measurement indicators to reflect the specific characteristics of
different posts. The five major criteria for performance appraisal for government
officials and civil servants are a case in point (see Table 4.1). The high level of
subjectivity is reflected in a sarcastic saying that is going round: 'If the leader says
you are good, then you are good even if you are no good. If the leader says you
are no good, then you are no good even if you are good.' This subjectivity

Table 4.2 Difficulties encountered in performance management – survey findings

Difficulties in performance management	% reported in the sample
Some tasks impossible to be measured objectively	82.4
Performance indictors were not given by superior and/or goal design was not fully communicated with employees	49.0
Employees' perceived subjectivity and incomprehensiveness of superior in handling performance evaluation	43.1
Difficulties in breaking down further the goals of performance indicators	41.2
Lack of scientific methods in setting performance assessment indicators	37.3
Ineffective in helping senior management team identify problems in enterprises	35.3
Lack of enthusiasm from employees in participating in performance management tasks	33.3
Others	11.8

Source: adapted from H. Chen (2003: 28).

encourages some people to pretend to be busy and cultivate their relationship with their superior to gain promotion.

Interventions in the appraisal process

Ironically, the biggest hurdle in making performance appraisal really effective is perhaps the adoption of the collective peer appraisal method. It requires colleagues from the same group/department to gather together to give a self-appraisal and to appraise each other's performance, including that of their superior, in a face-to-face meeting. The collective peer appraisal, known as a 'democratic life meeting' during Mao's era, is often no more than a show. It provides prima facie evidence of fairness and transparency in the process. In reality, peers are unwilling to say anything negative to each other face to face as a Chinese norm of face-saving for both parties. They are even less willing to criticize their superiors for fear of revenge.

Similar stories resonate in the author's interviews with government officials and civil servants. It is clear that fear of negative consequences of appraisal (e.g. revenge by superior if criticizing his/her conduct or reduced bonus as a result of self-criticism) is an important distortion factor in the performance appraisal process. It has been observed that annual appraisal report writing can be a literary exercise for supervisors and it may be the supervisor's literary skills, rather than the civil servants' performance per se, that determines the appraisal results. 'Moreover, supervisors were not held responsible for falsifying civil servants' performance records' (Chou 2005: 47).

In a similar vein, Hempel (2008) observed that the personal relationship between the supervisor and subordinate may influence the way the subordinate reacts to performance feedback. In other words, performance feedback may be seen as a covert statement of the quality of the relationship between the supervisor and the subordinate rather than a report of job performance. Hempel's (2008) study found that Chinese workers are not always sensitive to feedback. Nevertheless, they can respond to negative performance feedback positively and may be motivated to improve their performance if they feel that this feedback is given with good intent.

Lack of cooperation from employees

Employees may play an important role in preventing the effective implementation of a performance management scheme if they do not benefit from it. For example, a finance manager of a privately owned small hotel in a developed city in south-eastern China disclosed to the author during the interview in 2009:

> In our hotel, supervisors have performance-related bonuses but not the ordinary workers. So there is no incentive for employees to work hard to attract more business because they don't benefit from it. Also, if they don't

get on with the supervisors, then why should they work hard so that the supervisors can get more money?

A number of managers in the private firms interviewed by the author in 2009 also disclosed that some of their employees resent the significant gaps in the rewards between managers and employees. Where employee recognition is used without substantial financial incentive, the effect is limited and even negative. This is because employees are unlikely to subscribe to these exploitative mechanisms when employee recognition schemes are seen as a tactic used to elicit enhanced performance from them without adequate rewards. As Nishii et al. (2008) argued, the way firms adopt HRM practices has a significant impact on employees' perceptions of the intention of these practices.

Cultural barriers to adopting western performance management practices

Despite emerging trends of cultural change and receptiveness to western perform- ance management practices, as noted above, existing studies of performance management have highlighted cultural difference as a key challenge to adopting western-styled performance management schemes in the Chinese context (e.g. Hempel 2001; Cooke 2008e; Taormina and Gao 2009; Poon et al. 2010). For example, Wang and Wang's (2008) study found that whilst performance management was positively related to organizational performance, adopting it as a strategic HRM technique in China could be a serious challenge due to the Chinese traditional culture of harmony and egalitarianism.

Similarly, K. Huang's (2008) study of four sets of acquisitions of Chinese IT firms by US-owned MNCs revealed that attempts to initiate changes in the appraisal system by the acquiring firms have met with stronger resistance in the acquired firms. As a result, the foreign acquirers have not been able to diffuse their performance management system to the acquired firms. Prior to the acquisition, the acquired firms had already adopted performance appraisal methods in order to compete with the more powerful foreign rivals. Despite this, the foreign acquirers have noted that there were some gaps between the performance appraisal system used by the acquired firms and that adopted in the parent firm. More specifically, the Chinese firms tended to use rating results to distinguish good and poor performers, but neglect the planning and communica- tion process. The rigorous planning and evaluation process and procedure adopted by the foreign parent firms were considered by the Chinese managers as 'too inflexible and time-consuming' to be suitable for the dynamic Chinese market. Instead, managers from the acquired firms continued with their own way of managing performance. The complexity in linking performance with the analysis of training and development needs of employees adopted in the foreign parent companies also led to resistance from the acquired managers who lacked relevant skills to implement the scheme. Consequently, the new parent companies merely identified financial objectives for the business units as a whole, leaving it to the acquired firms to decide the performance indicators for the individuals and the departments.

Interestingly, K. Huang's (2008) study found evidence of reverse diffusion from the acquired firms to the foreign acquirers in the management of performance review. The main driving force for this diffusion was the positive views held by the managers from both sides towards the implementation of performance appraisal in the acquired firms. In one of the four firms studied, the performance practice based on a 360-degree appraisal recommended by a foreign-owned consultancy firm had been used for only six months before it was abandoned. One reason was that the Chinese managers in other subsidiaries felt very uneasy about giving their staff detailed behavioural feedback and were uncomfortable to be evaluated by their subordinates. Moreover, the lack of skills in conducting appraisal by the Chinese managers made the appraisal process time-consuming. As a result, this acquiring parent firm, and a couple of others in the study, have adopted the performance appraisal schemes that were developed by the acquired firms to other subsidiaries in China because the acquiring parent firms felt these schemes were more appropriate for the Chinese context.

K. Huang's (2008) study further revealed a salient central tendency (DeNisi and Griffin 2001) in performance assessment and the consequent narrow differentiation in rewards. In all the four acquired firms, 80 to 85 per cent of employees were rated 'satisfactory' (mid-range) in the performance scale. The role individual performance played in determining pay differentials and bonus distribution was therefore relatively moderate. More significantly, the central tendency in performance evaluation means that the pay levels of employees were indeed more determined by other criteria such as job positions, length of service and qualifications rather than a combination of these factors and performance levels. The role of individual performance in compensation was also constrained by the focus on team or departmental performance in the acquired firms. With insufficient performance differentiation among employees, the phenomenon of 'small rice pot' (i.e. everybody in the team sharing from the same pot) was fairly common in the bonus distribution within the departments, as was reported in Zhu's (2005) study. This finding suggests that even in the high-tech and competitive sector, an egalitarian approach, rather than an individualistic approach, remains widespread in performance appraisal and reward distribution. This is perhaps to do with the fact that in the IT firms a team-based approach to management is crucial for the successful management of projects, so project teams form the basic structure of the firms.

Conclusion

This chapter has provided an overview of the historical development of performance management and appraisal systems in China. It showed that some form of performance appraisal has long existed in a Chinese style, with a narrower purpose and a different focus in its content (e.g. moral behaviour) than that promoted in western literature as performance management systems. In recent years, performance management as a modern western HRM concept and technique is being embraced unquestioningly by an increasing number of Chinese firms. It is now evident that Chinese employees in enterprises are becoming more receptive towards performance-oriented rewards and welcome career development opportunities through the implementation of a performance management system.

However, the implementation of a performance appraisal system in China is challenged by a number of factors that are generic or cultural-specific. In particular, Chinese cultural values seem to have a profound and enduring influence throughout the various stages of the performance management system. This is especially the case in government and civil service organizations where state intervention remains relatively strong and performance outcomes are more difficult to quantify. It is perhaps in this sector where performance appraisal is seen more as a formality and punctuated with a greater level of subjectivity, compared with the reward-driven performance appraisal system in enterprises. A most notable difference between the Chinese-styled performance appraisal and that promoted in western HRM literature is the narrow focus of the former. The adoption of the western approach in China is further hampered by the lack of strategic orientation of many Chinese firms and the deficiency of HR skills to design and implement an effective performance management system.

In general, the traditional performance appraisal system in China is reward driven (i.e. focusing on retrospective performance) and tends to focus on the person and behavioural performance. By contrast, the performance appraisal system promoted in western HRM literature takes a developmental approach (i.e. prospective performance-oriented) and focuses on the alignment between individual performance and organizational goals. Nevertheless, recent studies on performance appraisal practices in China have detected a discernible trend that an increasing number of Chinese organizations are adopting a western-styled performance management system. Whilst a total transfer of western practices is not found, or indeed possible, a unique blending of both modernizing and traditional forces is at play in shaping the new performance management practices in China (Bailey et al. 1997). The continuing trend of adaptation of western performance management practices is likely to lead to further behavioural changes from Chinese managers and employees that depart from traditional Chinese cultural norms exhibited in the Chinese-styled performance appraisal system.

5 Pay systems, pay gaps and employers' reward strategies

Introduction

Reward strategies and pay systems have been a major topic for study in the western literature on human resource management, employment relations and labour market studies. By contrast, with the exception of executive compensation, pay practices in China remain a relatively under-investigated topic (Li and Edwards 2008; Ding et al. 2009). This is despite the burgeoning body of literature on HRM in China since the late 1990s (e.g. Zhu 2005; Cooke 2009b; Warner 2009). Yet, marketization has led to fundamental changes in the pay system. As Wei and Rowley (2009) noted, China's traditional pay system has been transformed from a state-administrated reward system that is characterized by a low wage policy and flat wage structure into an enterprise-administrated and contract/performance-based system with diversified wage structures and flexible pay schemes in different ownership forms. The emergence of the new system and pay practices reflects not only employers' strategy on pay as part of their HR strategy, but also reveals the impact of the emerging labour market on individuals' earning potential, with some more advantaged than others.

The opening up of the economy has also created spaces for widespread opportunistic behaviours and practices from both individuals and organizations to generate grey income, despite continuing attempts by the government to prevent it. In addition, executive pay in both the public and private sector has been a key point of tension. On the one hand, the government wants to provide sufficient incentives to business leaders in order to turn around thousands of collapsing state-owned enterprises (SOEs) and to stimulate high levels of performance in the private sector. On the other hand, the autonomy and power enjoyed by the enterprise executives has led to the heavy loss of state assets and widening income gaps between the low-earning categories of workers and the elite professional and managerial groups (e.g. Wu 2009).

It is beyond the scope of this chapter to provide a detailed investigation of executive pay (see for example, Yuan et al. 2008; Yi 2009; Xue and Wu 2009). Instead, the chapter first examines a relatively less studied but significant phenomenon in the understanding of human resource management, employment and labour market studies in China – gender pay gaps and reasons that account for this. Through the investigation of the causes of gender pay gaps, we reveal how factors that determine wages may have evolved during the marketization process of the Chinese economy. The chapter then presents some of the emerging trends of pay practices in the private sector, including wage payment, welfare benefits and social security, and their HRM implications.

Characteristics of the pay system

The total pay package in China consists of three major components: wage, bonuses, and subsidies and benefits (see Table 5.1). Under the state-planned economy period (1949–78), the pay system in China exhibited a number of unique characteristics in the urban state-owned sector where nearly 80 per cent of urban workers were employed (Cooke 2005a). One was the rigidity of the pay structure that was centrally determined by the state and implemented at the organizational level with little autonomy for managers. A second feature was the broad coverage of the same pay scales and structures across a wide range of occupational groups with little consideration of the nature of the industry or the skill differences of the occupations. A third characteristic was the emphasis on non-productivity criteria at the expense of productivity concerns in the distribution of reward. In particular, seniority, effort, morality and egalitarianism are strong components in determining rewards (Yu 1998). A fourth feature was that whilst the basic wage level was low, this was heavily subsidized by all sorts of benefits, including canteens, housing, transport, medical care, schooling,

Table 5.1 Composition of a total pay package

Likely components of a total pay package

Wages	*Bonuses*	*Benefits*
• Skill-based wage • Position wage • Performance-based wage • Project-based wage • Seniority wage • Overtime wage	• Performance/profit-related bonuses • Stock options dividend • Monthly, quarterly, annual bonuses not related to individual performance • Other types of bonuses (e.g. being a model worker, safety production awards)	• Statutory benefits (i.e. five forms of social security: pension, maternity, work-related injury, sick pay, medical care) • Company-based voluntary benefits (e.g. subsidies of food, transport and housing, paid holiday entitlement, social events, entertainments, additional social security benefits, holiday tours, company-sponsored education, training and development opportunities, other benefits in kind)

Source: compiled by the author.

paid maternity leave, sick pay, pensions and so forth (Warner 1997; Cooke 2005a).

In general, the pay system in the state sector in China has been heavily influenced by the socialist ideology of redistribution in which wages are seen as a necessity to maintain an acceptable living standard for employees and their families rather than as a motivational strategy to enhance productivity. This dominant ideology of wage distribution is reflected in its relatively narrow wage differentials across and within occupations. In particular, wage policy in the public sector and government organizations has been, and still is, heavily influenced by two factors: political ideology and cultural belief. Both emphasize the need for egalitarianism in which material rewards are officially subjugated to altruistic ideology and unpaid contributions are often praised and encouraged by the state employer.

The opening up of the economy in the late 1970s has led to some radical changes in the pay system as a result of the ongoing reform within the state-owned sector since the mid-1980s and the dramatic growth of the private sector since the 1990s (see Table 1.1). In the state-owned sector, bonuses have become an increasingly substantial part of the total wage income. The rising cost of living, the increasing amount of autonomy devolved to the organization and the continuing tight control of the wage structure and low level of basic wages translated into pressure on managers to find ways to generate revenue for bonuses in order to satisfy their employees who have learned to benchmark their income and make wage demands. Nevertheless, egalitarianism remains the norm in redistribution (e.g. Korzec 1992; Yu 1998).

In the private sector, wage composition is relatively simple. Performance-related pay is the norm, and the provision of work-related social security tends be limited, and in some cases non-existent (see below and Chapter 8 for further discussion). Wage levels are largely determined by the employers with little scope for bargaining or workers' involvement. In theory, the state requires employers to set up a collective negotiation system with their employees to negotiate terms and conditions collectively with the assistance of trade unions. In practice, only a small proportion of the larger firms have done so and the extent of its effectiveness remains questionable (Clarke et al. 2004). Generally speaking, neither the trade union nor employees have any real input in wage setting. Whereas employees in the state sector can exert pressure on their managers for higher bonus income, workers in the private sector may be much less able to do so due to the fear of job losses (Cooke 2005a). A key feature in pay determination in the private sector is the strong emphasis on responsibility and performance at individual and/or group level. For example, Child (1994) observed that by the 1990s, job responsibility had replaced seniority as the most significant predictor of employee earnings. This trend is supported by the studies of Björkman and Lu (1999) and Benson et al. (2000) who found that all companies studied had some elements of individual performance built into the wage system.

These characteristics in wage determination across different ownership sectors have been evolving as a result of the deepening marketization process.

It is important to understand the changes in the process. This is because the wage-setting structure may have a significant impact on gender pay gaps and therefore changes in the structure are important when analysing changes in the gap over time or when comparing the gap across countries (Blau and Kahn 1997). We will now turn to the more detailed discussion of patterns of gender pay gaps. In doing so, we highlight how some of the key factors that had influenced pay levels may be giving way to new factors that are more market oriented, with new implications for the gender pay gap.

Gender pay gaps and likely causes

A defining feature of the Chinese socialist state's commitment to gender equality has been the full participation of women in economic activities and the significant improvement of their political, economic and social position in the last five decades. Whereas women in some countries have a relatively low employment participation rate, with a large proportion of them engaging in part-time and/or contingent work, women in China tend to have continuous full-time employment for economic as well as political reasons. The proportion of women participating in higher education and in professional and managerial jobs at all levels has been rising since the 1990s (see *China Statistical Yearbook 2009*). However, despite this progress, gender discrimination in employment and career advancement remains a constant feature which Chinese women seem to share with their counterparts in other parts of the world (see Chapter 6 for further discussion). A direct consequence of this discrimination is the gender pay gap, despite the fact that this gap is relatively small compared with that found in some other countries. Given the narrowing difference in the human capital endowments between men and women in urban China, the effect of discrimination has been seen as a significant residual factor that is attributed to the persistent, and for some widening, gender wage gap.

Whilst gender inequality to the disadvantage of women, particularly certain groups of women, may be an undisputed fact, the process through which this outcome is produced may differ markedly across countries as a result of the interactions of unique historical, institutional, cultural and labour market conditions in each country (Beggs 1995; Rubery et al. 1999; Blossfeld and Drobnic 2001; Wang 2005). In addition, market reform has had diverse impacts on the gender pay gap in transitional economies (e.g. Brainerd 2000). Existing studies on gender pay gaps in China have primarily been quantitative studies from the economic perspective. Whilst they have made a significant contribution to improving our understanding of the patterns of pay gaps since the 1980s, they only offer a limited explanation, mainly from an economic perspective, of the causes that account for the gaps. In this section, we draw together existing literature on women and employment in China to highlight forces that are at play in shaping the patterns of gender pay gaps in contemporary China. In doing so, it offers a more comprehensive account of the institutional and cultural factors that may be responsible for gender pay gaps.

It is important to note that statistical information on employment and wages for men and women in China is limited (Maurer-Fazio et al. 1999; Gustafsson and Li 2000; Zheng 2001). National annual statistics do not provide a gender breakdown on wage levels, making studies on gender aspects of earnings a very difficult task. Despite these constraints, a number of statistical studies on gender pay gaps in the earlier part of China's economic reform period have emerged. This section builds on these scholarly studies to provide a qualitative analysis of how the evolution of established institutional factors and the emergence of new forces are reshaping the process of gender pay gaps since the 1980s. Transformation in economic structures and ownership reforms make this period an important one to study gender issues, during which rural workers have been gaining employment in urban areas on the one hand and the once dominant state sector has been experiencing a continuous contraction of employment through downsizing and privatization on the other. Due to space constraint, this chapter will focus mainly on issues related to gender wage gaps in the urban sector, as they are significantly different from that in the rural sector.

Patterns of gender pay gap

The closing gender gap in educational attainments, and the continuous full-time employment of women, have not been fully reflected in a simultaneous narrowing in gender pay gaps. The availability of a number of national data sets and survey results in the 1990s has led to the publication of a number of scholarly articles on gender pay gaps in the urban sector (e.g. Gustafsson and Li 2000; Shu and Bian 2003; Appleton et al. 2005; Bishop et al. 2005; Wang 2005; Chi and Li 2008; J. S. Zhang et al. 2008). A major focus of these studies is to investigate what factors influence gender pay gaps and whether, and the extent to which, political and economic changes that took place during the reforming period have led to any changes in the influencing factors and in the pay gap. Whilst it remains debatable as to what the actual gender pay gap is and whether economic reform since the late 1970s has resulted in a widening gap, scholars on the subject tend to agree that the gender wage gap in China is relatively small compared with that found in other countries (e.g. Maurer-Fazio et al. 1999; Gustafsson and Li 2000; Nie et al. 2002).

For example, in terms of the level of gender pay gap, Gustafsson and Li's (2000: 316) comparative analysis of the national sample survey data sets from the 1988 and 1995 Chinese Household Income Projects revealed 'a modest increase in the gender earnings gap' – while women earned 15.6 per cent less than men in 1988, this figure rose to 17.5 per cent by 1995. The gender wage gap 'is even smaller among the youngest wage-earners and those with longer educations' (Gustafsson and Li 2000: 326). Shu and Bian's (2003: 1117) analysis of the same data sets shows that 'gender gap in earnings remains remarkably stable' between 1988 (83.9 per cent) and 1995 (83.8 per cent). However, Shu and Bian (2003) observed that there was a larger gender disparity in the amount of increase in earnings between 1988 and 1995 for those with less education than for those with more education. Using the same data sets, Bishop et al.'s (2005: 258) analysis points to 'a small increase in the earning gap between 1988 and 1995'. However, they argued that on average, there was 'a slight decrease in discrimination between 1988 and 1995'. By contrast, Appleton et al.'s (2005) study shows that while men earned 12 per cent more than women in 1988, this gap had risen to 15 per cent in 1995 and then to 22 per cent in 1999. This, they argue, is an indication of the erosion of gender equality that was achieved during the state-planned economy period. However, Appleton et al. (2005) observed from the 2002 results that this trend of a widening gender wage gap might have been halted and perhaps even put into reverse at 19 per cent. Increased wage discrimination against women in this period is seen as the cause for the widening gap compared with the state-planned period.

In comparison, Wang's (2005) analysis of a national survey conducted in 1996 reveals a wider gender wage gap than those suggested by the above studies. Wang's (2005: 28) analysis shows that women only made 73 per cent of men's earnings 'after holding constant the effects of human capital, political capital, family structure and work unit as well as occupational characteristics' and that little of this gender wage gap 'can be explained by gender differences in endowments'. Two more recent studies by J. S. Zhang et al. (2008) and Chi and Li (2008) that cover the period 1987–2004 suggest that the gender earnings gap in urban China has increased substantially in this period, with the mean female/male earnings ratio declining from 86.3 per cent to 76.2 per cent (J. S. Zhang et al. 2008). In particular, women at the lower skill levels have been more adversely affected in the whole period, indicating a stronger 'sticky floor' effect (Chi and Li 2008). J. S. Zhang et al. (2008) further revealed that gender pay gaps at the upper end also widened greatly in the period 2001–4.

Two opposing arguments have been put forward in explaining the likely impact of China's economic transformation on gender pay gaps. The Mercerian school of thought argues that marketization should in principle diminish the gender wage gap because of the greater emphasis on human capital endowments as competitive imperative, thus reducing gender discrimination (e.g. Liu et al. 2000; Shu and Bian 2003). Some authors (e.g. J. S. Zhang et al. 2008) also argue that the higher return to education has been the major cause of widened gender pay gaps at the lower skill level, although gender discrimination plays a role. The other school argues that the level of gender discrimination may actually be increased in the process of marketization due to market imperfection on the one hand and the erosion of state power to enforce the socialist ideal of gender equality on the other (e.g. Nee 1989, 1991; Kidd and Meng 2001; Wang, 2005). For example, Li and Gustafsson's (1999) study revealed larger gender wage gaps and a higher level of unexplained residual gap in the economically more developed geographical areas where market forces were more prevalent. Similarly, studies by Maurer-Fazio et al. (1999) and Liu et al. (2000) found that both the gender wage gap and the size of the unexplained residual gap were greater in the private sector that was more exposed to market competition. However, the findings of some studies remain inconclusive. For example,

Rozelle et al.'s (2002) study lends no support to either the human capital theory (Mincer and Polachek 1974) or the socialist ideology argument. In a similar vein, Shu and Bian's (2003) study concludes that substantial marketization has not altered the existing gender gap in earnings. Nevertheless, the sources of gender wage differentials are changing, reflecting the growing significance of human capital and market power.

Causes of gender pay gap

Gender wage differential is an outcome of a combination of factors that are universal as well as country-specific. These factors may have varying effects on different groups of people in different countries and over time. In western societies, gender difference in productivity-related characteristics, occupational segregation by sex and wage discrimination have been seen as the major sources of gender pay gaps (Polachek and Siebert 1993; Petersen and Morgan 1995; Rubery et al. 2005). Existing studies on gender wage gaps in urban China (e.g. Meng and Miller 1995; Walder 1995; Hughes and Maurer-Fazio 2002; Shu and Bian 2003) have highlighted a number of contributing factors. These include: experience/seniority, political capital, educational attainment, organizational status, marital status, labour force placements (including occupation, industry and sector placement), employers' autonomy, enforcement of employment law, gender norms and discrimination against women. In the text that follows, we discuss the extent to which these factors play a role in the gender pay gap, and how their interactive influences may have changed during the period of economic reform.

Experience and seniority

Under the state-planned economy regime, seniority formed an important component of reward. It is believed that experience, often measured by age and tenure, was over-rewarded whereas 'returns to education were suppressed earlier in China's transition' (Appleton et al. 2005: 15). This factor is now giving way to qualification and performance level. However, seniority remains a tacit aspect of consideration when organizational leaders make decisions on promotion and reward. This is particularly the case in the public sector and government organizations where performance is often not readily quantifiable.

Political capital

It has been observed (e.g. Bian 1994; Walder 1995; Zhou 2000; Bian et al. 2001) that political capital has an important bearing on one's financial reward in China because 'the communist state rewards political loyalty more than competence' (Zhou, 2000: 1144). Membership in the Chinese Communist Party (CCP) is a significant credential of political capital which is often a prerequisite for career advancement in the state sector. Party members are more likely than non-party members to be selected for promotion, to receive sponsorship for training and development, and consequently to receive higher wages and benefits in kind and subsidies associated with the status (Bian et al. 2001; Li and Walder 2001; Shu and Bian 2003).

It is important to note that since the mid-2000s, CCP membership has become a hotly sought after credential for university graduates to differentiate themselves from fellow job seekers in the light of rising levels of graduate unemployment as a result of the dramatic expansion of higher education in the early 2000s. This latest development may have implications for Marini and Fan's (1997) finding which revealed that 'education has surpassed seniority to become one of the three most important sources of gender gap in earnings, while the significance of Communist Party membership has slightly declined' (cited in Shu and Bian 2003: 1135).

Given the fact that Chinese women are significantly under-represented in CCP membership, making up less than 15 per cent of the total membership nationwide and 25 per cent of urban membership (Solotaroff 2003), we can reasonably conclude that the failure to develop political capital partially explains the gender pay gap (Wang 2005). This is particularly the case in the state sector where political capital continues to play an important part in career progression and earnings. Indeed, women are significantly under-represented in government organizations – less than 28 per cent of women worked in government organizations in 2007, despite a considerable increase from less than 23 per cent in 1995 (*China Statistical Yearbook 2008*). More broadly, only 0.5 per cent of women in employment worked as heads of organizations in 2007, compared with 1.8 per cent of men (*China Statistical Yearbook 2008*). This is despite their significant advancement in educational levels and inroad into professional/technical positions.

Educational attainment

Perhaps the most significant change in the sources of pay determination during the economic reform period is the increasing return to human capital. For example, Zhou's (2000) study that examined changes in income determinants between the pre-reform and reform eras shows significant changes in the return to education. Walder et al. (2000) observed that educational credentials have become the single most important factor for obtaining high-level professional positions. Shu and Bian (2003: 1117) also noted that 'the higher the education, the smaller the gender gap in earnings'. Since the overall educational level of the women's workforce is slightly lower than that of men, lower educational attainment is one of the sources of gender pay gap. A number of studies have pointed out that education has surpassed seniority to become one of the three most important sources of gender gap in earnings. By contrast, the significance of CCP membership has slightly declined (e.g. Liu et al. 2000; Hughes and Maurer-Fazio 2002; Shu and Bian 2003; Bishop et al. 2005; Chi and Li 2008; J. S. Zhang et al. 2008).

A number of studies have shown that the return to education for women is greater than that for men (e.g. Wang 2005; Chi and Li 2008; J. S. Zhang et al. 2008). In addition, Chi and Li (2008: 252) found that 'the earnings advantage of professional and managerial employees over production workers was greater for females than for males'. While women have to rely on education to get higher pay, men appear to have more alternatives and are more favoured by emergent labour markets (Shu and Bian 2003; Wang 2005). However, increased human capital alone is not sufficient to eliminate the gender pay gap amongst those who are highly educated. In rural areas, possessing a high level of educational attainment may not guarantee jobs of relevant status. As Meng and Miller's (1995: 143) study revealed, 'better educated women are systematically excluded from senior positions in the TVP [township-and-village private] labour markets'.

Marital status

Interruption to labour market participation is one of the major reasons accounting for the lower earnings experienced by married women in many developed countries due to their career breaks for childcare responsibilities (O'Reilly and Fagan 1998; Blossfeld and Drobnic 2001), or as a result of the 'marriage bar' that leads to their exclusion from the mainstream labour market (e.g. Moon and Broadbent 2008; Nakata and Takehiro 2002). By comparison, marital status and presence of young children appear to have a limited negative effect on women's earnings in China – an outcome largely due to the socialist intervention that is aimed at reducing gender inequality (Shu and Bian 2003).

Nevertheless, Hughes and Maurer-Fazio's (2002: 147) study shows that 'despite the fact that Chinese women exhibit strong and continuous labour force attachment, married women in urban China still experience larger total gender wage gaps than single women'. The effect is not uniform across different ownership forms. Whilst married women earn 5 per cent and 3 per cent more than single women in state-owned and collectively owned enterprises (COE) respectively, married women earn 12 per cent less than single women in joint-venture firms (JVs) 'after controlling for differences in human capital characteristics' (Hughes and Maurer-Fazio 2002: 148). It is interesting to note that 'the marriage premium is maintained for men but disappears for women' in this most competitive ownership sector such as foreign-invested enterprises (FIEs) (Hughes and Maurer-Fazio 2002: 148) where wage level is amongst the highest of all ownership forms.

Hughes and Maurer-Fazio's (2002) findings reflect the different characteristics of employment relations between the state-/collectively owned firms and JVs and FIEs. For the former where employment relations tend to be more stable and market forces have not fully permeated, traditional values (e.g. seniority) still play an important role. As the majority of Chinese women tend to get married when they are in their twenties and thirties, married women tend to be more 'senior' than single women. For women in professional and managerial positions in blue chip JVs and FIEs, there are increasing reports that women choose to remain single or postpone their motherhood in order to progress with their career. This is partly because the ability to perform and exceed targets is the main criterion for retention and progression (Cooke 2009a). By contrast, some sweat-shop FIEs deliberately screen out women of marriage age (above 23 years) when they recruit workers in order to maintain productivity. Married women may also work fewer hours in these factories, hence earning less.

Working hours

It should be noted that women tend to work slightly fewer hours than men in full-time employment. The national average working hours per week in urban areas since the mid-2000s have fluctuated around 45.5 hours and men on average work two hours more than women per week (*China Labour Statistical Yearbook 2008*).

Gender segregation by industrial sector, occupation and ownership form

An important source of gender gap in earnings in many countries is the sex segregation in industrial sector and occupation in which women are overcrowded in lower-paid industries and occupations with less training and fewer benefits and promotion opportunities (Charles and Grusky 1995). Even when men and women are in the same occupation, women are often assigned to different job titles that imply a lower status than that held by men (Bielby and Baron 1986). By comparison, gender segregation is arguably less prominent in the Chinese labour market. While women tend to be over-represented in certain industrial sectors such as education, health care, finance, wholesale, retail and catering in part because these jobs are traditionally seen to be more suitable for women, they are present in all sectors and occupations in a relatively even pattern (see Table 5.2).

However, women tend to be significantly under-represented in certain industrial sectors and types of construction industry due to the high risk and physically demanding nature of the jobs (the employment law bans women from working in mines or in deep water). Similarly, women are under-represented in government and Party organizations where power and control continue to be dominated by men (Cooke 2009a), as is the case in most countries. Government organizations have the third lowest proportion of women employees, after the mining and construction industry. The majority of women who are employed in government organizations are in administrative roles or work as officials in the lower ranks (Cooke 2009a). This is in spite of the fact that the education level of women is very close to that of men in the sector.

In some countries, it is the concentration of women in low paying jobs, rather than unequal pay for equal work, that produces large gender wage gaps (Oaxaca 1973). This is not quite the case in China. Those industries where women have a higher presence than men are not necessarily more lowly paid than those dominated by men. In fact, both men and women are found in the lowest paying

Table 5.2 Proportion (%) of female employees by selected ownership and sector and annual average wages for all employees in urban units (end of 1995 and 2008)

Item	Proportion (%) of female employment by ownership and sector in urban units								Annual average wage for all employees in urban units (yuan)	
	Total		State ownership		Collective ownership		Other ownership			
	1995	2008	1995	2008	1995	2008	1995	2008	1995	2008
National total	38.6	37.6	36.1	37.3	44.6	35.4	48.3	38.2	5,500	28,898
Farming, forestry, animal husbandry, fishery	37.6	36.3	37.8	36.5	31.9	28.3	37.2	33.4	3,522	12,560
Mining and quarrying	25.9	19.4	24.4	21.5	42.1	21.7	22.8	17.4	5,757	34,233
Manufacturing	45.2	42.1	40.9	32.8	53.1	43.4	49.7	43.7	5,169	24,404
Electricity, gas and water production and supply	31.4	29.4	31.5	29.6	32.1	31.6	28.8	28.8	7,843	38,515
Construction	19.4	13.9	20.7	16.3	17.8	15.2	14.2	12.6	5,785	21,233
Traffic, transport, storage and post	26.5	27.3	25.9	26.9	29.4	31.6	24.2	27.8	6,948	32,041
Wholesale & retail and hotel and catering*	46.3	46.1	44.9	38.4	47.5	41.7	56.4	51.2	4,248	25,818
Finance	40.0	50.1	39.3	47.2	41.9	43.3	46.0	54.3	7,376	53,897
Real estate	33.7	33.9	34.1	35.5	33.2	33.7	31.9	33.3	7,330	30,118
Resident (community) services and other services	–	43.6	–	37.8	–	44.1	–	52.3	–	22,858
Social welfare**	44.1	50.4	43.0	49.6	55.1	56.6	59.0	62.4	5,860	27,619
Health care**	56.9	60.3	58.1	60.8	49.7	55.1	57.8	62.5	5,860	32,374
Education**	41.9	49.5	41.8	49.4	48.9	51.7	42.5	53.1	5,435	29,831
Culture and art**	40.1	45.9	40.2	46.2	39.2	40.3	42.6	44.0	5,435	27,854
Governmental and party agencies, social organizations	22.6	27.7	22.5	27.7	35.0	40.8	30.0	45.2	5,526	32,296

Sources: compiled from *China Statistical Yearbook 1996*: 101–2; *China Labour Statistical Yearbook 2009*: 20–3, *China Statistical Yearbook 2009*: 177–80.

Notes

* Figures in 1995 were combined as one entry 'Wholesale, retail and catering', but separated in 2007 as entries under 'Wholesale and retail' and 'Hotel and catering'.
** Wage figures for the social welfare and health care sectors were in the same combined category in 1995 but separated in 2007. Wage figures for the education and culture and art sectors were in the same combined category in 1995 but separated in 2008.

Figures contained in this table include only urban workers and not rural migrant workers working in the urban units. Gender statistics on rural migrant workers working in urban industries are not available. However, it is known that the majority of workers in the construction industry are male rural migrant workers, whereas the majority of workers in the catering industry tend to be female rural migrant workers.

Women are specified by law to retire five years earlier than men of the same occupation. This partly accounts for their lower proportion in the total workforce in employment.

industries (e.g. construction, manufacturing and catering). Whereas low productivity is a main reason for the low wage level in the state-owned and collectively owned manufacturing firms, the combined effect of low level of human capital and the absence of bargaining power in the saturated labour market is the main cause for low pay in the construction and catering industry where over 70 per cent of those employed are rural migrant workers (*Workers' Daily* 9 November 2004). Where wage level is relatively high, women also make up a relatively high proportion of the workforce (e.g. finance and insurance, social welfare, health, culture and arts) (see Table 5.2). However, this prima facie evidence of equality disguises the fact that women in these industries tend to be in the lower positions in the organizational hierarchy with resultant lower levels of pay. For example, all nurses are women who are most likely to be earning less than doctors in general. In education, women tend to be over-represented in junior and senior schools and are under-represented in universities where they also tend to occupy lower positions.

A unique feature of gender segregation in the Chinese labour market is the over-presence of women in certain types of business ownership that are less well paid. Historically, a relatively high proportion of women work in the collectively owned sector where wage levels have been the lowest compared with those of the state-owned and the private sector. For example, in 2002, the average monetary wage in the state-owned units and units of other types of ownership was 12,422 yuan and 13,212 respectively, compared to 7,667 yuan in collectively owned units (*China Statistical Yearbook 2003*). Workers were allocated to their workplaces by the state during these periods. The disproportional placement of women workers to the collectively owned sector has been a significant source of the gender pay gap (Bian and Logan 1996; Zhou et al. 1997; Shu and Bian 2003). Since the mid-1990s, the proportion of women working in the collectively owned sector has declined due to the rapid shrinkage of the sector through downsizing and privatization. However, we cannot be over-optimistic of the likely effect this reversing trend may have on reducing the gender pay gap. There are increasing gaps in the wage level across different types of ownership within the private sector. For example, employees working in the 'Cooperative Units' (the second lowest paying ownership units of all after COEs) earned just 60.4 per cent of that earned by their counterparts working for the highest paying enterprises – shareholding corporations in 2007 (*China Statistical Yearbook 2008*). Those privatized former collectively owned enterprises may continue to be the lower paying firms within the private sector, as poor productivity and lack of competitiveness now present even greater challenges to a large proportion of the privatized SOEs and COEs.

Employers' discriminative practices

The effect of employer discrimination has been held accountable for a substantial amount of gender pay gap worldwide. This is no exception in China where employer discrimination against women in recruitment and promotion has been a major source of 'the persistence and pervasiveness of gender inequality within the labour force in urban China' (Bauer et al. 1992: 362). Although working full-time throughout their adult lives has become the norm for women, their opportunities for career advancement or access to certain sectors and occupations remain limited (Bauer et al. 1992). If the dominance of the state sector and the direct intervention from the state during the planned economy period had led to significant achievements in gender equality at workplaces in the urban area (Liu et al. 2000; Stockman et al. 1995), then these achievements have arguably been eroded since the 1980s. As a result of marketization, employers are granted greater autonomy in operating their businesses and human resource practices. This monopsony power in a slack labour market is partially translated into the more explicit expression of gender discrimination that was previously suppressed by the state with some effect. As Zhou (2000: 1168) argues, work organizations 'are being transformed into new institutional forms whose governance is not necessarily consistent with the principles of either redistribution or markets. Thus it is unlikely that organization-based income inequality can be lessened, let alone eradicated, by the presence of labor markets'.

Discriminative practices exist in recruitment, job allocation, training, promotion, redundancy and retirement (Cooke 2005a). Organizations that violate equal opportunity regulations either deliberately or due to ignorance are rarely punished. Few organizations have an equal opportunity policy and/or a career development policy in place as part of their human resource management policy. Where a clear career development and promotion policy is absent or ineffectively implemented, employees may have to rely more on the informal organizational career structure and networks outside the organization to advance their careers. This presents additional barriers to women due to the patriarchal structure and gender norm (see below for further discussion). This is particularly the case in government organizations where promotion criteria may be more elastic and promotion processes less transparent, despite the existence of a standard set of promotion criteria and procedures nationwide (Cooke 2009a). The low proportion and low rankings of women in government organizations where positional power and privilege prevail is ironic because these organizations should be the forerunners in implementing the state policy and legislation on gender equality. Instead, organizational leaders in these government bodies continue to suppress women's entry to these organizations and their subsequent career progression. Even when women have managed to gain the same official rank as their male counterparts, they are often placed in less lucrative departments and in deputy positions with less organizational resources allocated to the posts. This further handicaps women's ability to network to obtain political and social capital within and outside the organization needed to perform their tasks and to gain further promotion (Cooke 2009a).

Social value on gender roles

Whilst differences in education levels in the older workforce may go some way in explaining why a much smaller proportion of women than men are in leadership positions, the Chinese patriarchal cultural value and gender discrimination at workplaces that reflects societal values are far more significant factors attributing to the lower proportion of women in management positions. The conventional family norm is for the husband to deal with the external affairs and the wife to look after the internal affairs (see Chapter 6 women auditors for example). The husband's career also takes precedence, even though most couples are dual workers. It is not expected, or in some cases tolerated, that a wife should be more advanced in her career than her husband. However, this mindset is to a large extent influenced by the deeply embedded institutional convention of rewarding a family based on the man's rather than the woman's achievements and the social expectation of how a (married) woman should behave (Cooke 2005a; Lu and Zhao 2002).

The above analysis suggests that there is a relatively low level of gender segregation in industries and occupations with the exception of a couple of industries. The gender pay gap is moderate compared with that in many countries. When assessed in the global context, it can be concluded that China has fared relatively well compared with many other countries in terms of gender equality and pay equity (Cooke 2010b). However, a level of gender discrimination has always existed, and the achievement during the earlier era of socialism has been eroded by the process of marketization in which the state is less able and/or willing to intervene with employers' practices and market forces. The retreat of the redistributive state and the emergence of a market economy have given rise to new institutional forces (Nee and Cao 2004; Zhou 2000) that are creating a new combination of influencing factors that account for new patterns of gender discrimination and pay gap.

For example, the rising significance of human capital and business ownership forms in the gender pay gap indicates that market forces are playing an increasingly important role in the gender pay gap that is convergent with that in developed countries (Shu and Bian 2003). Meanwhile, positional power and organizational hierarchy remain important factors in shaping earning opportunities (Zhou 2000) where men continue to have the advantage over women. Whilst the increasing level of market competition across different ownership sectors and industries has resulted in rising wage levels in the private sector and in the expanding industries (e.g. finance and education) where women have a large share of employment, women tend to occupy lower positions in the organizational hierarchy. Equally, in government organizations, state policies in HRM that favour education and youth in career development in the reform period may arguably present more equal opportunity for well-educated women. This is unfortunately not the case in reality because gender discrimination and segregation which exist throughout the career ladder have resulted in persistent, and arguably more significant, gender gaps in earnings. Party membership as a form of political capital has shown signs of a comeback in the light of fierce competition in the graduate job market. In short, marketization has not eliminated gender wage gaps but has altered some of the processes, and political credentials remain an important factor that determines earnings, directly or indirectly.

In this section, we have examined the extent to which characteristics of the pay system have changed and how key factors that determined pay level may have evolved as a result of marketization. We use gender pay gaps as a focal point to illustrate some of the changes at a macro level. In the next section, we provide empirical examples of the pay practices adopted by well-performing/high-growth private firms in China. We explore why firms adopt particular pay practices (or not) and the extent to which these pay practices achieve the employer's objectives and meet the demands/expectations of the employees.

Emerging trends of pay practices in the private sector

As discussed in chapters 2 and 3, pay is considered to be a low order motivator in the high-performance/commitment model of HRM. Employers are urged to adopt HRM practices that will enhance employees' intrinsic rewards in order to retain talent and elicit their engagement with the organization. Interestingly, Rynes et al. (2004) observed that although 'pay is not equally important in all situations or to all individuals' (p. 381), the broad practical use as well as symbolic value of pay suggests that, 'far from being a mere low order motivator, pay can assist in obtaining virtually any level on Maslow's motivational hierarchy, including social esteem and self actualization' (p. 385). Rynes et al. (2004: 386) continued, 'research suggests that individual pay-for-performance schemes … are most important to high academic achievers, high-performing employees, and individuals with high self-efficacy and high needs for achievement … – just the types of people most employers claim to be looking for!' A number of other studies on the effect of financial incentives on organizational effectiveness also point to the fact that benefit packages help companies to attract, motivate and retain more competent employees and improve service quality (e.g. Coff 1997; Shaw et al. 1998; Baron and Kreps 1999; Lee et al. 2006). The effects of this are more apparent in high-tech firms (Gionfriddo and Dhingra 1999).

Performance-related pay and stock options as popular reward schemes

As noted above, one unique characteristic in the Chinese pay system has been the relatively large proportion of bonuses in the overall pay package (Cooke 2005a). An increasing number of firms in China are adopting variable pay systems, including profit-related bonus and stock options in order to retain key talent. The author's (Cooke 2009c) study of 65 private firms in 2007–8 and her study of 27 private firms in 2009 in a wide range of industries, including manufacturing/processing, finance, trading, commercial and professional businesses, reveal that stock options and profit-related bonus schemes were the top HR mechanism for motivation and retention (see Chapter 2).

These two studies found that the heavy economic orientation of private firms influences the way they allocate resources for the HR function. The HR practices they adopt are heavily geared towards maximizing the company's financial return through rent-sharing with employees. By tying individuals' financial rewards to the firm's profit level, firms are putting individuals on the front line of business competition and transferring the risk to them. This strategy attracts those who are motivated by money and success and hence match the individuals with the firm. Whilst the role of financial reward in retaining and motivating talent remains controversial, and proponents of high-commitment HRM argue that money is only a hygiene factor (e.g. Pfeffer 1998a), these two studies by the author indicated that financial rewards remain the most used and most effective HR mechanism to attract and retain talent in the private sector in China. This supports the findings of Björkman and Lu's (1999) study which showed that a competitive salary is an important mechanism to attract and retain managerial and professional talent in China. It is also in line with that of Horwitz et al.'s (2006) comparative study, which revealed that financial benefits and empowerment initiatives are the two distinctive HR methods for firms in Singapore and South Africa to attract and retain knowledge workers. While empowerment is not a key feature in HRM in the Chinese firms in this study, opportunity of promotion to the senior level, and its associated pay rise and organizational power, are the most important reasons for the turnover of managerial staff.

In addition, employees in these two studies conducted by the author have a strong preference to those HRM practices that will directly enhance their labour market prospects and ultimately financial returns, for example, human capital development through company-sponsored training. They also prefer short-term financial incentives instead of being tied to the firm for the longer term. By contrast, employers prefer to reward employees for their current performance and are unwilling to invest in training for their future performance for fear that these efforts will be undermined by market processes. Here, the efforts–reward tension between the employer and the employees is most evident. The materialistic orientation of individual employees and the economic orientation of the firm suggest that employment relations in these private firms are largely of a transactional nature. It indicates a sharp departure from the traditional Chinese values that are characterized by paternalism and reciprocal loyalty. It also calls into question the practical utility of the high-commitment model of HRM in the Chinese context. MNCs that wish to transfer their western HRM practices that are humanistic oriented may not succeed without the support of a strong financial rewards policy.

However, there is a limit to the motivational effect of financial rewards. Managers interviewed by the author in the two studies reported that some highly paid employees become complacent and lose motivation and aspiration, hence damaging the morale of other employees and team spirit. Equally, resentment emerges when employees feel that the profit-sharing scheme designed by the firm does not reflect proportionally the growth of the firm. For example, the annual profit growth of a finance company was ten times in the last three years between

2006 and 2008, but employees' annual profit sharing had grown by only seven times. Employees complained to the top managers and threatened to resign collectively unless adjustments were made. A view commonly shared by managers interviewed is that whilst the bonuses and stock options income of the key employees has been escalating rapidly in the last few years, the motivational effect of these incentives seemed to be in decline dramatically. Some managers also reported that who should receive how much bonus is often a decision arbitrarily made by the chief executive officer (CEO) in secret. This reward secrecy engenders suspicion and mistrust amongst the colleagues and between the CEO and the rest of the key staff.

For some companies, handsome financial rewards may not be sufficient to prevent employees' corrupt behaviour. For example, an owner CEO of a private automotive component manufacturing firm that employed over 1,500 employees in northern China revealed his predicament in the interview with the author in 2009:

> We have four managers responsible for purchase and sales. Two of them are very competent but are dishonest. They take thousands of yuan commissions privately in both selling products and purchasing materials each year. But their sales volume is high and therefore bringing in good revenue for the company. They have worked for the company for many years and are two of the longest serving employees of the firm. The other two managers have worked for the company for just a few years. They are not as competent and have much lower sale volume. But they are honest and resent the corrupted behaviour of the other two managers. They reported these incidents to the company. This creates a big problem for me. I cannot sack the two dishonest managers because the company is having difficulty in recruiting competent sales managers due to shortage of good candidates, and we have been expanding very rapidly in the last five years. I cannot understand why these two managers have to behave like this. The company has treated them very well and they receive performance-related bonuses, in addition to company stock options. The company has been making good profit in the last ten years, so the overall income of these managers is very handsome. The company has a clear rule which says that taking commission is a violation of company rule and serious offenders will be dismissed. If I don't deal with them, others will be very unhappy and may start doing the same. The company is losing a lot of money each year due to this behaviour.

In fact, dishonest behaviour is not uncommon amongst sales employees. Wilkinson et al.'s (2005) study also revealed the problems of HRM and relationship management encountered by the 47 sample British MNCs which have sourcing partnerships with 77 indigenous Chinese supplier firms. Difficulty in recruitment and retention, corruption behaviour, cultural and communicational problems, and poor working practices of supplier firms are some of the major problems in managing their key staff in the purchasing function.

As an HRM practice, the use of employee stock options to incentivize performance may trap companies into a path which is costly for them to break away from in order to redesign HRM practices to suit their new strategic needs. The leading Chinese IT MNC Huawei Technologies Ltd is a case in point (see Box 5.1).

Box 5.1 Reward strategy at Huawei Technologies Ltd

Financial reward system

Fairness and competitiveness (against potential competitor employers) are the two fundamental principles running through Huawei's reward system (as noted in Chapter 2, Huawei was founded in 1988 and employs over 60,000 employees world-wide). Performance-based reward comprises a significant part of an employee's total pay package. Reward distribution is based on individual employee's competence, achievement and contribution to the firm rather than his/her personal factors such as gender, age and length of service. For example, in a product design department, employees' total pay package consists of six components: basic wage, welfare, subsidy, bonus, company stock option and performance-related pay. Basic pay contains a number of grades which differentiate an employee's seniority and experience. Welfare consists of two parts. One is a fund that is accredited to the employee's staff card on a monthly basis which the employee can spend on transport, canteen meals or commodities in Huawei's shop. The other component is a pension which amounts to 15 per cent of one's monthly basic pay.

Benchmarking to maintain competitive edge

Huawei adopts a competitive reward strategy through regular benchmarking with its competitors and makes adjustments to its wage level annually based on market information and Huawei's financial performance. International HR consultancy firms such as Mercer and Hay Group are used to conduct a salary data survey regularly. An individual bonus system is adopted in which the bonus plan of a Huawei employee is closely linked to his/her level of responsibility, performance and tasks completed in each quarter.

Stock options

In addition, Huawei is privately owned and about 80 per cent of its stocks are held by its Chinese employees who joined the company in its early

---

years of development. The stock option scheme is no longer available to new employees. However, this option, which was initially adopted to boost morale in the firm's early days, had served its function in Huawei. It has become a problem in motivating the longer-serving staff and the new employees. For the former, their profit-sharing income is far higher than their salary income, so they see no point in working hard. By contrast, the new employees work harder but are earning much less than the older group of employees; they are therefore aggrieved for not being given the options. In late 2007, Huawei forced over 8,000 long-serving employees to resign (with handsome redundancy pay) and then rejoin the company as new employees. This took place as the controversial Labour Contract Law was about to be implemented (see Chapter 8 for more discussion). It was reported that Huawei did this in order to pre-empt the constraints imposed by the new law. However, Huawei maintained that this radical action was needed to break the culture of complacency amongst the longer-serving employees and harmonize the HRM practices across the workforce.

Employee welfare and engagement with family and local communities

Huawei provides additional welfare benefits to its employees as well as the provision of social insurance specified by local employment laws. For example, over 20,000 of Huawei's employees work in its Shenzhen head-quarters. Single employees are provided with accommodation, though subject to availability, at low rates in a holiday resort-like environment on site. The accommodation compound has the capacity to house over 3,000 employees, with comprehensive sports and fitness facilities, hotels, clubs and other facilities for social functions. There are three football pitches for training and competition matches. Chinese food is delivered to overseas sites for Chinese expatriates to improve their living standards, especially for those in hardship places like remote areas of Africa. This is typical of the Chinese paternalistic style of employee care. In addition, Huawei HQ has a wide range of employees clubs that are aimed to enhance the social life of its employees and achieve a work–life balance. These clubs are responsible for organizing picnics, dancing parties, sports meets, photo-graphing, song contests and other activities. Huawei has a 'Family Day' event that enables the families of employees to develop a deeper under-standing of and bonding with the company. Huawei's employees' clubs also encourage employees to become the conduit of its corporate social responsibility policy implementation through their participation in local community development activities, including donations for relief funds and educational sponsorships.

Problems of performance-related pay

A major problem of Huawei's performance-related pay is that individuals are competitive and unwilling to help each other out. Relationship between employees and line managers may be somewhat distanced due to the perceived high level of control by employees to meet targets. Some twenty managers and employees from Huawei whom the author has interviewed agreed that the majority of employees were satisfied with their overall reward package. Whilst all managers felt that reward should be related to individual performance, just over half the employees shared the same view. Employees interviewed felt that performance-related pay alone does not motivate them to work harder. Instead, the perceived need to enhance one's capability, competence and skills level, and the prospect of promotion and pay rise remain the key reasons that motivate hard work.

In addition, performance appraisal is conducted by line managers and employees may question the level of fairness in the managers' judgement (subjectivity). There appears to be no formal mechanism through which employees can participate in the design and implementation of the performance appraisal scheme or to challenge managers' assessment outcomes. This affects the perceived equity of the policy at the firm level. As one employee observed, 'Huawei is non-unionized. Everything is very paternalistic and top-down. Performance-related pay is used as a strong management control mechanism to regulate employees' behaviour unilaterally'.

Source: interview data collected by the author in 2008, also see Cooke 2009e.

Company-based welfare benefits

Company-based welfare benefits remain an enduring component in an employee's total financial reward package in China. For some companies and groups of employees, this component may constitute a significant part. Welfare benefits provisions may take a wide variety of forms, including: subsidies for meals, housing, transport and medical care, holiday tours, gifts for festivals, top-up social securities, sponsorship of education and training, entertainment and social events, paid holidays and so on. Some firms also extend their welfare activities to sending employees birthday presents, visiting them when they get married or when there is a bereavement in the family and providing hardship funds to employees whose families are going through difficult times. Unlike contributions to the social security provision which is statutorily required (see Table 5.1), company-based benefits provided by employers are on a voluntary basis.

There are several reasons for the centrality of company-based benefits in the reward package. Traditionally, taking care of employees, particularly when they are experiencing difficulties and hardships, is considered a moral duty and a social obligation of the employer. Employee welfare is one of the essential ingredients of organizational culture management (Cooke 2008b, also see Box 5.1 for Huawei's practices). It focuses on the material welfare and physical well-being of employees. Attention is paid to improving employees' quality of life by improving their living standards and working conditions. The objective of an extensive welfare provision is to alleviate employees' non-work-related worries and let them feel the warmth of the company so that they can concentrate on their work. It reflects the Chinese paternalistic value with a humanistic orientation. Such paternalistic value also informs the philosophy of management in the state-owned sector in socialist China.

What is interesting is that private firms are adopting more varieties of workplace welfare benefits than they used to in order to attract and retain talent. It is expected that the psychological outcome (e.g. enhanced commitment, motivation and morale) will be achieved through material support to satisfy employees' physiological and environmental needs. In high-paying jobs in private firms, workplace benefits are used as an effective means to top up employees' total income with less tax constraints, up to a limit, when wage increases are suppressed by the government.

More broadly, the emphasis on material provision to enrich employees' material and spiritual life is important in China because it is a relatively poor country and the majority of its workers can only earn enough for the most basic living. Firms are able to source materials and consumable products in large volume more economically than individuals, making it more cost-effective for firms to provide benefits. In export-oriented manufacturing plants (some are known as sweatshops), it is common for employers to provide subsidized accommodation and meals to the workers. The primary objective of this provision is to control labour mobility, to achieve economies of scale in social reproduction and to maximize the productive time of the workers (e.g. Cooke 2004; Lee 2007; Pun and Smith 2007). For the workers, this may be seen as a win-win solution as they are able to live very efficiently and maximize their earnings potential. It also provides them with a network of social support which is important when they are working far away from home. Of course, this mode of labour management has its inherent social problems (e.g. a series of suicides in Foxconn) and may become a natural and effective space for labour organizing during labour-management disputes (see Chapter 7 for more detail).

Another important reason for the adoption of company-based benefits instead of pay rises is that it gives employers flexibility in reward management. Since most of the benefits are decided unilaterally by the employer on a contingency basis, firms are able to withdraw or reduce the benefits according to their financial situation, employees' mood and changes in the market. The reluctance of employers to make longer-term financial commitments to their employees is also evidenced in their unwillingness to contribute to their employees' social security premium as required by law. As we have seen in Chapter 2 and will see in Chapter 8, employers are seeking innovative ways, often in collusion with other institutional actors in the labour market such as the employment agencies, to bypass the constraints of the Labour Contract Law. In the next section, we will discuss briefly the scope and level of social security provision for those in informal employment, which accounts for the majority of (rural) migrant workers employed in the urban area and a significant proportion of those who work in the private sector.

Scope and level of social security provision

As we have noted in Chapter 2, a significant proportion of Chinese workers are engaged in informal employment, although what classifies as 'informal employment' remains a concept of much debate. Rodgers (2002) argued that the lack of social protection is not only a defining feature of the informal economy, but also a critical aspect of social exclusion to those who have never had access to formal mechanisms of social protection or are losing the protection they once had through the state and/or their workplace. This is especially true in developing countries where social protection for workers in the informal sector is either rudimentary or non-existent and where compulsory coverage, even when it exists, is often not complied with in practice (ILO 2000). Yet it is these workers in informal employment who are most in need of social protection, not just because of their job and income insecurity but more importantly, 'because of the greater likelihood of their being exposed to serious occupational safety and health hazards. Such exposure impairs the health and productivity as well as the general well-being and quality of life of informal workers and their families' (Rodgers 2002: 54).

Prior to the enactment of the Labour Contract Law in 2008 (see Chapter 8), a rudimentary system of social security had emerged to cover workers in the formal sector, gradually extending to those in informal employment (Zhang 2007). However, the main problem is the absence of social security schemes affordable by those in low pay. For example, Jiao (2008) reported that in 2004, only 15,000 workers in informal employment in Yangzhou – a developed city on the eastern coast – participated in health insurance schemes. This was less than 5 per cent of the 303,000 rural migrant workers working in the city in the same year.

Although a series of social security policy regulations have been issued by the Ministry of Human Resources and Social Security, the implementation of these schemes remains problematic and is heavily biased towards urban residents. Local governments are trying to address the situation through piloting various innovative social security schemes tailored for the low-wage workers. For example, Cooke's (2008c) study found that a municipal trade union in southern China was facilitating the local government to introduce a low-cost medical care scheme for workers in financial difficulty. The scheme provides subsidized medical care for registered workers at local hospitals. Another medical care scheme involves insurance cooperatives where workers' participate in the insurance against specific types of illnesses such as breast cancer.

The municipal governments of Shanghai and Beijing adopted different insurance initiatives tailored for workers in informal employment. In Shanghai, workers employed in informal labour organizations can participate in all sorts of social security schemes. Both employees and employers are given a lower rate of contribution, but the employees can enjoy the same benefits as those social security participants in formal employment. The objective of this favourable policy is to encourage the growth of informal labour organizations through government subsidy of contributions (Jia 2007; Ren 2008). This scheme is considered not efficient due to the high cost to be borne by the government. It triggers opportunistic behaviours of informal labour organizations which provide employment opportunities mainly to unemployed urban citizens, particularly the laid-off workers, instead of rural migrant workers (Ren 2008).

In contrast to the 'Shanghai Model' (Jia 2007; Ren 2008), the 'Beijing Model' (Jia 2007) targets rural migrant workers by providing special regulations for their health insurance. According to the 'Temporary Regulations on Basic Health Insurance for Rural Migrant Workers in Beijing' (2004), contributions to the basic health insurance scheme for rural migrant workers is to be borne by their employer instead of the workers. Rural migrant workers who suffer from major illnesses enjoy the same insurance benefits as others during their insured period, disregarding the number of years they have been insured. This model essentially shifts the financial burden from the rural migrant workers to the employers (Jia 2007), making some low-profit businesses unsustainable.

It is clear that how to strike the balance between fairness and efficiency through the reasonable allocation of the insurance cost among the individual, employer and government remains a challenge to local governments. Each of them is coming up with its own initiatives, often implemented in a trial-and-error manner with varying degrees of success. What needs to be noted here is that we cannot assume that local governments will always act in the interest of the workers in policing employers' compliance to legal requirements. On the contrary, local governments, in order to achieve their other priorities, may create opportunities for employers to bypass the laws promulgated by the state, as we can see in Chapter 8.

Conclusion

It is now acknowledged that there are widening income gaps and economic disparity among different groups of employees employed by firms in different ownership forms in China as a direct result of marketization. The opening up of the Chinese economy has also led to the evolution of values and preferences/ expectations in the exchange of effort and rewards. In this chapter, we have examined reasons for the widening wage gaps at firm and industrial level. We have also investigated what new pay schemes are being adopted by firms in order to contain costs, motivate the workforce and retain talent. In particular, we have explored the extent to which performance-related pay and stock options may be effective as motivational and retention mechanisms. It is clear that pay level remains an important factor in the Chinese labour market that is sensitive to skill and unemployment levels, and that pay determination is perhaps the most crucial and challenging aspect of HRM that firms have to grapple with in attracting and retaining talent. Research evidence suggests that firms are primarily rewarding existing performance instead of investing in their employees for development and future productivity gains. This short-term orientation of the reward strategy is not conducive to human capital development for both the individuals and the firm in the long term. Perhaps not surprisingly then, stock options as a popular incentive scheme is not yielding the desired motivational effect sought by employers. This is in spite of the fact that employee stock options have been advocated by strategic HRM writers (e.g. Bhattacharya and Wright 2005) as one of the mechanisms for firms to retain employees.

It is clear that many private firms are still non-strategic in their reward management and that their motivational mechanisms are simplistic, non-systematic, lack variety and perceived fairness. For key staff, incentives rather than punitive mechanisms are adopted to discipline behaviour. There is insufficient consideration of what employees desire in order to match the reward practices with their expectations (e.g. Ding et al. 2009). Nevertheless, there are clear signs (Cooke 2009c and 2009e) that private firms are beginning to commission market surveys, via HR consultancy firms, to benchmark their wage levels. This is particularly true in the finance, IT and real estate industries where business expansion and wage increase are both rapid. This benchmarking exercise enhances the transparency of the pay level of the firm in comparison with its competitors in the same industry. It not only helps diffuse employees' suspicions that they are worse off than their counterparts in other firms, but also enables firms to adjust their pay level accordingly to remain competitive. Moreover, benefits as an important component in employees' reward packages are used more strategically to elicit higher levels of performance and as a way to control labour cost in a more flexible way, and not simply as paternalistic gestures derived from Chinese culture.

It is important to note that paternalism and egalitarianism, the two enduring values that influence the reward system in China, are not just traditional Chinese cultural values, but also socialist values that have informed many management practices (also see Chapter 6). Employers are expected not only to take care of their employees but also to do so in a fair manner. As Confucius articulated in his Analects, 'he is not concerned lest his people should be poor, but only lest what they have should be ill-apportioned' (不患寡而患不均) (Waley, 1995, cited in Wu 2009: 1038). Ironically, the Chinese people are found to be more tolerant of income inequality. Wu's (2009) study showed that Chinese people believe in individual effort and merit-based disparities. They are more willing than people from other societies to accept the fact that some people are earning more because of their merit-based attributes, including education and skill levels. Nevertheless, there is a strong perception that farmers and workers are underpaid and that 'senior government officials and executives in large state-owned companies are overpaid by a large amount' Wu's (2009: 1051). And much of the social unrest and discontent has been fuelled by this growing income disparity and distributive unfairness (see Chapter 7).

Considerable space has been devoted in this chapter to assess the level of gender pay gaps and the likely causes of these gaps, including the role of gender discrimination, because so far this issue has attracted little attention in the literature of HRM in China. Given the fact that women make up nearly 38 per cent of the full-time workforce, this is a significant gap that needs to be filled. The understanding of gender pay gaps also enables us to understand more fully other related aspects of gender (in)equality in employment and HRM. This is because employers' strategy plays an increasingly crucial role in shaping HRM practices at the workplace level within the wider institutional and cultural context. In the next chapter, we will continue to examine issues related to equal opportunities in the labour market and HRM practices, including the awareness and understanding of diversity management and work–life balance as part of the corporate social responsibility of employing organizations.

6   Equal opportunity and diversity management

Introduction

The concept of diversity management (DM), popularized in the USA in the 1990s, is increasingly promoted as a strategic people management technique that will enhance organizational competitiveness (Cooke 2011a). Some US-owned MNCs also roll out their domestic-designed DM programmes to their global operations (Nishii and Özbigin 2007). This is in spite of the fact that the utility of DM as a US-originated concept in other societal contexts has been questioned by some researchers (e.g. Agocs and Burr 1996; Ferner et al. 2005; Healy and Oikelome 2007; Nishii and Özbilgin 2007). The intention of promoting DM in global operations is to address the talent shortage problem and to enhance employees' engagement by accommodating the diverse needs of individuals and social groups (Cooke 2011c).

Existing studies have revealed unique societal contexts in which diversity issues are embedded; as such, diversity may be manifested in different meanings and substantive issues across national boundaries (Cooke and Saini 2010). For example, in the USA and the UK, workforce diversity may include: gender, race, ethnicity, religion, age, disability, immigration status, social class, political asso-ciation, marital status, parental status, sexual orientation, ex-offenders and so on. Many of these differences are accepted by the society, protected by law and accommodated in company policy. However, some of these diversity character-istics may not be acceptable legally and/or socially in oriental countries like China, where age, gender, disability and place of origin (e.g. rural v. urban) are the main causes of social inequality (Cooke 2011a). Similarly, ethnic groups in Japan and Korea are relatively homogenous and as a result, gender, women's marital status and their related employment status may be the key sources of workforce diversity (Cooke 2010b). These societal differences undoubtedly present significant challenges to western multinational firms that wish to design and implement a global DM programme to retain and harness talent.

This chapter examines the institutional and cultural context of equal opportunity (EO) and diversity management in China. It identifies what the key issues are in managing diversity and investigates the extent to which legislation, government policies, organizational initiatives and management attitudes have been conducive to achieving a fair work environment. It should be noted that despite growing academic interest in DM, 'diversity management' is a poorly understood, increasingly slippery and controversial concept that is used 'in an all-embracing fashion to include not just the social categories of AA [affirmative actions] such as race and sex but a wide range of personal characteristics' (Ferner et al. 2005: 309). For the purpose of this chapter, we adopt a broad definition of DM put forward by Arredondo (1996) and adopted by Wentling (2000): 'diversity initiatives are defined as specific activities, programmes, policies, and any other formal processes or efforts designed to promote organizational culture change related to diversity' (cited in Wentling 2000: 436). Examples of DM initiatives at the organizational level we examine here include: flexible working arrangements, work–life balance initiatives, training programmes to raise cultural awareness, and equal opportunity policies and practices.

Diversity management as part of strategic HRM

The concept of managing diversity has its origins in the USA and emerged as an HR intervention in the mid-1980s. It was primarily a response to demographic changes (e.g. more immigrants and women) in the workplace as well as the customer/client base (Agocs and Burr 1996). It was also a response to corporate discontent with the affirmative action approach imposed by the US government. Diversity management was seen as a way to address retention, integration and career development (Agocs and Burr 1996). Growing demands from ethnic minorities, women, and older, disabled, and gay and lesbian groups for equal rights and the consequent human rights legislation in the 1990s and 2000s gave further drive to the need for recognizing, accepting and valuing individual differences at the workplace and in society more widely (Mor Barak 2005).

In Britain, the concept of managing diversity has undoubtedly become more influential since the mid-/late 1990s in part due to the demographic change of the workforce, but more so because DM is seen as a more comprehensive and sophisticated approach to equal opportunities management that adds value to business. The Chartered Institute of Personnel and Development (CIPD), a British national association for HR practitioners and academics, defines diversity as 'valuing everyone as an individual – valuing people as employees, customers and clients' (CIPD 2006: 2).

It is suggested (e.g. Cox 1993; Soni 2000) that the objectives of DM are for organizations to increase awareness of cultural differences; to develop the ability to recognize, accept and value diversity through organizational intervention in order to minimize the patterns of inequality experienced by those not in the mainstream; and to modify organizational culture and leadership practices so that 'members of all socio-cultural backgrounds can contribute and achieve their full potential' (Cox 1993: 225). It is argued that there are three important reasons for DM: effective people management, tackling market competition and enhancing corporate reputation (e.g. Jayne and Dipboye 2004; CIPD 2006; Konrad et al. 2006). DM is regarded as a better approach than equal opportunity management as it 'focuses on valuing people as unique individuals rather than on group-related issues covered by legislation' (CIPD 2007: 6). In line with proponents of the importance of strategic HRM to organizational performance, enthusiasts of DM argue that organizations committed to DM outperform those that are not (e.g. Cox 1993; Soni 2000; Jayne and Dipboye 2004; CIPD 2006; Konrad et al. 2006). Indeed, existing studies have provided some evidence to support the assumption that strategic DM can lead to enhanced HR outcomes, such as the attraction of talent (e.g. Ng and Burke 2005).

However, other studies have revealed that the benefits of DM rhetoric can be overstated (e.g. Williams and O'Reilly 1998; Wise and Tsehirhart 2000), and that DM initiatives may actually undermine efforts in EO programmes (e.g. Subeliani and Tsogas 2005). Kochan et al. (2003) questioned whether or not the business case rhetoric of DM has run its course. Nevertheless, they argued that while we may be sceptical about the positive impact of DM on organizational performance, diversity is a labour market imperative as well as a societal value and expectation. Therefore, 'managers should do their best to translate diversity into positive organizational, group and individual outcomes' (Kochan et al. 2003: 18).

In short, workplace diversity is becoming a core issue for study in management theories and practices in western countries (Konrad et al. 2006), marked by a burgeoning body of literature that spans a number of disciplines (e.g. psychology, sociology and management) with different research methods (e.g. interviews, case studies, surveys, ethnographic studies and laboratory-based studies). By contrast, DM as a management concept has been hardly heard of by most people in China, and is even less featured in its management talks. This is not to suggest that Chinese societies are not diverse and that there is no legal provision to protect some of the basic rights of those socially disadvantaged, or that managers at workplaces do not have the task of managing the diverse needs of their workforce. Rather, it is argued here that diversity in China may exist within a significantly different historical, institutional, social and cultural context, and that organizations have yet to realize the strategic importance of managing a diverse workforce effectively to gain competitive edge. In addition, a low preference for diversity management may well be linked to the low level of countervailing power possessed by the disadvantaged groups in these countries.

In the next two sections, we discuss the cultural and institutional background, ideology, process and outcome of equal opportunity and diversity management in China. We do so with reference to western DM literature (see Table 6.1) and assess the extent to which the western notion of managing diversity is compatible with Chinese culture, and how managers manage (or not) their workforce diversity. It must be noted that the concept and moral soundness of DM is still a contentious issue in western literature. It is beyond the scope of this chapter to go into detail about these debates (see Lorbiecki and Jack 2000 for an overview of the conceptual premises and critique of DM). For comparison purposes, we draw on the USA/UK perspective (loosely defined) as the context for the discussion of diversity issues in China.

Table 6.1 Diversity management issues in the USA/UK and China

Issues of diversity management	Country	
	USA/UK	China
National cultural values and institutional environment as societal context for managing diversity	Individualism; increasing emphasis of human rights, broadening framework of employment legislation; changing demographics of workforce; heightened global competition; influences of well-developed professional associations and consulting firms on HR matters	Collectivism, respect of hierarchy, endurance, diligence, paternalism, egalitarianism; basic but increasing level of employment regulation, high level of government intervention; relatively high level of women in employment, large number of rural migrant workers in urban employment, skill shortages, high level of repatriation of western-trained graduates; rapid expansion of business opportunities in last two decades
Sources of diversity/discrimination as recognized by the society and, in some cases, protected by law	Gender, ethnicity, religion, age, disability, immigration status, social class, political association, marital status, parental status, sexual orientation, ex-offenders, experience	Gender, migrant rural workers, age, disability, ethnicity, overseas graduate returnees
State intervention in diversity management/equal opportunity	Equal opportunity regulations, affirmative action plans, administrative policy	Equal opportunity regulations, affirmative action policy (e.g. minimum quota for women in management in government organization)
Reasons for diversity management at organizational level	Legal compliance to avoid financial and reputation cost, business case (widely publicized but not necessarily embraced by firms)	Legal compliance (not always stringently enforced), business case (yet to be made aware of to firms)
Approaches to diversity management/equal opportunity at organizational level	Equal opportunity regulations, business case, HR/diversity management initiatives (e.g. fast-track promotion programme for ethnic minorities, family leave, job sharing, language courses)	Equal opportunity regulations (not always adhered to), HR policy (often not available), ad hoc and informal practices (sometimes adopted by managers at operational level)
Methods of implementation at organizational level	Communication, training, involvement	No formal implementation mechanism (as reported by interviewees)
Measurements of diversity management outcome at organizational level	Measurement techniques available but not always adopted by firms	Measurement techniques not designed and outcome not measured (as reported by interviewees)

Source: compiled by the author.

Contexts and sources of workforce diversity and inequality in China

China has a markedly different societal context for diversity management from the USA and UK (see Table 6.1). It is a relatively homogeneous country, with about 95 per cent of its population belonging to the *han* race. Whilst over 50 ethnic minority races coexist, they are mainly populated in the peripheral area of the country where the economy is generally much less well developed compared with the eastern region. Mandarin is the official language, although thousands of local dialects are spoken for daily communication. Religious practices are not widespread in part due to the restrictions imposed by the Communist Party, especially prior to the social and economic reform period starting from the late 1970s. For thousands of years, successive Chinese rulers have emphasized unity at the expense of diversity and multiculturalism, sometimes achieved through military force. Under the socialist regime, the ideology of 'pursuing universalism (sameness) with tolerance to differences' (求大同，存小异) prevails. As a result, the major sources of diversity in contemporary China come from gender, age, differential residential status of rural v. urban origin and geographic differences.

Indeed, existing evidence suggests that residential status (i.e. urban v. rural residential status, local v. non-local residential status), gender and age are the three most significant sources of discrimination in the Chinese labour market (see Tables 6.1 and 6.2; also see chapters 5 and 8). Women, non-local residents and older workers are amongst the most disadvantaged groups of workers which may be subject to various forms of discrimination throughout the labour market process. In some cases, age, gender and residential status intersect with each other, further disadvantaging certain groups of workers, notably women (Cooke 2011d).

Women workers: opportunities and barriers

Women engaging in full-time employment is a relatively new phenomenon in many western countries as a result of the changing structure of their economy (e.g. from manufacturing to service oriented), the feminization of certain professional occupations (e.g. banking) and the increased availability of women to work part-time or even full-time. By contrast, one distinctive feature of the labour market in China is the high participation rate of women, as noted in Chapter 5. This is in spite of the fact that the proportion of women in the workforce has experienced a small but steady decline since the 1990s. In 1995, women made up 38.6 per cent of the workforce; this was reduced to 37.6 per cent in 2008 (*China Statistical Yearbook 2009*). In fact, both men and women experienced a considerable decline in the employment rate, from 97 per cent for both genders in 1988 to 89 per cent for men and 81 per cent for women in 2004 (J. S. Zhang et al. 2008). This decline is mainly attributed to the ongoing large-scale downsizing in the state-owned and collectively owned enterprises since the mid-1990s.

Table 6.2 Forms of inequality and types of workers affected

Types of workers affected	Forms of inequality
Gender	
• Women	• Disproportionally laid off in the SOEs • Inaccessibility to certain professional groups and career progression • Wage discrimination
Age	
• Young workers	• Recruitment discrimination due to lack of experience
• Older workers	• Disproportionally laid off • Age bar in recruitment • More likely to be forced into informal employment
Residential status	
• Rural migrant workers	• Confined to informal employment and to certain industrial sectors and occupations (e.g. construction, manufacturing, catering, community services) • Poor employment terms and conditions • Inaccessibility to social security • Job insecurity
Gender and age	
• Women in the state-owned sector	• Earlier retirement age • Older women less likely to be promoted
• Women in privately owned/ foreign-funded manufacturing plants	• Age bar in recruitment
Gender and residential status	
• Rural female migrant workers	• Secondary earner of the migrant family
• Female university graduates with non-local residential status	• Recruitment discrimination

Source: Cooke (2011d).

Protecting women's employment rights and interests has been a mission of the Chinese Communist Party as the foundation for realizing gender equality, at least in principle. Since the 1950s, the state has made efforts to promote women's participation in employment through legislation, administrative policy and affirmative action programmes. Significant investment was made in childcare facilities to relieve the burden of working mothers. These interventions have led to significant advancements in pay and social equity for female workers. Research studies have found that gender discrimination is less of a problem in certain employment aspects in China than in some other countries such as the USA, Britain, Japan, Korea and India (e.g. Stockman et al. 1995; Cooke 2007; Lam and Graham 2007).

However, despite achievements in gender equality, gender inequality exists in various stages of the labour market process and is exhibited to a different degree across sectors (see Tables 5.2 and 6.2). For example, in the SOEs and COEs, women have been disproportionately selected for retrenchment and are experiencing more difficulties than men in regaining employment (Zhang and Zhao 1999; Appleton et al. 2002; Cooke 2005a). A large proportion of women are taking up informal employment as the last resort and women are more lowly paid than men in general (Cooke 2005a). For example, 45 per cent of the workers employed in community services and self-help bases in 2004 were women (*China Labour Statistical Yearbook 2005*: 180). Indeed, the deepening of China's economic transformation has led to a rising level of informalization of employment – a growing form of employment that has yet to be protected effectively by employment law (see chapters 2, 7 and 8). Both policy makers and officials in organizations that are charged to facilitate women's re-employment (e.g. labour authorities, trade union organizations and All-China Women's Federation (ACWF) branches) appear to focus on getting laid-off women re-employed rather than creating opportunities for them to find decent jobs (e.g. measured by pay level and working time). Some of them criticize laid-off women for being too picky and ambitious in what (quality) jobs they can hope to get instead of being 'more realistic' and accepting *any* jobs.

Discriminative criteria are often spelt out in recruitment advertisements and selection processes (e.g. Cooke 2005a, 2011a; Woodham et al. 2009). There appears to be persistent recruitment discrimination against young women who have yet to become mothers due to the perceived cost of maternity (e.g. downtime and reduced commitment to work). Lack of progress in social insurance for maternity has been a major stumbling block for younger professional women to seek meaningful employment and career progression. Many professional women postpone their maternity in order to hold on to their career. In many firms, not having a child in the first few years of employment has become an unwritten rule for young female employees. Some firms set an annual quota system and request women to queue for their turn to have children (this information was disclosed to the author by a female informant who worked in a state-owned bank branch in May 2010).

Seniority in organizational position and pay equity are two important indicators of gender equality. But existing evidence suggests that there remain some gaps in these two dimensions. Women continue to be under-represented in organizational leadership positions in China. Despite their significant advancement in educational attainments and a respectable inroad into professional and technical positions, only 0.5 per cent of women worked as heads of organizations in 2007, compared with 1.8 per cent of men who did so (*China Labour Statistical Yearbook 2008*). Gender discrimination is also a source of gender pay gaps, although the precise proportion is difficult to specify (see Chapter 5 for further discussion).

At the national level, a higher proportion of women than men work in the informal sector. For example, according to a report issued by the Chinese State

Council in 2003, over half those in informal employment in the urban sector were women (cited in Zhao and Ma 2007). Other studies (e.g. Xu 2000; Jin 2006; Liu and Li 2007) also point to the gendered pattern of informal employment in which women are more likely to be employed in this sector, concentrated in the manufacturing and service industries, and receive a lower wage than men on average (see chapters 2 and 7 for further discussion on informal employment and rural migrant workers).

Residential status: discrimination against rural migrant workers

One major contribution to China's burgeoning urban economic development since the mid-1980s has been the extensive participation of rural migrant workers. According to national statistics, there were some 50 million rural migrant workers working in urban areas by 1995, representing one-quarter of those working in the urban area (Chen et al. 2001). By 2003, there were over 98 million rural migrant workers working away from their hometown (*Workers' Daily* 12 October 2004). In some developed cities, there are more rural migrant workers than urban citizens. Rural migrant workers made up over 46 per cent of the workforce in the industrial and service sectors (*Workers' Daily* 9 November 2004). Despite their indispensable contribution to China's urbanization and rapid economic development, rural migrant workers enjoy very few labour rights, and where rights exist they are often not effectively enforced (Cooke 2005a, also see chapters 7 and 8).

In fact, residential status has been an enduring source of discrimination and social inequality. The *hukou* system has privileged urban citizens against rural citizens and local residents against non-local residents in the enjoyment of education, health care, social security and employment opportunities as well as other rights. Rural migrant workers are by far the largest and most disadvantaged group of workers of this rigid, albeit relaxing, system. Initially working in manufacturing plants, on construction sites and as domestic helpers, they are now working in a wide spread of industries and occupations, but primarily in private firms, foreign-invested sweatshop plants and the informal sector where labour standards are low and employment regulations often violated. The vast majority of rural migrant workers have no written employment contract, little training, few rest days, no social security and minimal health and safety protection. They work extremely long hours, live in poor conditions and are largely unorganized and unrepresented (e.g. Chan 2001; Gallagher 2005; Lee 2007; Pun and Smith 2007). Despite high-profile government campaigns in the mid-2000s, delays of wage payment remain common, especially in the construction industry (Cooke 2008d).

In dangerous jobs, the near absence of social security and health and safety protection has had damaging consequences for workers and their families. Over 70 per cent of the major industrial accidents occur in non-state-owned small enterprises as a result of the lack of training, employers' negligence in health and safety protection, and the dilapidation of the technology and equipment deployed for production (*Renmin Daily* 2 December 2004). Many minor accidents and workplace-related health problems go unreported or are not dealt with, despite the constant media exposure of workplace health and safety hazards.

The adversarial employment condition endured by rural migrant workers is a legacy of the non-egalitarian socialist development strategy adopted by the government in which urban development has been achieved ironically at the expense of the rural population (e.g. Solinger 1999; Meng 2000; Shue and Wong 2007). Institutionalized discriminative practices continue when rural migrant workers enter urban employment. Although efforts have been made by the government to eliminate discriminative practices since the 1990s through regulatory and policy intervention, the lack of comprehensive legislative coverage and effective enforcement in the private and informal sectors means that these workers remain largely unprotected (Cooke 2008d). The enactment of the Labour Contract Law in 2008 has not brought real protection (i.e. employment security and social security) to the majority of migrant workers. This is because employers have found ways to bypass the law effectively. Eager to attract business investments to generate tax revenue and achieve their performance targets, local governments often turn a blind eye to employers' malpractices. Some local governments have even introduced administrative policy regulations to dilute the impact of the Labour Contract Law.

Adversarial labour standards, the absence of labour protection and organization, and social discrimination and exclusion have resulted in rural migrant workers voting with their feet en masse, causing severe labour shortages (known as *mingong huang* 民工荒) in the developed economic areas where factories cluster, between 2004 and 2008. Although the wage level of some factories are not low in a relative sense, the poor working and living conditions and aggressive management style cause retention problems.

The government has recognized the problem and is introducing new regulations to eliminate the inequality experienced by rural migrant workers, including the enactment of the Labour Contract Law and the Labour Disputes Mediation and Arbitration Law in 2008. However, implementing these regulations at organizational level remains a challenge (see Chapter 8). In the longer term, workplace inequality against rural migrant workers is likely to be more problematic for employing organizations, as the second generation of rural migrant workers are more highly educated compared with their parents' generation. They are more aware of social injustice problems, demand fair treatment and seek better employment and career opportunities, as evidenced in the series of strikes in foreign-invested plants in 2010 (see Chapter 7).

Employment-related migration brings a major source of diversity to the workplace because different geographic origins give rise to different habitual traditions, dialects, cultural preferences and lifestyles, especially for a large country like China. Since cross-region migration (e.g. from poorer provinces and cities to richer provinces and cities and from rural to urban areas) has become very common for individuals to seek employment and advance their careers, how to manage the diverse groups of workers remains an HR issue. This is particularly the case among the lower level of workers. For example, Cooke's (2004) study of a toy manufacturing plant which employed primarily rural migrant workers revealed that inter-region differences can be a main source of conflicts and grievances amongst migrant workers, especially when production pressure is high. According to Chan and Goto (2003: 455), geographic origin is an important source of group identity for collectivists such as Chinese who 'are particularly sensitive to the ingroup/outgroup distinction'. When involved in a conflict, Hong Kong Chinese tend to categorize themselves as ingroup members and those from Mainland China and the USA as outgroup members. Undoubtedly, similar issues occur in the Indian context where internal migration for work is also common.

Age discrimination

Given the higher proportion of young people in the population, the relatively early retirement age for Chinese workers and the redundancy and early retirement schemes adopted by organizations in part to ease unemployment pressure, workers in China are relatively young. Still, ageism is a widespread form of discrimination in China. Age disadvantage manifests itself in two ways in the labour market. Discrimination against older workers is widespread across sectors and ownership forms. For instance, it is a common practice for job advertisements to specify age limits to job candidates, in addition to gender preferences as noted above. Older age is also a negative factor for promotion in mid-senior ranks for government officials and civil servants. In the private sector, employers often specify the gender and age limits of job candidates even though this is unlawful as stipulated in the Labour Law of China (Cooke 2005a). In the state-led redundancy programme in state-owned and collectively owned enterprises in the late 1990s, age was a common criterion for selection or for dismissal. Women above the age of 40 and men above the age of 50 were mostly likely to be laid off or forced to take early retirement. These displaced workers then encountered significant barriers to regain employment due to their obsolesce skills and age disadvantage compared with rural migrant workers and young school leavers.

It is important to note that labour market discrimination is not confined to older workers and those who are relatively low skilled and lowly educated. The rapid expansion of the Chinese higher education sector since the early 2000s has led to a rising level of university graduate unemployment, particularly of those who have no work experience. Increasingly, employers only hire job candidates who have at least two years of work experience. The costs of training and retention problems are the main reasons for employers' unwillingness to employ inexperienced university graduates. The highly controversial Labour Contract Law enacted in 2008 further deters employers from hiring graduates to try them out, as the law imposes a number of restrictions on employers in wage payment and termination of contract (Fu 2008).

Gender, age and residential status factors may intersect, further disadvantaging certain groups of workers in different segments of the labour market, as we shall see below.

Double disadvantages: gender and age

Since 1951, China has pursued a retirement policy in which female workers in general retire five years earlier than their male colleagues in the same occupation (at the age of 50 for manual female workers and 55 for female professionals). This policy was introduced initially as a preferential treatment for women who have to bear the strain of childbearing and caring. The enforcement of the one-child policy since the mid-1980s has increased the affordability of childcare and domestic help, and technological advancements mean that work is less strenuous and that the burden of family care is significantly reduced for women. The dramatic increase in educational level also helps many women develop a successful career (Cooke 2005a). However, despite repeated campaigns by women's pressure groups for the government to change the differentiated retirement policy on economic and equity grounds, no change has been made to the policy formally. Nevertheless, industrial/occupational-based policy documents have been issued in recent years which request employing organizations to extend women's employment age where conditions permit. In government organizations, older women cadres are less likely to be promoted than men of similar age bands and are often allocated to positions/departments with fewer resources (Cooke 2009a).

For migrant women workers, the age bar comes much earlier in their working life, particularly for those who work in the privately owned or foreign-funded manufacturing plants with a high level of production intensity. In the interests of maintaining productivity premium (delivered by young and able workers) and avoiding the responsibility imposed by the local government to monitor the birth control of their women workers, employers target women between the ages of 16 and 23 for recruitment. Once they are married and become pregnant, they will be dismissed. Some employers even compel women workers to sign an (unlawful) agreement that they will not get pregnant during their employment with the firm or they will be dismissed. When labour shortages are encountered, employers may be willing to consider recruiting older women (e.g. those in their late thirties or forties) who have passed their most active reproduction period. However, employers may choose to recruit these workers via employment agencies in order to pass on the birth control monitoring responsibility – employment agencies simply dismiss these workers when they are found to be violating the birth control policy.

The transient nature of rural migrant workers' employment, as perceived by factory managers, further deprives these 'maiden' workers of any career progression prospects. As Lee's (1995: 385) study revealed, 'management only groomed male recruits to acquire firm-specific technical skills. The promotion track from repair worker to technician, assistant foreman, and supervisor was denied to women workers'.

Double disadvantages: gender and residential status

Gender and residential status undoubtedly have a compound negative effect on women and their opportunity to seek quality employment and wage earning. This affects women at both the lower and upper end of the labour market. For example, a report released by the ACWF in 2006 showed that over 50 per cent of female rural migrant workers were engaged in informal employment compared with 40 per cent of men (cited in Wei 2007). Gao's (2006) survey of 1,916 migrant workers in five major cities in 2003 revealed that men on average earned a much higher hourly wage (4.8 yuan) than women (3.4 yuan). In particular, the industrial sector plays a more important role in accounting for the wage differentials than the small differences in age and educational level between the genders.

Liu and Li's (2007) study revealed an M-shape pattern in the age of women rural migrant workers, indicating the need for them to remain in the rural family home during the childcaring period. In addition, a much higher proportion of women (45 per cent) than men (23 per cent) migrate with their spouse. Wang (2006) observed an increasing trend of family migration instead of single migration amongst rural migrant workers. As 'trailing' spouses, the wives of migrant families with childcaring responsibilities are more constrained than single female migrants in their mobility and job opportunities. They tend to play the home carer role, often taking some casual and short-time jobs to supplement the family income instead of being the main income provider. This primary–secondary earner family model breaks away from the modern Chinese dual-earner family model established in the urban area where husband and wife are co-earners with shared, albeit not always equally divided, family responsibility. This migration model in which the wife moves as a 'tied migrant' conforms to the international migration patterns identified in other countries (e.g. Spitze 1984; Boyle et al. 2001). In this sense, the allocation of work–home responsibility amongst Chinese rural migrant families living in urban areas converges to that in other countries such as the UK, USA and Japan (e.g. O'Reilly and Fagan 1998; Kreimer 2004; Broadbent and Ford 2008) rather than to that of urban Chinese families. In other words, married female rural migrant workers enjoy less equality than their urban counterparts in general (Cooke 2008d).

In the graduate job market, while discrimination against women graduates in recruitment has long existed (Cooke 2005a), this problem is exacerbated by the dramatic increase in university graduates in recent years. The compounded disadvantage of gender and residential status has put women university graduates with non-local residential status and no work experience in the least marketable category of graduates seeking employment in large cities such as Beijing, Shanghai and Guangzhou. The ranking order for groups of graduates is: local male, non-local male, local female then non-local female graduates.

Changing values of the workforce

Meanwhile, the economic reforms of China since the 1980s, during which SOEs have changed from providing a job-for-life and extensive workplace welfare to a market approach, have led to the divergence of work-related values between the older and younger generation of workers. For example, Liu's (2003) study of two generations of employees in SOEs revealed a generation gap in which the younger generation of workers is more receptive to performance-related rewards and resents the typical egalitarian approach adopted by Chinese managers in bonus distribution. They are also less loyal to the company and welcome the adoption of employment contracts based on competence and performance. By contrast, the older generation prefers egalitarianism in reward distribution in order to maintain harmony. They value loyalty, job security and even bureaucracy. The changing values of Chinese workers have also been noted in Chapter 2. Well-educated Chinese young workers are ambitious and eager to reach to the top of their careers. They not only expect lucrative financial packages, but also demand early promotion and (overseas) career development opportunities from their employers. Where these demands are not met or where there are better offers elsewhere, they are ready to switch employers. This creates a need for more tailored HRM practices that are sensitive to individual diversity.

Cultural characteristics

China exhibits some cultural characteristics that are typical of oriental societies, such as India, Japan and the Republic of Korea, and may not be conducive to DM in organizations. For example, China is a highly hierarchical society and people are conscious of their status in the social order in contrast to a more informal and egalitarian approach favoured by the Americans (Lam and Graham 2007). Superiors are seen as the ultimate source of authority who should not be challenged, and decision making is often left to the most senior person in a group. China has a collectivist culture, although modernization has seen the rise of individualism in the younger generation. The need for social harmony through egalitarianism and mutual respect (to gain and save face) is an important part of the Chinese culture informed by Confucian philosophy (Crookes and Thomas 1998). This means that group-based equality rather than individual differentiation is the key to manage workplace relationships (see also chapters 4 and 5). In addition, endurance, diligence and devotion to the organization (as one's family) are the cultural norms taken for granted and expected by employers, just as employees are expected to be well treated by employers (see below for further discussion on paternalism). Homosexuality is neither socially accepted nor legally recognized in China. Divorce and co-habitation are far less common than in the West. Childcare and domestic services are more accessible to working parents through extended family networks and low-cost commercial services. These characteristics diverge from the western DM ideology that is founded on the need to respect individuals' rights and the need to design organizational policy to accommodate their family commitments. Nevertheless, social diversity does exist in China and the need for harmonization and social inclusion of the wider society is reflected in the need to manage diversity at the organizational level.

We now turn to the issue of how diversity is perceived and managed at the organizational level through the lens of managers. We do so by drawing on information from interviews with over 120 Chinese managers and professional employees on HRM in general and which covered diversity management and equal opportunity issues as part of the investigation (see Cooke and Saini 2007; Cooke 2009c; Cooke and Jin 2009 for more details).

Key issues in diversity management at the organizational level

Most Chinese managers interviewed had not heard of or thought about the concept of 'managing diversity'. They began to understand what it was about after the author's explanation at the beginning of the interview and were then able to analyse the Chinese situation against the concept. According to these managers, the sources of diversity in China come from gender, age and cultural diversity (mainly from MNCs). With the exception of one Chinese-owned MNC, none of the Chinese firms have a formal HR policy or affirmative action plan to promote gender equality or diversity. Discrimination against older and rural origin workers remains an issue. For example, a manager who worked for a prestigious Chinese MNC disclosed that in order to raise its corporate image further, this MNC dismissed all its rural migrant workers who had low levels of skills and education, and replaced them with young college graduates in 2003. The company also dismissed all its workers above 45 years of age in 2005. The company then boasted of a young and well-educated workforce. All its employees were below 35 years of age. However, this practice had actually back-fired by attracting bad publicity for the firm instead of enhancing its reputation as it had desired.

Managers who work in the MNCs identified two aspects of cultural diversity at their workplace. One is between foreign expatriates and Chinese employees. The other is from the Chinese overseas graduate returnees who are keen to work for, and are favourite candidates of, MNCs. According to a Chinese HR manager who had worked in a number of large private firms including an international HR consulting firm, 'all foreign employees [expatriates] emphasized their cultural shock when they come to China. But [Chinese-owned] MNCs have not developed a formal policy to manage these cultural shocks'. For example, a typical welfare measure offered by Chinese firms to their single employees is to provide dormitories. In large cities where housing is expensive, this often takes the form of a bedroom shared by two or three employees of the same sex (for rural migrant workers, this situation is far worse where ten or more people crowd in a room). While this arrangement is acceptable to the Chinese employees (Chinese students also share their dormitories in schools and universities), it is not acceptable to employees from western countries because of the lack of privacy. This has led to the turnover of a few foreign employees and the company has made no efforts to retain them, perhaps due to the reluctance to create a precedence of differential treatment between Chinese and foreign employees. Different management styles are also a source of cultural shock for foreign employees and become one of the reasons for turnover.

According to the managers who work for MNCs, they employ a large number of overseas graduate returnees. These repatriated western-trained graduates bring with them different lifestyles and expectations. They expect high salaries and fast promotion. They tend to feel superior to their home-grown fellow graduate employees and cause friction at work. How to recruit and manage overseas graduate returnees is an important issue for MNCs operating in China. Companies are now reportedly more cautious in recruiting and managing these returnees because they are seen as 'demanding' employees who are difficult to retain.

Apart from the need to manage the differences between the western and Chinese cultures in order to accommodate the needs and expectations of foreign employees and Chinese overseas graduate returnees, managers observed regional diversity amongst their employees. In general, it is believed that people from the northern part of the country are easier to manage. They are more diligent and more able to endure hardship than their counterparts from the south. Some firms also like to recruit university graduates from rural origins because they are easier to manage and retain. 'Their rural characteristics get diluted after years of university education and living in the city, so these [rural-urban] cultural differences will not cause any conflict at workplace' (a Chinese manager from a private IT firm). It must be noted that there are firms which do not want to recruit graduate employees of rural origin, believing that they are less well educated and more money oriented, as noted in Chapter 2. Interestingly, managers also believe that regional differences may be reduced and become less of a source of tension among highly educated employees. This is partly because years of higher education and living away from their hometown tends to dilute the regional habitual style of the individuals and homogenizes the workforce.

Most Chinese managers interviewed felt that diversity was not an issue in their organization and therefore there was little need to manage diversity. Some of them are insensitive to diversity issues and hold biased perceptions of women, believing that they are less productive and more family oriented than male employees. Not surprisingly, hardly any activities on DM in their companies were reported. This included one of the Chinese-owned MNCs that took over a large section of a highly reputable foreign business in the mid-2000s. Nevertheless, the manager from this MNC had a better understanding of diversity management compared with other managers interviewed. This MNC is also more advanced in its DM thinking in part because of the influence of its acquired foreign business unit. Below is the manager's account of its DM situation.

Diversity is not a key issue in the workforce in China. So it is not a priority of our company. Our major task is post-acquisition integration to align our organizational cultures and become a truly international company.... Before the takeover, we had more women at the senior management level. Now the proportion of women in senior management has actually reduced because we are now part of a bigger international operation. There are fewer senior women managers from our acquired business unit. Also, when new managers are recruited, it is not the equal opportunity that we consider; rather it is organizational politics. You need to be competent as well as well connected to get the senior manager's job.... We do emphasize the need for employees to respect other employees' rights and privacy. Aggressive or discriminatory remarks or behaviours are forbidden, even as jokes. These are written in the business conduct guideline for employees. But we don't have specific equal opportunity or diversity management programmes to enforce these clauses. There was an initiative about grouping women at the international level together to have a global forum to discuss diversity issues last year, but budget constraint means that the plan has been put aside. We do have a scheme called 'Improvement Email Account' for complaints from employees and customers. It is confidential. A team monitors and deals with these complaints. This was adopted and is still used by the Chinese operation but has not yet been rolled out to our international operation because of the low priority. Our acquired business unit also has good HR practices, for example, work–life balance and managing diversity. These have not yet been transferred to our Chinese operation due to staff shortage. Our priority is talent management. A new scheme called 'Mobility Plan' has just started to be implemented at the international level. The purpose of the Plan is to give managers an opportunity to work overseas to gain international experience to be able to lead at global level. It is not aimed at Chinese managers in principle, but in reality, it is about sending Chinese managers to the US for development.

In general, avoiding conflicts and cultural clashes seems to be the reason for managing diversity as perceived by Chinese managers. In other words, they see the need to manage diversity from a problem-solving point of view instead of seeing it as value-adding to the business.

Western DM literature recommends that organizations should have an overall strategy to managing diversity that is integrated with other aspects of the organization's strategy and supports its business goals. Communication, training, employee involvement and senior management support are seen as important for the initiative to succeed (e.g. CIPD 2006). It is clear that the Chinese firms have not reached this level in their DM, although arguably few western firms have either, judging from existing research findings (e.g. CIPD 2007). Generally speaking, Chinese firms have not yet adopted a systematic approach to managing HR. It is also worth pointing out that Chinese managers, at least those interviewed by the author, are not receptive to the idea of having a formal HR policy on flexible work arrangements for employees. They prefer to deal with it informally on a case-by-case basis rather than institutionalizing the arrangements which may be taken advantage of by misbehaving employees. They believe that it is important they retain the power to exercise their discretion to reward employees who are deemed loyal and well behaved. At the same time, they prefer to adopt an egalitarian approach to treat all employees the same in order to avoid resentment of differentiated treatment. This finding is similar to that of Nathwani et al.'s (2007) study.

To a large extent, the approach adopted by Chinese managers is paternalistic in dealing with diversity, often in the way of handling individual employees' needs and requests. Paternalism is one of the most salient characteristics in the Asian national culture (Pye 1986; Aycan 2006). It is a form of relationship, and an indication of the quality of the relationship, between employees and managers at the workplace. The functioning of paternalism requires several behavioural ingredients: authority, hierarchy, care, obedience, loyalty and dependence. According to Aycan (2006), paternalism in Asian culture is that of a benevolent (dictatorship) nature. It focuses on the well-being of the employees, whereas the new-found paternalism that has emerged in western HR policies as a means to elicit enhanced employee commitment and performance is of an exploitative nature. From this point of view, managing diversity in the oriental context is relationship driven and may be a means as well as an end in itself. By contrast, the agenda of managing diversity dominated by the western business case approach is outcome driven and therefore a conscientious means to an end. Given the different motives of DM and levels of awareness of the need to manage diversity, it is not surprising that there is little evaluation of the effect of DM in Chinese firms.

According to CIPD (2007), there are a wide range of measures that organizations may use to monitor diversity. These include: employee attitude surveys, the number of complaints and grievances, labour turnover, employee performance appraisals, absenteeism, the ability to recruit, the number of tribunal cases, impact assessment, the level of customer satisfaction, employee commitment surveys, business performance, balanced scorecard, diversification of customer base, improvements in problem solving and decision making and psychological contract issues. None of the Chinese managers interviewed believe that their firm has a formal mechanism in place to measure the effect of DM. This is not surprising given the low priority afforded to the issue by the firm and the absence of a formal DM policy. It must be noted that diversity and productivity enhancement should not be taken as a definite and positive relationship. Academic studies on diversity-performance relationships have so far yielded non-conclusive results (e.g. Cox et al. 1991; Tsui et al. 1992; Lau and Murnighan 1998; Richard et al. 2004).

Work–life balance initiatives

Work–life balance is one of the key components in western DM literature. Work–life/family-friendly initiatives, such as flexible working arrangements, have been promoted as good HRM practices to accommodate (women) workers who have family commitments and to reduce the work intensity of managerial/professional employees. Work–life conflict (WLC) in China derives from a range of sources that may be different from those manifested in western societies and therefore require different HR initiatives in the Chinese context. Whilst family commitment remains a key source of work–life conflict, work intensity, including long working hours, appears to be the main HR issue amongst managers and professionals in MNCs and private firms in China (Cooke 2011c). This is largely due to the heightened market competition and the rapid growth of firms, particularly those in the fast-growing industries such as telecommunications, IT, consultancy, finance and real estate. Work intensification has led to health problems, retention issues and labour disputes.

For example, PricewaterhouseCoopers (China) (hereafter PwC China) experienced a serious labour dispute incident in 2004. Employees in several major cities went on strike in protest against the unbearable working hours and the unacceptably low levels of overtime pay. At the time of the strike, the average working time for an employee was seven days per week with no more than five sleeping hours every day. After the dispute was settled, PwC China introduced a dedicated employee care programme, called 'We Care', to look after its employees. Activities of the programme include: free movie tickets, discount tickets to concerts and musicals, yoga and tai chi classes in offices, numerous sports and fun days such as 'PwC China Cup', family days, stress management seminars, health talks, a free influenza vaccination programme and focus group meetings to identify areas for improvements (PricewaterhouseCoopers website, accessed in 2008). Other foreign MNCs also have similar programmes in place to address work–life conflict problems.

Xiao and Cooke's (2010) study of 69 auditing professionals and managers from five accountancy and consultancy firms in the private sector in the cities of Shanghai, Hangzhou and Hefei revealed that the demanding nature of external auditing (long hours and business trips) discouraged many female auditors from continuing with the profession or moving upward with their careers. In general, male auditors are reported to have much stronger career motivation and orientation than female auditors in the consultancy industry. Conventional gender roles imposed on women outside the work sphere (i.e. women as the main home carer) and the lack of work–life balance support from the employing organizations are the main reasons for the lower level of career motivation and advancement of women auditors compared with men. A considerable proportion of female auditors also choose to exit the auditing consultancy industry or the auditing profession after they have started a family – some of them are under pressures from their families to do so.

Similarly, Cooke and Jin's (2009) study of 122 CEOs, managers and professional employees revealed that despite the fact that the one-child policy has led to the reduction of childcare work for married couples, childcare and elderly care responsibilities continue to fall upon women disproportionately. Therefore, women are more likely to feel the pressure of WLC than men. Outsourcing their housework and family care, drawing on family networks for assistance or domesticating one spouse, usually the wife, seem to be the coping mechanisms. For some single career women, their WLC takes another form – the difficulty in finding a spouse and the fear of starting a family at the expense of their career. Higher earners are able to reduce their WLC by commercializing their household responsibilities and are more likely to complain to their company about working long hours and ask for compensation of one form or another. By contrast, those who are on low pay and in insecure jobs actually demand more working hours in order to increase their wage income, thus perpetuating the long-hours culture.

Cooke and Jin's (2009) study further showed that Chinese organizational leaders and to a large extent workers tend to accept work–life conflict as a fact of life without feeling the need for the organization to address it. Individuals adopt various coping strategies on their own. Whilst organizations are more likely to introduce HR initiatives to cushion the negative effect of long working hours on their key employees and their family, managers are far less sympathetic towards women's (and men's) childcare needs and are unwilling to introduce policies to accommodate family commitments.

Many of the HR initiatives adopted by organizations to help employees enhance their work–life balance are of a collective nature, providing bonding opportunities among employees and between employees and their family. In addition, money remains the main motivator and a de-stressor in that financial and material rewards have been the main mechanisms for alleviating employees' grievance of WLC inflicted by work intensification. This reflects China's current stage of economic development, that is, that people desire better living standards and extra material rewards are appreciated. It also reflects the Chinese collectivist and paternalistic culture in which a workplace plays an important role in providing social bonding activities to develop and maintain a harmonious relationship amongst employees and between the firm and its workforce. The provision of employee welfare and employee entertainment is traditionally seen by Chinese firms as an important ingredient to improve the morale and commitment of the workforce and to enhance the productivity of the firm (Cooke 2008b). The willingness of individuals and their families to endure WLC further reflects the traditional Chinese work ethic in which work and career achievement is given primacy over family life or self enjoyment (also see Choi 2008). Diligence and self-sacrifice, including family's well-being, for the public good are praised and glorified. Relaxation is only encouraged in the sense that it will contribute to the regeneration of energy for one to work more efficiently.

It needs to be noted that organizing and sponsoring social life for employees and their families has long been a workplace welfare provision in SOEs and to a lesser extent in private firms as part of the Chinese paternalistic culture. In the more individualistic nature of western culture, work–life balance means, amongst other things, giving employees more time to spend with their family in private. By contrast, involving family members in company-sponsored events is an important part of work–life balance initiatives in China. However, work–life balance alone may not be sufficient to retain talent. Well-educated Chinese young workers are ambitious and are eager to fulfil their career potential while beginning to develop a taste for leisure. They not only expect lucrative financial packages, but also demand early promotion and (overseas) career development opportunities from their employers. Where these demands are not met or when there are better offers elsewhere, they are ready to switch employers, as noted in chapters 2 and 5.

Conclusion

In this chapter, we have explored the institutional and cultural context against which equality and diversity issues may occur and are managed. We have identified a number of sources of discrimination against disadvantaged groups of workers based on gender, age and residential status. We have reviewed state policies and initiatives in advancing gender equality at the macro level. We also critically examined HRM practices and management attitudes at the organizational level, drawing on first-hand empirical data on diversity management and work–life balance practices. We did so by drawing on the western DM literature as the backdrop in order to highlight the similarities and differences found in China compared with the DM environment in western countries.

It is clear from the discussion that managing diversity is a softer approach to HRM and has yet to feature as an espoused HR strategy of Chinese firms. While managing diversity is featuring in organizational policy statements and becoming a pervasive topic in management research in advanced western countries, this term largely remains unfamiliar to Chinese managers. Inequality at workplaces and in society is often accepted and internalized without any serious challenge. In China, employment insecurity is relatively high and the provision of social security benefits is not extended to all. Certain groups of people are fighting for the very right to a basic living through low-paid employment. The fact that they are treated unfairly is much less of a social concern, although the issue of widening social inequality has been causing social unrest and is attracting an increasing level of attention from the government, the media and the academic community.

Nevertheless, given the persistent and somewhat institutionalized discrimination against women and migrant workers, the marginal effect of employment law and the general absence of bargaining power of workers and their representing bodies in the employment relationship (see chapters 7 and 8), it is unlikely that discriminative practices against these groups will disappear or be alleviated in China's marketizing economy in the foreseeable future. It is clear that strong state intervention is the most, if not only, effective means to achieve social equality, at least in the Chinese context, as was shown during its state-planned economy period for gender equality.

The intention of this chapter has been to highlight the historical, institutional and cultural context within which issues of diversity are embedded and (not) managed in China. The awareness of these societal differences has strong implications for western MNCs operating in developing countries such as India and China, as their approach to managing and assessing workplace diversity in these countries may need to be different from that adopted in their home country. While organizations, whether they are MNCs or domestic firms, operating in a diverse environment need to find new ways of generating trust, relevance and connection with their stakeholders, they need to do this in ways that are acceptable to the individuals, communities and nations.

Finally, for research implications, how different social groups interact with each other at workplaces, which groups they choose to identify with, and how groups establish and enhance their social identity are important socio-economic and management issues to study. For example, Chan and Goto (2003) found that Hong Kong Chinese feel closer to the Americans in social distance than they do with other Asians. The influence of socio-geographic subculture is therefore very important, but has not received sufficient attention in existing studies on diversity management. Given the fact that China, and indeed, many other developing countries are large countries in both geographic and population terms with a relatively high level of labour mobility, more detailed studies in this area will be beneficial to advance our knowledge. This is especially the case when an increasing number of MNCs are expanding in these countries and domestic firms are also spreading their businesses across regions within the country. These issues can be studied, and best studied, from an interdisciplinary perspective because the study of workforce diversity is necessarily an interdisciplinary undertaking.

7 Workers' representation and voice

Introduction

Effective representation is essential to protecting and advancing workers' rights and interests. In developing countries like China, effective representation may often be an aspiration rather than a reality due to flaws in the design and enforcement of the labour regulations, the weak bargaining power of the workers and the absence of effective organizing bodies such as trade unions to play the organizing and representation role. This chapter investigates the scope of workers' rights as defined in the labour legislation. It evaluates the role of various official bodies that may be involved in organizing and representing workers. In particular, the governance structure, regulatory role and perceived efficacy of the trade unions are critically analysed in the context of radical state-sector reform, the emergence of a market economy and the changing profile of union constituency. The chapter also investigates new initiatives and modes of organizing from the ACFTU in response to the new dynamics in employment relations and the rising level of labour disputes, notably in the export-oriented manufacturing sector. Finally, it examines the various forms of workers' self-organizing and their impact, with particular reference to the unprecedented number of strike events in foreign-funded manufacturing plants across the country in 2010.

Legal rights of Chinese workers

To understand the mechanism and effectiveness of workers' representation, it is important, first of all, to establish the scope of legal rights of the workers and their representing body. It has been argued that, with 'the major exception of freedom of association', the labour standards established by the series of labour laws and regulations of China 'are not markedly inferior to those of comparable countries and indeed many developed nations' (Cooney 2007: 674). Since the 1990s, a number of legislative and administrative regulations have been issued by the government that provide a basic framework under which the labour market and employment relations are regulated in principle (see Chapter 8 for detailed discussion). The rising level of labour disputes accompanying the privatization and marketization of the economy has made it imperative for the state to improve legal protection and labour standards; and the continuing growth of the economy has made it possible to do so (Chan 2009; Cooke 2009d; Cooney et al. 2007).

However, labour rights stipulated in these laws focus mainly on individual rights, such as contracts, wages, working conditions and social security; whereas collective rights, particularly 'the rights to organize, to strike, and to bargain collectively in a meaningful sense' are largely absent (Chen 2007: 60). Whilst the exercise of collective rights may not change 'the basic structural disadvantage of labour in a capitalist economy' where employers have the prerogative to 'determine the nature and availability of jobs', the existence of these rights is crucial for facilitating the development of a workers' power base to countervail state and managerial power (Chen 2007: 60). In this sense, labour rights in China are defective because the lack of collective rights is a contributing factor that 'render workers' individual rights vulnerable, hollow, unenforceable, or often disregarded' (Chen 2007: 77).

It should be noted that collective rights are not totally absent from China's labour legislation. 'Both the Labour Law and the Trade Union Law, for example, contain clauses on the rights to organize although they are defined vaguely and abstractly' (Chen 2007: 65). Collective bargaining is perhaps the most significant collective right of Chinese workers, although its implementation, like other regulations, remains problematic. For most of the socialist Chinese history, the trade unions did not have any role in collective bargaining, as employment terms and conditions were set unilaterally by the state employer. The notion of 'collective bargaining' was not introduced in China until the early 1990s, after the Trade Union Law (1992) authorized unions at the enterprise level to conclude collective contracts with the employer. The term 'collective consultation' instead of 'collective bargaining' is preferred by the state. It is believed that consultation is a more constructive approach than 'bargaining', as it conforms to Chinese cultural practice characterized by non-confrontation and conflict avoidance (Cooke 2010c).

In 1994, the Provisions on Collective Contracts was issued by the then Ministry of Labour which provided detailed regulations to support the Collective Contract provision outlined in the Labour Law (see Taylor et al. 2003 and Brown 2006 for more detailed discussion). Trade unions were given the official role of representing workers for consultations with employers. This position of the unions has been reinforced and expanded in subsequent labour laws. According to Article 20 of the Trade Union Law (amended 2001), a trade union shall represent employees in equal negotiation and in signing a collective contract. Matters that can be concluded in a collective contract may include labour remuneration, working time, rest and vacations, occupational safety and health, professional training and insurance and welfare. However, as noted earlier, without the right to organize independently and the right to strike, the right to collective bargaining is meaningless as it does not give workers any real power to bargain with employers (Chen 2007). As a result, the collective consultation and contracts system serve no more than a mechanism for the government to monitor the implementation of the labour regulations 'and hence avoid overt conflicts' (Clarke et al. 2004; Chen 2007).

The ACFTU's drive to promote the collective consultation system since the early 1990s and the signing of collective contracts in more recent years has been no more than a 'single-minded pursuit of numerical growth' with little substantive gains for the workers beyond what has been stipulated in the labour laws (*China Labour Bulletin* 2009: 39). Workers were rarely consulted, in some cases were not even aware of the terms and conditions agreed. The Wal-Mart (China) agreement for example is a case in point – the collective agreement was signed between Wal-Mart and the ACFTU at the regional level in 2008, with local stores having no idea of what they had been signed up to. When the local trade union officials requested managers at the store level to negotiate a collective agreement with the employees, the managers refused, claiming that an agreement had already been signed at the higher level (*China Labor News Translations* 2008).

The All-China Federation of Trade Unions as the official representing body of workers

As noted in Chapter 1, only one trade union – the All-China Federation of Trade Unions – is recognized by the government as the representing body of workers in China (see Warner 2008 for an overview). It operates under the leadership of the Chinese Communist Party. The union–CCP tie dates back to the 1920s (the union was founded on 1 May 1925) when grassroots union organizations served as party member recruitment bases and provided vital support to the CCP by mobilizing workers. Although the relationship between the CCP and the ACFTU has not always been smooth, attempts by the ACFTU to gain greater power and autonomy have been suppressed by the CCP (Sheehan 1999). Similarly, attempts to form autonomous workers' unions have been crushed, as was the case during the Tiananmen Square event in 1989 (Cooke 2010c, also see below for more recent developments on workers' self-organizing).

The roles and responsibilities of the unions are set out in a number of laws, namely the Trade Union Law (1950, 1992, amended in 2001), the Labour Law (1995) and the Labour Contract Law (2008). According to the Trade Union Law (2001), 'the basic function and duty of the trade unions is to safeguard the legal rights and interests of the employees. While upholding the overall rights and interests of the whole nation, the Trade Union Law provides that trade unions should, at the same time, represent and safeguard the rights and interests of employees' (Article 6). Article 7 further stipulates that the

> trade union shall mobilize and organize the employees to participate in the economic development actively, and to complete the production and work assignments conscientiously, educate the employees to improve their ideological thoughts and ethics, technological and professional, scientific

and cultural qualities, and build an employee team with ideals, ethics, education and discipline.

In reality, the most important function of the ACFTU at the grassroots level is to maintain stability in society, as admitted by union officials (Cooke 2011b). This means that they may have to perform a policing role on occasions. For example, ACFTU officials interviewed reported that they have had to divert demonstration crowds with their colleagues from government departments on several occasions. The second most important role is then to protect workers' rights. We need to be reminded that the trade union's role in labour disputes resolution is not to organize industrial action, but to monitor the labour standards and enforce labour regulations. When the labour disputes are a result of direct conflicts between the state (employer) and the workers, union officials typically play a mediator role and at times side with the management (O'Leary 1998; Clarke 2005). Nevertheless, 'the ACFTU is credited with its effort to promote the pro-labour legislation' (Chen, 2007: 65), particularly in drafting the Labour Contract Law and Labour Disputes Mediation and Arbitration Law.

The priority of the ACFTU's functions is necessarily a result of its lack of independence, both politically and financially. Local branches of the ACFTU are partly funded by the fiscal budget of the local governments, which oversee the union activities. The governance structure of the ACFTU branches are in the form of a vertical and horizontal reporting line (see Figure 7.1). ACFTU organizations are under the dual control (or 'leadership' as it is described) of the local government at their level and their organizational branch of a higher level. Senior union officials at each level are normally appointed by the CCP rather than elected. This is in spite of the specification of Article 9 of the Trade Union Law that 'trade union committees at all levels should be democratically elected at members' assemblies or at union representatives' congresses'. Some of the union officials have worked in government departments as part of their political career development. Government officials and ACFTU officials at local government level are managed in similar ways to civil servants as prescribed in the Civil Servants Law (Cooke 2011b).

This subordination to the CCP/local government means that incentives for union officials to perform well 'come from the party above rather than from workers below' and that union officials tend to be reluctant to confront their higher authority on the one hand and the powerful employers on the other (Howell 2008: 861). The way the ACFTU is set up and operationalized has attracted criticism from international trade union organizations, labour movement activists and scholars on the legitimacy of the ACFTU as a trade union (e.g. Taylor and Li 2007).

Research findings show that union officials generally lack resources, power, skills and legal knowledge to fulfil their collective bargaining role and to defend their members' rights (e.g. Warner and Ng 1999; Cooke 2010c). In spite of the high level of membership in unionized workplaces (see Table 7.1), trade unions are widely considered ineffective in representing workers' interests against

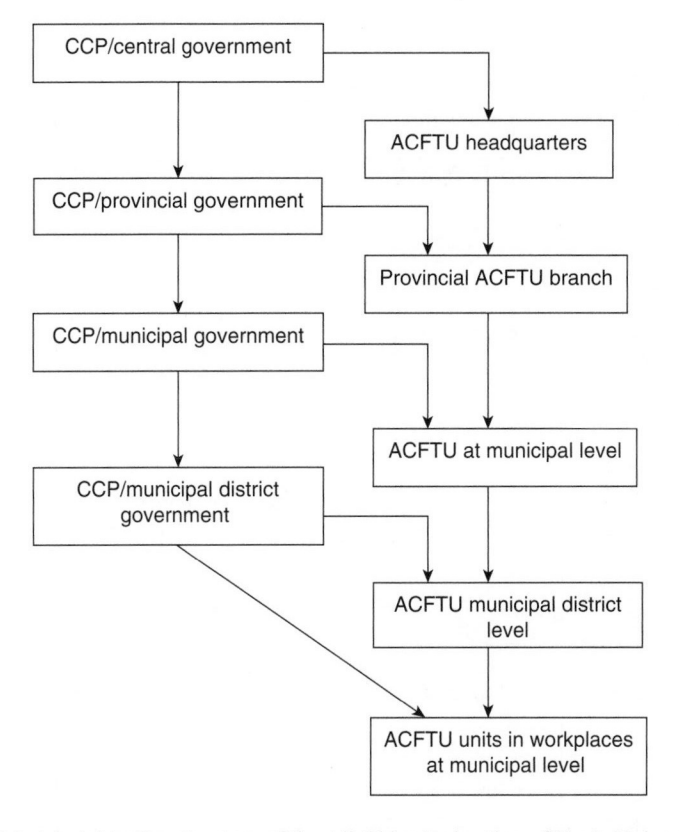

Figure 7.1 Administrative structure of the All-China Federation of Trade Unions.
Source: compiled by the author.

management prerogatives and at times side with the management (O'Leary 1998; Clarke 2005).

The Leninist 'conveyor belt' model of unionism has put the ACFTU in an increasingly awkward position between the Party-state, employers and workers during the economic reform period that began in the late 1970s (e.g. Howell 2008). The radical SOE restructuring that took place in the mid-1990s created conflicts between the workers and their state employer as a consequence of the displacement of millions, many of whom became jobless, and the erosion of employment terms and conditions for those who remain in work. More broadly, the divergence of labour–capital interests and the resultant conflicts that arise pose tremendous challenges to the ACFTU organizations to demonstrate their continuing value to employers, state and workers simultaneously. This requires them to reconstitute their traditional functions (Clarke and Pringle 2009), to gain identification from new bases of workers' constituency and to reduce resistance from employers in the private sector at the same time.

Table 7.1 Union membership level in unionized organizations

Year	No. of grassroots unions (1,000 units)	No. of employees (1,000 persons)	No. of female employees (1,000 persons)	Membership (1,000 persons)	No. of female members (1,000 persons)	Membership density (%)	No. of full-time union officials (1,000 persons)
1952	207	13,932	–	10,023	–	71.9	53
1962	165	26,671	–	19,220	–	72.1	86
1979	329	68,972	21,717	51,473	–	74.6	179
1980	376	74,482	25,186	61,165	–	82.1	243
1985	465	96,430	35,967	85,258	31,492	88.4	381
1990	606	111,569	42,910	101,356	38,977	90.8	556
1995	593	113,214	45,153	103,996	41,165	91.9	468
2000	859	114,721	45,345	103,615	39,173	90.3	482
2001	1,538	129,970	50,879	121,523	46,966	93.5	–
2002	1,713	144,615	51,576	133,978	46,652	92.6	472
2003	906	133,016	50,793	123,405	46,012	92.8	465
2004	1,020	144,367	55,026	136,949	51,353	94.9	456
2005	1,174	159,853	60,163	150,294	55,748	94.0	477
2006	1,324	181,436	67,193	169,942	61,778	93.7	543
2007	1,508	204,524	74,945	193,290	70,422	94.5	602
2008	1,725	224,875	81,688	212,171	77,738	94.4	705
2009	1,845	245,353	86,526	226,344	82,484	93.3	746

Source: compiled from the *China Statistical Yearbook 2010*: 885.

Note
Since 2003, statistical coverage of the number of grassroots trade unions has been adjusted (original note).

The declining level of union membership and funding from the government during the late 1990s and the mid-2000s, partly as a result of the state-sector restructuring, has led to the 'resource crisis' of ACFTU (Liu et al. 2011). For example, the total number of full-time union officials nationwide had dropped to 0.46 million in 2004 compared with 0.56 million in 1990 (*China Labour Statistical Yearbook 2009*; also see Table 7.1). Between 2001 and 2004, union organizations underwent a period of restructuring and downsizing as part of the state-sector reform. This retrenchment is in the context of the expansion of the union functions and the rising number of grassroots union organizations and members. Under the threat of job losses and financial penalty (e.g. deduction of bonus) for failing to achieve performance targets, union officials now work beyond their normal hours and duties. As the ACFTU chairman of a municipal branch revealed, 'Our trade union officials now work any time and whenever there is a call for help. They are all contactable by mobiles' (Cooke 2008c).

Financial constraints impair the opportunity for capacity building and solidarity for ACFTU grassroots organizations. Research findings (Cooke 2008c, 2011b) suggest that there were limited interactions between workplace union representatives and union officials at the municipal district branch level, with the main activity being to disseminate new policy documents and initiatives from the higher level of authorities. Financial constraints also affect the development of union officials and representatives, with those at the grassroots level being the most affected. Whilst training is provided to union officials in the ACFTU branches on a regular basis at various levels, there is much room for improvement in the quality and quantity of the training courses. Training opportunities for part-time union representatives within the enterprises are much more limited, largely due to lack of resources and management apathy (e.g. Cooke 2011b). To compensate for the inadequate skills of union representatives at the workplace level, the ACFTU attempts to 'professionalize' grassroots union leaders by parachuting in union officials from the higher level to participate in negotiation with the management at the enterprise level (Chen 2007).

Union membership level and changing constituency

The ACFTU is the largest national trade union body in the world, measured by its official membership (Warner and Zhu 2010), although the reliability of official union membership statistics is questionable. As we can see from Table 7.1, union membership level has been consistently high at over 90 per cent since 1990 at workplaces where union organizations were established. Women's membership level is also high and is less than 3 per cent lower than that of men's (see Table 7.1). It must be noted here that the high level of membership in recognized workplaces is not necessarily an indication of union strength. Once a trade union unit is established in a company, it is virtually mandatory for its employees to become a member. Some workers are not even aware of the fact that they have become a member (Cooke 2005a).

The expansion of union membership since the mid-2000s is a direct result of the ACFTU's national recruitment drive (in an attempt) to organize rural migrant workers. Reduced restriction in labour mobility across administrative areas since the 1980s as part of the government's policy to stimulate the marketized economy had attracted some 150 million rural migrant workers to the urban sector by the mid-2000s. They made up 58 per cent of the workers in the industry sector and 52 per cent in the service sector (The State Council 2006). The trade union's response to the growing presence of rural migrant workers as a potential group to be organized and represented was largely passive until the mid-2000s. This was in spite of the fact that the ACFTU at all levels was instructed by the government in late 1994 to launch a campaign 'to set up unions in all the non-unionized foreign-invested enterprises, with the ultimate declared purpose of implementing collective bargaining' (Chan 1998: 1223). Under the Chinese socialist administrative system, farmers did not fall within the constituency base of the ACFTU because they were not classified as 'the working class' which was a privilege reserved for urban workers. Since rural migrant workers working in the urban areas still carry their administrative status of rural residents, they failed to gain the trade union's attention as targets for organization (Cooke 2007).

Rampant exploitation and the rising level of health and safety problems in sweatshops and construction sites that accompanied the rapid expansion of the urban economy meant that organizing and representing rural migrant workers became an urgent priority. In August 2003 the ACFTU officially classified rural migrant workers in urban areas as 'members of the working class' and required union organizations to organize rural migrant workers (*Yangcheng Evening News* 8 August 2003). By the end of 2004, 20 million rural migrant workers had been recruited as union members (*Workers' Daily* 7 December 2004). This figure was increased to 70 million by the end of 2008 (*China Labour Bulletin* 2009: 32). The ACFTU's strategy was to recruit as many rural migrant workers as possible into the union, regardless of where they were from, what types of jobs they did, how long they had worked or whether they were in employment or not (*Workers' Daily* 25 February 2005). As such, the ACFTU was criticized for being 'more concerned with meeting quotas than establishing genuinely representative workers' organizations' for effective representation (*China Labour Bulletin* 2009: 32).

In China, the formal 'representative function' of the unions, according to the Labour Law, is supplemented by the trade union-guided Workers' Representatives Congress (Workers Congress hereafter) within enterprises. It is an official mechanism of worker participation, through the workers' representatives, in enterprise decision making and management. Initially introduced in the late 1940s, the Workers Congress has been given an enhanced role since the 1980s as a result of economic reform. Again, in reality, the role of the Workers Congress remains less than effective (Benson and Zhu 2010; Cooke 2005a). Interestingly, the author's ongoing research in China found that an increasing number of private firms have been setting up a Workers Congress forum in recent years as evidence of law compliance, although this rarely leads to the recognition of a trade union.

In practice, these Workers Congress forums serve as an extended HRM function in practice instead of playing an industrial democracy role on behalf of the workers.

Chinese workers are not a homogenous group. Instead, ownership forms and occupational characteristics shape the identity, needs and perception of the ACFTU as their legitimate representing body (Cooke 2008c). Existing studies on workers' organizing strategies have focused mainly on two categories of workers: workers in the state-owned enterprises and those in the privately-owned and foreign-invested firms (e.g. Chan 2001; F. Chen 2003a; Gallagher 2005; Chen 2006; Lee 2007; Nichols and Zhao 2010). It is true that these two categories of workers are amongst those most in need of representation. However, there are other categories of workers who could be organized and represented by the ACFTU. For example, employees in the public sector (e.g. hospitals and schools) are an important category who have received much research attention in other countries (e.g. the UK) but have rarely been studied in China. Civil servants (e.g. police force, legal institutions and government organization employees) are another category who are technically 'workers' falling within the remit of ACFTU's representation (Cooke 2011b).

Cooke's (2011b) study on Chinese women workers' representation needs and their perception of union effectiveness shows that there is clearly an issue of (lack of) identification with the trade union in general. Chinese women employees' attitudes and representation needs are also different across educational background, occupational class and industrial sector and ownership. More specifically, employees from government organizations categorically reject the trade union as their legitimate organizing body. This reflects the social hierarchy of Chinese society in which mandarins consider themselves amongst the elite class of the society, enjoying privileges not afforded to the mass. Civil servants disassociate themselves from the trade unions even though government officials and union officials often work in the same local government building and union officials are salaried by the local governments. They believe that trade unions are meant for enterprises and emphasize the fact that their needs are represented by *zuzhi bu* (personnel department for government officials) which is well above the trade union organization in the official hierarchy. This feeling of superiority is evident from some of the elite mandarins interviewed. In spite of the fact that women employees in government organizations are perhaps more heavily discriminated against compared with those in other types of organizations (Cooke 2005a), the trade union is not able to fight the battle for gender equality with limited representational legitimacy.

Compared with their civil servant counterparts, public sector employees are far more receptive to the welfare role and social functions of the trade unions. A general complaint is, however, that the trade unions are not doing enough to enhance their working and social life. In general, public sector employees are well educated to university degree or diploma level. They tend to have a stronger desire than shopfloor workers to develop art and cultural skills and participate in sports events. They also have better career prospects and hence career aspirations for which they want support. The union function in schools is welcome as teachers complain about headmasters not being familiar with HR policy and statutory maternity leave provisions. Similarly, the union function in hospitals is necessary to provide an extended HR function. Women union representatives are a welcome aid to male managers in dealing with women's issues. In the public sector where the dual role of the trade union – i.e. carrying out instructions from the state and looking after the welfare of the employees – remains less challenged by the market economy, there is still plenty of scope for the trade unions to improve their functions (Cooke 2011b).

Workers from SOEs and collectively owned enterprises are familiar with the concept of trade union but believe it to be useless in protecting rights other than carrying out a welfare and social function. Having experienced radical organizational changes with worsening employment outcomes, these workers clearly have representation needs that are mostly unmet and lead to a rising level of grievance and resentment (e.g. F. Chen 2003b; Lee 2007; Cooke 2011b).

The largest group of workers without a voice or any representational mechanism but most in need of protection is undoubtedly the rural migrant workers. As noted in other studies, many of them work in foreign-invested or private firms (e.g. Chan 2001; Gallagher 2005; Lee 2007). Despite the ACFTU's recruitment drive, few of them have heard of the phrase 'trade union' at all, even fewer were being represented, as trade unions face formidable barriers to recognition by employers (Cooke 2008c, also see below for further discussion).

This diversification of union constituency resulting from the marketizing economy presents different opportunities as well as challenges for trade unions. It also calls for the adoption of different roles, organizing strategies and activities at the grassroots level to address multiple issues if the trade unions are to maximize their utility. This poses significant challenges to grassroots union organizations as well as those at the policy-making level because the needs and grievances of these groups are framed distinctively within the boundary of class, educational level, and occupational and social identity that cannot be readily transcended (Perry and Selden 2000). What organizing strategies have the ACFTU adopted in response to these changes and challenges? In particular, what strategies have the ACFTU adopted in organizing the rural migrant workers? We examine these issues in the next section.

New ways of union organizing

Hyman (2001) advanced three models of trade unionism in the western economies:

- Market-orientation, for example, by seeking to improve members' well-being through collective bargaining,
- Class-orientation, for example, by promoting working-class interests in the society in a more radical approach and

- Society-orientation, for example, by strengthening 'the voice of workers in the broader society' and acting 'as a force for social, moral and political integration' (cited in Gospel 2008: 14–15).

Small traces of each of these three models can be found in the ACFTU's historical trajectory. For example, a radical class-oriented approach was adopted during the two decades of the revolutionary period that led to the CCP seizing power against the national party and the founding of socialist China in 1949. This class-oriented approach continued to be influential during the state planned economy period when the working class was hailed as 'the master of the country'. During this period, the ACFTU also assumed the social actor role by engaging in the education and moral teaching of workers in the state sector and providing welfare services. As China's economic transformation deepened in the last two decades, the market-oriented goal ascended in the ACFTU agenda. ACFTU grassroots organizations have become an active labour market broker, providing training and employment services to displaced SOE workers as well as migrant workers (also see Table 7.2). Meanwhile, the ACFTU has also become more fully aware of its responsibility to the Party-state in maintaining 'social harmony' by containing labour unrest.

To this end, a number of initiatives have been adopted by the ACFTU to organize workers outside the state sector, targeting especially rural migrant workers and foreign-invested firms. These initiatives take the form of both hard and soft approaches. As mentioned earlier, the ACFTU launched a national recruitment drive in 2003 that led to the recruitment of over 70 million rural migrant workers into the union by the end of 2008. In mid-2008, backed by the Party-state, the ACFTU launched an intensive three-month campaign to 'unionize the Fortune 500' whose unionization rate in China was significantly lower (less than 50 per cent) than the average unionization rate (73 per cent) in overseas-invested companies as a whole. This led to a rapid increase of unionization rate to over 80 per cent by September 2008 (cited in *China Labour Bulletin* 2009: 32). It should be noted that some high-profile foreign-invested firms recognized the trade unions in order to silence critics (e.g. K. Wang 2008). In addition, the ACFTU maintains that 'it would not allow companies to bypass the unionization process by setting up proxy-organizations such as "employee welfare clubs" and "employee entertainment clubs" funded by the two per cent of payroll that by law should go to the union' (*China Labour Bulletin* 2009: 32).

In conjunction with these high-profile campaigns, two major strategies have been adopted by the trade unions for organizing migrant workers (see Table 7.2).[1] One is 'workplace organization', i.e. to gain recognition at the workplace and then unionize the workers with the support of the company. However, gaining employer recognition remains a difficult task given the persistent resistance of private firms (Cooke 2007). The other way of organizing is 'distant organization', i.e. to recruit migrant workers (those already in employment or who are seeking jobs) outside the workplace with service packages as

Table 7.2 Characteristics of two models of unionizing migrant workers

	Distant organization	Workplace organization
Governing framework	• Labour regulations • Government administrative policies	• Labour regulations • Collective agreement • Company procedures
Recruitment targets	• Migrant workers seeking work • Migrant workers already in employment	• Migrant workers in the workplace
Methods of recruitment	• Public campaign to raise trade union profile • Attraction of free or low-cost services and advice • Collaboration with local government authorities and community bodies • Grievance-based recruitment • Word of mouth	• Use of labour regulations and mobilizing local government authorities to seek employer's recognition • Once employer's recognition is secured, then recruit members at the workplace en masse through employer's support and peer pressure
Activities	• Service provision (e.g. training, employment information, legal advice, counselling) • Representational function (e.g. negotiation with employers, representation in tribunal and court)	• HR function (e.g. organizing productivity enhancement initiatives, such as skill competition, problem-solving task force) • Welfare role (e.g. employee care programmes) • Representation function
Outcome/effect	• More costly • Recruitment and organizing not integrated • Possibility of recruiting a large number efficiently, e.g. in job fairs and employment and training centres • Possibility of disseminating the benefits of joining trade union through word of mouth across the country • More difficult to organize, retain and represent migrant workers collectively • Lack of continuity in communication • Individuals less likely to identify themselves with the trade union and only turn to the trade union when help is needed • Dependence on full-time union officials to undertake activities • Results more individual oriented rather than collective • Need to coordinate with other functional organizations (e.g. local labour authority, employment and training centres) • Potential competition with other functional organizations	• Less costly as part of the operating cost absorbed by employers • Integration of recruitment and organizing • Easier to organize workers once access is allowed by employers • Easier to maintain communication • Easier to represent collectively • Easier to identify key supporters to establish a core team to strengthen union presence and function • Shared problems and shared solutions to maximize the impact of trade union • Members more likely to identify themselves with the trade union • Less opportunity of disseminating the benefits of joining the trade union • Less competition from other functional organizations

inducement (see Table 7.2). This is usually carried out by operating in the labour market and in ways similar to what Kelly and Heery (1989: 198–9) classify as a 'distant expansion' recruitment strategy.

However, these organizing techniques are essentially logistic innovations, whereas a key issue here is for the trade union to gain power and be able to prevent rampant exploitation and mistreatment at the workplace. Without recognition by the employer, union effectiveness is questionable as it is more difficult for the union to represent workers collectively outside the workplace. In addition, workers' dependence on the trade union and union impact are likely to be weakened where union organizing attempts are duplicated and diluted by other functional bodies offering similar services in the labour market. Whilst this service-oriented mode of organizing has some tangible effects in increasing union memberships, the rural migrant workers may be unionized but not necessarily organized in the strict sense. Union density is not a reliable indicator of union strength, especially where the main function of the union is to provide services rather than organizing to press for improved working conditions (Cooke 2007). It is significant to note that in the strikes at the Honda plant in Foshan in 2010, ten trade union officials tried to physically shut down the workers' picket line, although a thin apology from the local government was made afterwards (Watts 2010a, also see below). This suggests that peace keeping rather than defending workers' rights is the main priority of the trade union function.

Workers' perception of union efficacy

The making and working of the union officials has been much criticized (e.g. Taylor and Li 2007; Howell 2008; Warner 2008). In spite of the widely held view of the ineffectiveness of the grassroots unions, research findings show that Chinese workers believe that it is necessary to have trade unions (e.g. Nichols and Zhao 2010; Cooke 2011b). In other words, workers are supportive of the idea of unionism and the associated ideology of collectivism and representation to safeguard their rights and interests. They are not necessarily critical of the union officials/representatives as individuals. Rather, they are critical of the powerless position of the trade unions in fighting for their rights and interests. In many ways, the findings of this study echo those in western economies (e.g. Healy et al. 2004) where union disaffection is a direct consequence of union's inability to organize. As Heery and Simms (2010) argue, union members may have higher expectations, a higher level of grievance and hence lower perception of the efficacy of unions. It is worth noting that in workplaces where workers are satisfied with their work environment and pay and conditions and where union representatives play an active role in organizing welfare services and social events (e.g. well-performing schools and hospitals in municipal areas), employees actually hold positive views of the trade unions and desire more services from them (Cooke 2008c, 2011b).

More broadly, it should be acknowledged that there are union representatives who play an active role in organizing/servicing workers at work, albeit within the traditional Chinese characteristics of unionism. Their efforts and positive impact, though rather limited, should not be dismissed altogether if we are to gain a more complete understanding of the role of the trade unions in China. While much effort has been made by union officials at the municipal and district branch level, most of their functions appear to be akin to that of the social services. The dual and contradictory role of workers' representation and implementation of state policy are manifested in full force in the union officials' work where state-owned firms used to dominate. Instead of fighting against redundancy and the inadequate provision of social security, they are there to pacify the workers and persuade them to accept any decisions. Union officials and representatives work within the principle laid down by the Party. They demonstrate the traditional cultural mentality of a Chinese mandarin in which diligence, endurance of hardship, maintenance of harmonious environment and obedience to the superior remain the core values. The tasks of defending the poor and the needy are then performed under this guidance (Cooke 2008c).

Alternative forms of organizing and representation

The fact that the ACFTU is the only union officially recognized by the government does not mean that it is the sole organizing body in the labour market servicing the workers. There are a number of organizations, both public and private, which have either existed for some time or are gearing up to organize (rural migrant) workers and provide somewhat similar services to them. These include: the All-China Women's Federation (ACWF), the local governments (mainly the labour authority), job centres/employment agencies, training centres and legal centres (see Table 7.3). It must be noted that these organizing bodies are targeting their work mainly at the laid-off state-owned enterprise workers, women workers and rural migrant workers as the disadvantaged groups in the labour market. Whilst ACWF has long existed, other bodies' functions have emerged over the last two decades or so.

The role of the All-China Women's Federation

Founded in 1949, the ACWF is a multi-tiered organization with local women's federations and group members at every divisional level of government. Its mission is to represent and to protect women's rights and interests, and to promote equality between men and women through its participation, education, representation, service and liaison functions (ACWF website 2005). The tight grip of the Chinese state in political and social organizations means that the ACWF is the only official women's organization at the national level in China (Judd 2002). As Judd (2002) argues, it is a very different type of organization from those in the West, but is one that is equally as legitimate and as effective as women's movements elsewhere, given the constraints in China. The ACWF's monopoly position is institutionalized by the 1998 Regulations which specify that 'identical or similar social groups cannot be set up within the same administrative

Table 7.3 (Emerging) forms of organization, representation and protection of workers

Organizing bodies	Major functions	Likely positive effects
All-China Women's Federation	• Representing women in workplaces and society • Providing training, counselling and welfare services • Organizing public events for information dissemination • Organizing social events	• Greater protection of women workers • Greater awareness of women's rights • Enhancing the skill level and knowledge of workers • Enhanced social welfare provisions for women workers • Social bonding amongst women workers
Local governments	• Employment information • Facilitating job selection • Training for laid-off workers and rural migrant workers • Social insurance schemes • Delivery of migrant workers from hometown to workplace • Sanctioning private job centres • Monitoring labour standards • Administrative policy for greater labour rights protection and social inclusion • Public service (e.g. legal advice centre, library, educational and cultural centre)	• Greater match of demand and supply of labour and skills • Enhancing the skill level of workers • Greater protection of workers • Greater social inclusion of rural migrant workers
All-China Federation of Trade Unions	• Training • Pursuing outstanding wage payment for workers • Employment services • Monitoring implementation of labour regulations	• Enhancing the skill level of workers • Greater protection of rural migrant workers • Greater match of demand and supply of labour and skills
Employment agencies and job centres (public and private)	• Employment information • Facilitating job selection • Becoming the employer to offer more job security and guarantee labour rights	• Greater match of demand and supply of labour and skills • Greater protection of workers
Training centres (public and private)	• Training • Employment information	• Enhancing the skill level of rural migrant workers • Greater match of demand and supply of labour and skills
Legal centres (mostly public)	• Education/training to workers on their employment rights • Protection and representation of workers in labour disputes	• Greater protection of workers • Greater awareness from workers of their legal rights
Workers' self-organizing network (e.g. *Tongxiang hui*)	• Organizing social events • Handling grievances and disputes amongst workers and with employers • Disseminating job-related information	• Some protection for workers • Support for each other • Providing a sense of identification and belonging amongst workers • Increased labour market transparency in terms of job vacancies and employment terms and conditions

Source: expanded from Cooke (2007: 585–6).

area'. In the late 1980s and 1990s, defending women's equal employment rights has become a priority for the ACWF, and it played a fundamental role in blocking the 'women return home proposal' (Zheng 2000: 68) advanced by some (male) academics and economists (Cooke 2008c). It must be noted that, similar to the ACFTU, the ACWF's activities take place mostly outside the workplaces and have little presence in the private sector. Local ACWF branches often join forces with the ACFTU or government departments to host events to maximize resources and impacts.

The role of local government

As we can see from Table 7.3, local government plays an important role in organizing laid-off and rural migrant workers, either through direct involvement in service provision or through the introduction of administrative policies and initiatives. In particular, pre-employment training has been a major function provided by local governments in response to the 'Sunshine Project' initiated by the government in 2003 which aims to deliver training to rural workers on a large scale.

Some local governments have a more comprehensive strategy that links training, employment opportunity and labour standards monitoring together. There are also signs that local governments are looking into providing a more diverse range of services to rural migrant workers. These include, for example, providing free health check-ups, holding job fairs to provide free employment consultations, setting up employment centres and training centres, inspecting profit-making job centres and publicizing a list of reputable ones (*Workers' Daily* 25 February 2005; *Workers' Daily* 15 April 2005). Public facilities and services (e.g. legal advice centres, libraries, educational and cultural centres) are also made available that are specifically tailored for rural migrant workers. Some local governments are also proactive in organizing their labour inspection teams to monitor labour standards at workplaces and introduce mechanisms to punish non-compliant employing organizations (see Chapter 8 for further discussion of this role).

The role of employment agencies and job centres

Employment centres/agencies represent an institutional presence in the labour market and are expected to play a number of roles specified by the government. These include: providing labour market information, training, screening, recruitment and placement of workers, influencing wage setting, regulating the contingent labour market, redistributing the risks associated with contingent employment and acting as employers. In the latter, it is believed that this form of employment relationship benefits both the worker and the user firm in that the worker enjoys a higher level of job security and labour rights protection, whereas the user firm will have a continuous supply of labour (*Workers' Daily* 22 February 2005). In practice, this triangular employment relationship proves to be complicated and prone to abdication of responsibilities due to ambiguity of status (Cooke 2006).

The Employment Centre/Agency Regulation promulgated by the state in 1995 stipulates that employment centres/agencies established by the local labour authorities should be non-profit making, whereas those set up by private firms or organizations unrelated to the labour authorities can be profit-making or non-profit making. In reality, most job centres and employment agencies make service charges, often beyond the price set by the local authority. Employment agencies have been criticized for their lack of professionalism, lack of up-to-date market information and lack of coordination between various organizations related to labour market services. Their training function is often under resourced and poorly equipped. Their training content is largely outdated and fails to reflect what is most needed by employers (Li 2000).

The legitimacy of employment agencies as a labour market broker remains questionable amongst job seekers. Y. B. Li (2003) reported that 70 per cent of laid-off workers had never visited an employment agency and only 3 per cent of re-employed laid-off workers found their job through employment agencies. Other research evidence shows that employment agencies are not a main channel through which rural migrant workers seek employment. For example, Liu et al.'s (2006) study of 1,424 migrant workers revealed that less than 5 per cent of the migrant workers found their job through technical colleges or government organizations. Only 10 per cent of them found their job through employment agencies, whereas 62 per cent found employment through their family and personal networks. The majority of employment agencies and job centres funded by local labour authorities are primarily providing services to laid-off workers. Rural migrant workers get their services from designated 'migrant labour market' organizations that provide services at a fee. There is little skill-training provision other than general training on occupational ethics and citizen's conduct (Mu 2003). Worse still, Mu's (2003) study revealed that the majority of rural migrant workers had never visited an employment agency, believing that they were dishonest organizations with a motive of exploiting them (see Chapter 8 for further discussion on the unintended consequence of the Labour Contract Law on employment agencies).

The role of legal centres

Legal centres, often supported by the trade union and local government, are set up to provide legal advice to rural migrant workers and handle labour disputes for them. These legal centres play an education, protection and representation role and have a tangible impact in protecting the workers' interests. For example, a legal centre set up under the auspices of the trade union in Wuyi City (Zhejiang Province) had dealt with over 3,000 cases in the four years from 2000 to 2004. It had represented, free of charge, workers in 167 cases in tribunals and helped them gain over 90 million yuan in compensation (*Workers' Daily* 8 March 2005). However, it must be noted that what legal centres can do is perhaps only a drop in the ocean, given the extent of violation of labour rights and the limited resources available to combat injustice. The promulgation of the Labour Contract

Law and Labour Disputes Mediation and Arbitration Law in 2007 has led to a sharp increase of labour dispute cases (see Tables 8.1 and 8.2). For example, a total of 317,162 and 350,182 dispute cases were accepted for arbitration nationwide in 2006 and 2007 respectively. Following the enactment of the two laws mentioned above, the total number of dispute cases accepted for arbitration in 2008 rose sharply to 693,465, almost doubling the figure of 2007 (*China Statistical Yearbook 2010*: 885). It is unclear, though, what additional resources have been provided nationwide to legal centres, and indeed other bodies involved in disputes resolution, to facilitate the handling of these cases.

In addition to the above formal domestic bodies that may play a role in organizing and representing workers to various effects, foreign client firms operating at the upper end of the product market and international NGOs are increasingly playing a role in monitoring labour standards and legislative compliance in China. This is particularly in the export-oriented manufacturing sector. Foreign client firms use corporate social responsibility (CSR) as their leverage to raise the labour standards of Chinese supplier firms. Some authors believe that this pressure has had both positive and negative effects on Chinese workers (e.g. Cooke 2009d; Harney 2009). Others critique that the discourse of CSR may be merely a hypocritical device to protect the western market (e.g. Howell 2008).

International NGOs and domestic ones under international patronage provide financial, medical, legal, educational and emotional support to workers in sweatshop plants through some forms of organizing primarily outside the workplaces (e.g. Murdoch and Gould 2004; Pun and Yang 2004; Kessler 2008; Lee and Shen 2008). These services are provided within an institutional environment that is largely absent of a civil society tradition and at times hostile to the embedment of non-CCP-led NGOs. Nevertheless, the promulgation of the Labour Contract Law and related regulations undoubtedly provide NGOs with more legal instruments to carry out their work.

Nonetheless, the emergence of these new sources of pressure and forms of organizations providing services and support to aggrieved workers, though small in scope of services and limited in effects, has forced the ACFTU to develop similar lines of services. For example, the ACFTU are now sponsoring/operating a significant proportion of the job centres, training centres and legal advice centres nationwide. Some local ACFTU organizations have reportedly approached NGOs and black lawyers for collaboration (Clarke and Pringle 2009). However, it is unclear if this is a genuine intent to collaboration or a disguised form of insurgence to seek control by the Communist Party.

Workers' self-organizing

Self-formed associations and networks

The inadequacy of the ACFTU and other official bodies in defending workers' rights has to some extent led to the reliance on a number of alternative routes, often unofficial and informal, for workers to voice their grievances, to resolve their disputes with employers, to share labour market information, and to provide peer support and a forum for social bonding (Cooke 2008c). In some workplaces and local areas where a large number of migrant workers work and live, workers set up their own *tongxiang hui* (loosely formed association of workers from the same region/village) to carry out a variety of activities. Whilst offering a level of protection and compassionate support to fellow rural migrant workers, *tongxiang hui* are unofficial, unprofessional and sometimes take extreme measures in handling disputes between groups of workers and between labour and management (Gao and Jia 2005). It is beyond the scope of this chapter to discuss these kinds of organizations in detail, but they do present a potential competing source of attention/identification against the ACFTU.

It has been noted (Gao and Jia 2005) that in developed cities such as Beijing, networks developed by rural migrant workers in informal employment prove highly efficient. They consist of a group of highly physically able workers in their prime age, and they are highly sensitive in capturing and responding to labour market information. Nevertheless, the self-organization of rural migrant workers tends to be precarious and largely inadequate in protecting their labour rights.

Spontaneous strikes, protests and negotiations

The inability of the ACFTU grassroots branches and other formal channels to organize workers to protect their employment terms and conditions has also led to various forms of industrial actions such as wildcat strikes, street protests, walkouts and collective resignations by aggrieved Chinese workers (e.g. Chan 2001; F. Chen 2003a, 2006; Lee 2007; Chan and Pun 2009). It is important to note that these continuing attempts at self-organizing have taken place in spite of the strong suppression of labour unrest by the government. These industrial actions are often spontaneous and event specific, targeted at the workplace or local government level. These labour protests are not confined to rural migrant workers in sweatshop plants or to workers in the state-owned enterprises who have either been displaced or are suffering from low wages due to financial deficits of the firm. Other occupational groups such as taxi drivers in major cities and school teachers in remote/poor areas have also taken to the street as the last resort to protest against their low income as a result of harsh taxation by the taxi companies or wage arrears by the local government employer (*China Labour Bulletin* 2009). It is interesting to note that workers' applications for setting up unions (e.g. aggrieved taxi drivers) have been rejected by the ACFTU branches with the reason that 'unions should be organized by the enterprise' (*China Labour Bulletin* 2009: 35).

Whilst Lee's (2007) study depicted a pessimistic regional picture of the powerlessness of workers in sunbelt and rustbelt China, Chan's (2009) in-depth study of a Taiwanese-invested factory in Shenzhen showed that workers have been able to act collectively (strikes) and mobilize labour laws successfully to increase their wages and social security benefits. It needs to be noted that the fulfilment of these labour rights was aided by a tight labour market where the recruitment and retention of labour presented a major problem for employers in the region in the mid-2000s.

The year 2010 marked the turning point of the labour–capital power imbalance through a string of high-profile strike actions organized by workers themselves in a number of foreign-invested manufacturing/brewery plants in various major cities. These include, for example, Honda in Foshan and Zhongshan, Hyundai in Beijing, Toyota in Tianjin, Brother in Xi'an, Panasonic in Shanghai and Carlsberg in Chongqing. Demands for higher wages and better working conditions were the main reason for the strikes. According to the ACFTU, a quarter of Chinese workers have not had a pay rise in the past five years (Wasserstrom 2010). These strikes have yielded positive results – all employers have agreed to a substantial pay rise of between 20–40 per cent after rounds of negotiation (Watts 2010a).

In Foxconn (Shenzhen), young workers in their twenties took a more extreme form to put an end to their miserable working life – suicide by jumping off the building. The Foxconn factory in Shenzhen is one of the largest electronics factories in the world, employing over 300,000 workers. The factory is run by a large multinational company from Taiwan and produces electronic components for the most famous brand names in the global IT industry such as Apple, Hewlett-Packard, Dell, Nokia and Sony. For seven consecutive years it has ranked as the number one export corporation on China's mainland. The tragic series of suicides among young workers of the 'Foxconn City' factory in 2009 and 2010 attracted worldwide publicity and criticism of the firm. Poor labour standards, in part due to the low-cost contracting in the supply chain of electronics manufacturing, are the major reason. In mid-2010, Foxconn was forced to implement a number of decisions to prevent further tragedies and to pacify worker discontent. As a result, Foxconn's employees received a pay rise of 66 per cent if they met certain conditions and were also guaranteed a weekly rest break. In addition, a number of HR initiatives, such as counselling, were introduced to enhance the physical and psychological well-being of the workers. At a deeper level, the Foxconn case reveals the exacerbating physical and mental health problems experienced by millions of rural migrant workers as a result of their poor working and living environments and the institutional and social barriers that prevent them and their families from being integrated into the urban society (Cooke 2007).

The successive industrial action of various forms that have taken place across a number of industries and the country since the 1990s suggest that Chinese workers are becoming more aware of their rights and more ready to fight for the improvement of their terms and conditions. Emboldened by the promulgation of the Labour Contract Law and the Labour Disputes Mediation and Arbitration Law, they 'have demonstrated the ability to organize large-scale and effective protests' (*China Labour Bulletin* 2009: 31). Despite being illegal, strikes remain a highly effective way to resolve labour disputes, in part due to the government's eagerness to see disputes settled to avoid the eruptions of larger-scale labour unrest. However, this may not be without cost to those who organize the collective actions, particularly in the state sector (e.g. F. Chen 2003a, 2006). Whilst strike actions against foreign MNC management/owners are also likely to result in victimization of strike leaders, it is much less likely to attract a hail of police batons on protesting workers, thanks to the government's willingness to indulge nationalist sentiment.

In the past, the government has mobilized forces to curtail protests and strikes and suppressed media coverage of these events. In the string of strikes in foreign-owned plants in 2010 as noted above, the Chinese authority verged on the supportive, claiming that the workers' demands were 'reasonable' (Milne 2010). Another reason for the authority's tacit support of the strike action was the pressure the government has been facing to increase wages in order to address the growing inequality in income and to stimulate internal demand for consumption to offset a fall in exports as a result of the 2008 global financial crisis. It was reported that in a speech in 2010, Premier Wen Jiabao said that in return for their contribution to China's economic take-off, migrant workers deserved to be 'cared for, protected and respected' (Wasserstrom 2010).

Not all collective actions are of a confrontational nature. For example, Li and Edwards's (2008) study of small garment factories in Guangdong Province owned by worker-turned entrepreneurs revealed that skilled workers in these factories have considerable bargaining power in wage negotiation. There are three important factors for this. One is the concentration of small factories in the same location competing intensively for business contracts, making it vital for owners to secure skilled workers and their cooperation. Skill is a second important factor which gives workers substantial bargaining leverage to be mobilized at crucial timing. A third factor is the social organization of the firms. The small firm size and existence of personal networks through which recruitment is made engender an informal nature of workplace relations with a considerable amount of give and take between owner-managers and workers. In addition to accepting wage bargaining, owner-managers grant autonomy to skilled workers. It must be noted that these bargaining units are based on work groups who are engaged in the same production activities and receive the same pay structure. Both employers and workers use market rates to benchmark their wage-efforts bargaining, which is a common practice in production zones where similar businesses are clustered.

All this evidence suggests that there are 'embryonic forms of freedom of association in China' (Clarke and Pringle 2009: 99). However, industrial action taken by Chinese workers is essentially 'livelihood struggle' instead of 'class struggle', to borrow Lee's (2007: 29) classification, or in Watts's (2010b) words, it was more of a stealth movement than a Solidarity moment of Chinese labour in global production. As such, these collective actions are transient, event-specific and unlikely to form a congruent part of the international labour movement. This is particularly in view of the hostile attitude of international labour organizations towards the ACFTU in the past, the limited role of international NGOs in

China so far, and the limited resource, capability and political legitimacy of Chinese workers for self-organizing. Nevertheless, the series of strikes in 2010 revealed signs that Chinese workers are organizing more effectively. In Honda, disgusted by the response of the trade unions, as noted earlier, striking workers hired a top industrial relations professor in China (Chang Kai from Renmin University, Beijing) to advise them on pay negotiation. They are asking not just for pay rises but more importantly structural reforms such as independent and elected union chairpersons to represent them in collective bargaining (Watts 2010a).

Conclusion

This chapter has reviewed the legal rights of Chinese workers and the ACFTU as their official organizing and representing body. It also drew attention to the emergent organizing and representing role of other formal representing bodies from both the domestic and international arena. When assessing the functions and impact of the ACFTU organizations, it is important that we take a balanced and multi-level view to evaluate both their legislative and policy role at the national level and their servicing and representing role at the grassroots level within and outside the enterprises. As a number of authors have noted (e.g. Taylor and Li 2007; Chan 2009), the role the ACFTU plays in influencing pro-labour legislation has not been given sufficient credit. Similarly, the positive attitude and efforts of at least a proportion of the union officials need to be acknowledged instead of simply branding them as an incompetent and even corrupt group indifferent to workers' needs and sufferings. Outside the workplace, they work closely with the local government and labour authorities to monitor law enforcement and provide a range of services. Within enterprises, they play a welfare and extended HR role such as in counselling and training. These activities are necessary to harmonize workplace relations and enhance individual workers' well-being.

More generally, the ACFTU is responding, albeit belatedly and slowly, to the changing nature of employment relations by adopting new initiatives and strategies for organizing workers, with particular reference to rural migrant workers. These include, for example, collective negotiation, collective contract system, tripartite consultation system and welfare and other services. However, political, institutional and organizational constraints largely determine how far these changes can go (Liu et al. 2011). As Warner (2008) observed, the ACFTU plays multiple and at times conflicting roles, including being labour market actors, vehicles of anti-capitalist mobilization and agents of social integration. The absence of legality of collective actions in the collective negotiation, collective consultation and collective agreement process (Feng 2006) is perhaps the biggest constraint of the ACFTU in representing workers. This image of the trade union as inefficacious devolves into a more grotesque view when grassroots union officials play an active role in preventing strike action from the workers, as was evidenced in the Honda case reported above.

In spite of the fact that strikes and collective actions are often suppressed by the state, these activities have taken place on a number of sites across the country with some positive effects in redressing workers' grievances. Although many of the strikes were workplace-based, they often triggered similar actions in other workplaces, thus transgressing the barriers of locality and workers' origin (Chan and Pun 2009). However, these collective actions were largely spontaneous and non-industry-based actions that have not formed part of a sustained countervailing force against the capitalists/management. They are primarily ad hoc economic rather than political struggles. Without the freedom of association and the right to strike, these forms of locally based and event-specific activism are unlikely to be transformed into a more conscious and strategic labour movement. If the labour movement in the earlier part of the ACFTU history was informed by any level of class consciousness, this is largely absent in the labour movement of the post-Mao era despite the rise of capitalism in areas where the level of labour disputes are also high. It must be argued that the ACFTU's role as the CCP agents in suppressing collective actions is detrimental to China's labour movement in the absence of an alternative legal organizing body.

Finally, in view of the ineffectiveness of the ACFTU, the role of international organizing bodies remains a crucial force to protect Chinese workers' rights. These include: the role of the International Labour Organization in promoting labour standards and decent work, the role of international media in reporting human rights issues, the role of foreign client firms in pressing for corporate social responsibility and the role of NGOs in providing support to workers. But one should not have any illusion that any independent organizing bodies could emerge to become a mainstream organizer of labour movement without the backing of the CCP-state. Given the political role of the ACFTU and fundamental ideological differences, the prospect of strengthening relationships between the ACFTU and the labour organizations of other countries remains unclear. In the meantime, 'with any fundamental trade union reform still in the distant future, we can expect workers increasingly to find their own ways to organize and resist workplace exploitation' (Howell 2008: 863).

8 Employment laws and regulations

Introduction

The healthy operation of labour markets and the achievement of harmonious employment relations require an effective regulatory system. From the workers' point of view, effective labour market regulation plays an important redistributive role in a marketizing economy such as China's where the majority of workers do not have any form of labour market advantage. However, over-regulation may reduce the competitiveness of firms and industries where the flexible deployment of labour constitutes an important part of the competitive strategy. It has therefore been argued that promoting efficiency and equity are the two key objectives of labour market regulation (e.g. Buchanan and Callus 1993; Fudge and Vosko 2001). Another goal 'is to stop recreating and exacerbating labour market segmentation through the various forms of legal regulations' (Fudge and Vosko 2001: 332).

As mentioned in Chapter 7, a number of labour laws and regulations have been promulgated by the Chinese government since the early 1990s (also see Brown 2009). Major laws and regulations include, for example:

- The Labour Law of the People's Republic of China in 1994 (enacted on 1 January 1995, hereafter the Labour Law), which was the first most comprehensive piece of labour legislation in China.
- The Labour Market Wage Rate Guideline (1999), which is aimed to increase labour market transparency and at the same time allow the labour market to have a fuller role in wage determination.
- The 'Regulation on Labour Market Management' (2000), which was superseded by the Employment Promotion Law (2008, see below).
- The special regulation on minimum wages (2004), which is a revision based on the 'Enterprise Minimum Wage Regulation' issued for the first time in 1993 (see Cooke 2005a for further discussion). A key feature of the revised regulation is that it divides wages into two types: monthly and hourly, respectively applying to full-time and non full-time workers.
- The Regulations on Employment Services and Management (2008), which is a set of implementation rules for the Employment Promotion Law.

In 2007, dubbed as the 'legislative year of China', the government stepped up its legislative activities and passed three major pieces of employment-related laws to take effect from 2008. They are:

- The Labour Contract Law of the People's Republic of China (enacted on 1 January 2008, hereafter the Labour Contract Law).
- The Employment Promotion Law of the People's Republic of China (enacted on 1 January 2008, hereafter the Employment Promotion Law).
- The Labour Disputes Mediation and Arbitration Law of the People's Republic of China (enacted on 1 May 2008, hereafter the Labour Disputes Mediation and Arbitration Law).

These three pieces of new labour legislation are interconnected and cover different stages of the employment relationship, i.e. from recruitment to the termination of employment contract. More specifically, the Employment Promotion Law aims to promote employment and secure the employment rights of workers; the Labour Contract Law seeks to regulate the rights and responsibilities of employer/labour user organization and the worker; and the Labour Disputes Mediation and Arbitration Law is a procedural law that aims to ensure the fulfilment of these rights. The promulgation of the Labour Disputes Mediation and Arbitration Law is to support the implementation of the Labour Contract Law.

The legislative necessity and urgency of the above laws arises after a gap of more than 12 years since the introduction of the Labour Law. During that period, significant changes took place in the economic structure and employment environment. These changes have led to a divergence of goals and interests between the actors in employment relations, a heightened level of conflicts between these interests and the surge of power of the employers. The promulgation of the three laws signals the government's renewed and stronger determination to raise the level of protection for its workforce and to counterbalance the prerogative of employers. Employees are afforded greater power to seek justice through legal channels when these laws are violated by employers. Together, these labour laws and their supplementary regulations provide a legal framework within which the employment relationship is to be governed and labour market regulated (see Figure 8.1). The primary objective of their implementation is to achieve a more efficient and equitable labour market. In parallel, a system for labour disputes resolution is formed, albeit one that is far from robust.

As noted by Cooney (2007), the labour standards defined by the series of labour regulations compare favourably with some developed countries. What remains most problematic is the lack of effective enforcement (Taylor et al. 2003; Cooney 2007). While implementation failures are characteristic of all regulatory systems (Cooney 2007), the Chinese system is frustrated by the multiplicity of employment-related laws, directive regulations and administrative policies issued at central, provincial and municipal government level, the ambiguous status of some of these regulative instruments, and the confusing channels through which workers can seek to secure compliance of laws (Cooney 2007).

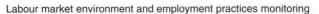

Labour market environment and employment practices monitoring

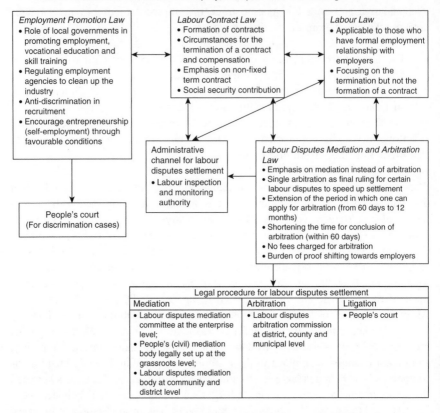

Figure 8.1 Major employment-related laws and their interconnections and impacts.
Source: compiled by the author.

The promulgation of the three laws by the central government therefore raises an important set of questions that have not been addressed. What is the legislative environment and what are the institutional barriers for introducing employment regulations in China? Given the brief history and limited experience of the Chinese state in employment legislation, does it have sufficient legislative capacity to provide an effective regulatory framework for the labour market and employment relations? Are these laws able to bring to an end the fragmented authoritarianism that has been an enduring and key feature in the economic and social development characteristic of the central state control in the post-Mao era? Similarly, will these laws be tight enough to circumvent the growing ability of employers, particularly since the 1990s, to bypass or override regulatory constraints in pursuit of their business objectives? What may be the impact of these regulations on the workers and other institutional actors? What new actors may have emerged in the regulatory process and how do the interactions of these institutional actors shape the legislative outcomes?

This chapter aims to address these questions. Using the Labour Contract Law and the Labour Disputes Mediation and Arbitration Law as the focal point for discussion, the chapter examines the response of employers, workers and the trade unions to the new regulations and the emergence of 'new' institutional actors in the regulating process. These 'new' actors are not necessarily 'new' in a sense because some of them have existed for a number of years. What is new is their more direct and active role in employment relations at the workplace/ organizational level as an unintended consequence of the enactment of the labour laws in 2008.

This chapter consists of four main sections in addition to this introduction. The first main section describes the background, key focuses and intended legislative progress of the three laws. This is followed by an investigation of the impact of the laws on the main actors, such as the employers, workers, local governments and the labour authorities. It also examines their tactical responses and dynamic interactions. The third section then examines the emerging roles of the new actors in the implementation of the new laws. It investigates how they establish themselves through collaboration and alliance with other actors, officially and unofficially. The chapter concludes that whilst the three laws signal a significant advancement in China's employment legislative domain, the legislative power of the state has been undermined by other institutional actors at the local level, who interact and permeate each other's sites and spatial boundaries in acknowledgement of and to complement each other's resource/capacity constraints.

Background, key focus and intended legislative progress of the three laws

1. Employment Promotion Law

There are two reasons for the promulgation of the Employment Promotion Law: to promote employment and to regulate the labour market. First, there has been mounting pressure for the government to create employment opportunities for the newcomers in the labour market (e.g. rural migrant workers, school leavers and university graduates) and for those who have been displaced by their employer as a result of technological advancement, intensifying global competition, industrial structural change and ownership reforms. In particular, university graduate unemployment is becoming a serious social concern. The rapid expansion of the Chinese higher education sector since the early 2000s has led to a rising level of unemployment amongst university graduates. A second reason for the need for the law is that the absence of laws on employment rights, which is arguably a precondition for other labour rights, has led to a disorderly labour market management situation. In the absence of a central law, local administrative policies and regulations proliferated. They are often confusing, contradictory, unprofessional and with low enforceability (Han and Liu 2008). The Employment Promotion Law was therefore promulgated in 2007 to take effect from 1 January 2008.

The Employment Promotion Law is essentially a regulation that promotes employment security. It contains nine chapters and 69 articles. Key aspects covered include: policy support, fair employment, employment services and administration, occupational education and training, employment assistance, monitoring and inspection, and legal liability.

There are four key foci in the Employment Promotion Law (see Figure 8.1). First, it emphasizes the role of the local governments in promoting employment, vocational education and skill training through a range of measures and mechanisms. These include, for example, funding vocational education and training institutes; initiating training programmes for rural migrant workers; monitoring training budgets and activities of enterprises; and applying penalties on non-complying firms. Second, the Employment Promotion Law seeks to create a healthy labour market by cleaning up the employment agency/job centre industry. A number of rules are introduced to define the scope of services of employment agencies and to regulate the behaviour of employment agencies and user firms. Forced closure and/or financial penalty may be applied to agency operators who violate the law. A third focus of the Employment Promotion Law is fairness in employment, a point that is also specified in the Labour Contract Law. The Employment Promotion Law specifies that employers cannot discriminate on the grounds of ethnicity, race, gender, religious belief, disability or against carriers of infectious pathogens and candidates of rural origin. Although equal opportunity rights have been stipulated in the Constitution (1954, 2004) and the Labour Law, it is the Employment Promotion Law that makes the most specific and comprehensive statement on the types of workers who should not be discriminated against. The expanded categories of vulnerable groups of workers indicate that China's employment laws are not only becoming more liberal in recognizing changing social characteristics in the labour force, but also converging to international trends of enhanced legislative protection relating to equal opportunity and diversity management (Cooke 2011a). In addition, a remedial channel is outlined for legal liability. A fourth focus of the Employment Promotion Law is to provide employment assistance through the provision of favourable policy conditions for setting up self-employed businesses (e.g. Han and Liu 2008; Liu 2008).

2. Labour Contract Law

There were two main reasons for the introduction of the Labour Contract Law. First, the legal system that governs employment relations had been flimsy, relying largely on the Labour Law which applies mainly to those in the formal employment sector with formal employment relationships (Hu 2004; Cooney et al. 2007; Dong 2008). It failed to address the growing tensions emerging from the privatized economy and the growing informalization of employment, through casual work and agency work (known as labour dispatch in China). There is considerable ambiguity as to whether certain laws and regulations should apply to the informal sector and workers in informal employment. Employers tend to take advantage of these regulatory loopholes and argue for exemption (Cooke 2008f). Despite the lack of consensus on its definition, it is agreed that informal employment has become a significant form of employment in China, employing an estimated 20 per cent of the total workforce (e.g. Peng and Yao 2004; Shi and Wang 2007; Wu 2008). Again, the legislative void is partly filled by a range of administrative regulations and legislative instruments adopted by local governments (Cooney et al. 2007). Whilst these interventions have had some effect, they are essentially administrative regulations that have limited consistency, authority and enforceability (Hu 2004).

A second and related reason is that the number of labour dispute cases and the number of workers involved in disputes have been rising significantly in recent years (see Tables 8.1 and 8.2; also see Cooke 2008f for a detailed analysis). For example, in 2001 154,621 cases were accepted for arbitration, this rose to 350,182 in 2007. In 2001, a total of 467,150 workers were involved in the labour disputes cases; in 2007, this figure had increased to 653,472 (*China Labour Statistical Yearbook 2008*). A notable parallel development is the increasingly individualistic nature of the disputes. In 2001, collective labour disputes cases (i.e. cases that involved three or more people in each) made up 6 per cent of the total cases and 61 per cent of the total number of workers involved in the disputes. In 2007, collective labour disputes cases made up 3.7 per cent of the total cases and 42 per cent of the total number of workers involved in the disputes (*China Labour Statistical Yearbook 2008*). This indicates that collective organization is poor.

Main forms of non-compliance from the employers include: non-provision of employment contract, under-payment of wages, wage arrears, excessive overtime and non-contribution to social insurance premiums. According to the statistics from labour inspections, fewer than 20 per cent of the small and medium-sized private firms had signed contracts with their workers. This figure was much lower in the self-employed business sector (cited in Chang 2008). Since the Labour Law only covers those in formal employment, this leaves the majority of workers in de facto employment relationships unprotected. For those who have signed employment contracts, the majority of contracts were for one-year duration. The short-term nature of the contractual relationship renders employment relations unstable at the macro level. Some contracts include unlawful clauses that allow the employers to evade responsibilities on sickness and work-related injuries (Qiao 2008). About 70 per cent of migrant workers have experienced wage arrears (Dong 2008). According to a survey conducted by the labour authority in April 2005, nearly 13 per cent of the workers were paid below the local minimum wage level. Some firms reduced the real wage by unilaterally reducing the unit price of production or raising the production targets which forced workers to work unpaid overtime to complete their tasks. Wage arrears and unlawful deduction of wages were the most common violation cases revealed in the labour inspections (cited in Chang 2008). A primary objective of the Labour Contract Law is therefore to create a formal and stable employment relationship between the workers and employing

Table 8.1 Trends of labour disputes in China (1994–2009)

Year	No. of cases accepted		Increase from previous year (%)		No. of employees involved		Increase from previous year (%)		Cases settled	Means of settlement					
	Total cases	Collective cases	Total cases	Collective cases	In total cases	In collective cases	In total cases	In collective cases		Mediation		Arbitration		Others	
										cases	% of total	cases	% of total	cases	% of total
1994	19,098	1,482	–	–	77,794	52,637	–	68	17,962	9,362	52	3,465	19	5,135	29
1995	33,030	2,588	73	75	122,512	77,340	58	63	31,415	17,990	57	7,269	23	6,156	20
1996	47,951	3,150	45	22	189,120	92,203	54	49	46,543	24,223	52	12,789	27	9,531	20
1997	71,524	4,109	49	30	221,115	132,647	17	60	70,792	32,793	46	15,060	21	22,939	32
1998	93,649	6,767	31	65	358,531	251,268	62	70	92,288	31,483	34	25,389	28	35,155	38
1999	120,191	9,043	28	34	473,957	319,241	32	67	121,289	39,550	33	34,712	29	47,027	39
2000	135,206	8,247	13	–9	422,617	259,445	–11	61	130,688	41,877	32	54,142	41	34,699	27
2001	154,621	9,847	15	19	467,150	286,680	11	62	150,279	42,933	29	72,250	48	35,096	23
2002	184,116	11,024	19	12	608,396	374,956	30	63	178,744	50,925	29	77,340	43	50,479	28
2003	226,391	10,823	23	–2	801,042	514,573	32	37	223,503	67,765	30	95,774	43	59,954	27
2004	260,471	19,241	15	78	764,981	477,992	–5	–7	258,678	83,400	32	110,708	43	64,550	25
2005	313,773	16,217	20	–19	744,195	409,819	–3	–14	306,027	104,308	34	131,745	43	69,974	23
2006	317,162	13,977	1	–14	679,312	348,714	–9	–15	310,780	104,435	34	141,465	46	64,880	21
2007	350,182	12,784	10	–8	653,472	271,777	–4	–22	340,030	119,436	35	149,013	44	71,581	21
2008	693,465	21,880	98	71	121,4328	502,713	86	85	622,719	221,284	33	274,543	44	126,892	20
2009	684,379	13,779	–1	–37	101,6922	299,601	–16	–40	689,714	251,463	36	290,971	42	147,280	21

Sources: compiled from *China Statistical Yearbook 1995 to 2010*.

Table 8.2 Labour disputes appealed and settled by arbitration committees in China (1995–2009)

Year	Cases	Appealed by employers		Appealed by employees		Cases settled	By result of settlement					
		Cases	% of total	Cases	% of total	Cases	Cases won by employers		Cases won by employees		Cases partly won by both parties	
							Cases	% of total	Cases	% of total	Cases	% of total
1995	33,030	–	–	–	–	31,415	6,189	20	16,272	52	8,954	28
1996	47,951	6,254	13	41,697	87	46,543	9,452	20	23,696	51	13,395	29
1997	71,524	2,751	4	68,773	96	70,792	11,488	16	40,063	57	19,241	27
1998	93,649	4,446	5	84,829	91	92,288	11,937	13	48,650	53	27,365	30
1999	120,191	6,039	5	114,152	95	121,289	15,674	13	63,030	52	37,459	31
2000	135,206	5,985	4	120,043	89	130,688	13,699	10	70,544	54	37,247	29
2001	154,621	7,840	5	146,781	95	150,279	31,544	21	71,739	48	46,996	31
2002	184,116	11,863	6	172,253	94	178,744	27,017	15	84,432	47	67,295	38
2003	226,391	10,879	5	215,512	95	223,503	34,272	15	109,556	49	79,475	36
2004	260,471	11,136	4	249,335	96	258,678	35,679	14	123,268	48	94,041	36
2005	313,773	20,063	6	293,710	94	306,027	39,401	13	145,352	47	121,274	40
2006	317,162	15,929	5	301,233	95	310,780	39,251	13	146,028	47	125,501	40
2007	350,182	24,592	7	325,590	93	340,030	49,211	14	156,955	46	133,864	40
2008	693,465			650,077		622,719	80,462		276,793		265,464	
2009	684,379			627,530		689,714	95,470		255,119		339,125	40

Sources: compiled from *China Statistical Yearbook 1996 to 2010*.

organizations through a tighter definition of labour contract arrangements, as stated in Article 1:

> This law is enacted and formulated in order to improve the labour contract system, to specify the rights and obligations of both parties to the contract, to protect the legitimate rights and interests of employees, and to construct and develop a harmonious and stable employment relationship.

The Labour Contract Law includes clauses on probationary period, redundancy, liquidated damage, severance pay, non-competition and labour dispatching (agency work). It offers a more comprehensive guidance than the Labour Law on the employment relationship, from the formation of contracts to circumstances for the termination of a contract and compensation (see Figure 8.1). It restricts employers' autonomy to dismiss workers at will by introducing the non-fixed-term labour contract. It is anticipated that tighter regulation will lead to the formalization of employment relations and a reduction of the number of those in informal employment, particularly agency workers and hourly rate workers. In the meantime, workers are given more freedom of mobility by forbidding the use of bonds – a strategy commonly deployed by employers to chain their workers to the firm. The Labour Contract Law also requires employers to make contributions to the social insurance premium for the employee (a requirement that is also stipulated in the Labour Law). In addition, the regulatory role of the trade unions has been strengthened through the right of joint decision making in management practices. The legislative intent is to provide greater protection of workers' substantive rights and increase the costs of non-compliance for employers. From this perspective, the Labour Contract Law is seen as a progress from the Labour Law. Local governments have been given more responsibility to monitor the compliance of the Labour Contract Law.

3. Labour Disputes Mediation and Arbitration Law

The labour disputes arbitration system of China was resumed in 1987. With the promulgation of the 'Regulations on Enterprise Labour Disputes Treatment' in 1993 and the Labour Law in 1994, a system of consultation, mediation, arbitration and litigation was established, albeit a rather fragile one. In order to support the enactment of the Labour Contract Law, the Labour Disputes Mediation and Arbitration Law was designed, approved and enacted within a year. Such speed was rare in China's law-making history but was deemed necessary, as stated in Article 1:

> This law is formulated in order to resolve labour disputes in a fair and timely manner, to protect the legitimate interests of the parties concerned, and to promote a harmonious and stable employment relationship.

The Labour Disputes Mediation and Arbitration Law contains several important changes from the previous disputes resolution system, which in principle makes justice more accessible to workers. These changes include:

- 'One Arbitration, Final Ruling' for certain labour disputes (e.g. a claim for wage arrears, medical expenses relating to work injuries, unpaid overtime or social insurance) instead of going through the previous 'one arbitration and two trials' procedure which was time-consuming. Compared to the procedures of other types of disputes in China, the mediation and arbitration of labour disputes involved the most complicated procedures and had been widely criticized. The Labour Disputes Mediation and Arbitration Law is intended to reduce this procedural complexity (Liang 2008; Tong 2008; Wang and Zhang 2008) through the following provisions;
- Extending the application for arbitration from 60 days to one year to give workers more time to understand their situation and take action;
- Once the arbitration commission accepts the case, it must be dealt with within 45 days or with an extension of up to 15 days for a complicated case. This has shortened the time for concluding arbitration;
- Shifting the burden of proof as well as the consequences for failing to provide certain evidence to the employer in circumstances 'where the evidence related to the disputed matter is in the form of records kept by the employer' (Article 6);
- Removal of fees charged for arbitration and reduced fees for litigation and
- Adding a mediation stage prior to arbitration in order to shift from a judicial to a voluntary approach to labour disputes resolution.

A new emphasis of the Labour Disputes Mediation and Arbitration Law is the role of mediation. By adding the mediation stage prior to the arbitration stage in the labour disputes resolution procedure, the government hopes to resolve labour disputes in an efficient and peaceful manner in line with its ideological objective of building a harmonious society. More specifically, the Labour Disputes Mediation and Arbitration Law (Article 10) has expanded the provision of labour disputes mediation bodies to include three types:

1. Labour disputes mediation committee at the enterprise level;
2. People's (civil) mediation body legally set up at the grassroots level and
3. Labour disputes mediation body set up at the community and district level where there is mediation capacity (but what qualifies 'having mediation capacity' is not defined).

This multilayer labour disputes mediation mechanism provides workers with several channels to seek settlement. However, there exist some loopholes in the design of the law. First, there is no specific or legal requirement for the establishment of a mediation committee at the enterprise level. Employers are left to make a choice as to whether they 'have the conditions' to set up a committee or not, and if so, how it is to operate. As a result, many employers have not set up a mediation committee. Where one exists, it is more in name than in substance. The absence of an independent third party in the committee is a common phenomenon. Next, the second and third types of mediation bodies lack authority, legal position and power, a problem exacerbated by the deficiency in legal competence of the mediators whose rulings are often perceived unfair and challenged by those involved. This situation is not conducive to the promotion of mediation as the main means of labour dispute resolution (Lin 2008).

The promulgation of the three major pieces of employment-related laws has in principle significantly streamlined China's legal framework for employment protection and labour disputes resolution. However, the implementation of these laws has so far been frustrated by a number of serious challenges due to conceptual ambiguities in the clauses, structural problems in legal channels, system abuse by both employers and workers and resource constraints in handling disputes. These issues are discussed in the next section.

Challenges to implementation and the role of/impact on the main institutional actors

Local authorities, labour dispute resolution bodies, employers, workers and trade unions are the traditional main actors in the enforcement of labour regulations (see Chapter 7 for more detailed discussion of workers' representation). This section investigates the impact of the laws on them, their tactical responses and dynamic interactions between them (see Table 8.3 and Figure 8.2). The Employment Promotion Law is a much less influential and controversial law than the Labour Contract Law and the Labour Disputes Mediation and Arbitration Law, as it is directed mainly at local governments. By contrast, the consequences triggered by the implementation of the Labour Contract Law and the Labour Disputes Mediation and Arbitration Law, many of which were not foreseen, are unfolding and having a strong impact on the existing positions of the institutional actors.

Employment Promotion Law

The Employment Promotion Law has been criticized for being ambiguous in its wording and sounding more like a government policy statement than a serious piece of legislation. There is little clarification in terms of what legal responsibility should apply to unlawful behaviour, making it impossible to enforce (e.g. Han and Liu 2008; Ma 2008). For example, Article 62 stipulates that 'In the event of any employment discrimination in violation of the provisions of this Law, the relevant worker(s) shall be entitled to initiate legal proceedings in the people's court'. However, there is no clear guideline on what constitutes discrimination, what and how evidence should be used and what compensation/remedial actions should/can be taken to facilitate its enforcement. Similarly, there is no

Table 8.3 Impacts of the Labour Contract Law and the Labour Disputes Mediation and Arbitration Law on institutional actors and their responses

Institutional actors	Impacts	Responses
Employers	• Increased labour costs • Inflexibility in labour deployment	• Strong opposition to LCL and request for amendments • Dismissing workers, hire freeze or (re)hiring workers through agency firms • Accepting unlawful employment terms and conditions • Refusing to sign contract • More ready to file labour dispute applications • Pursuing innovative ways to access justice (e.g. administrative litigation)
Workers	• Job losses • Wage losses due to contribution to social insurance fund • Easier to file labour dispute cases against employers	
Trade unions	• Expanded power through joint decision making	• Welcoming the new laws • Involvement in setting up mediation committee at enterprise level
Local governments	• Tension between attracting investment and supporting business on the one hand and protecting labour rights on the other • Increased financial burden for labour dispute arbitration and litigation	• Developing innovative local policy regulations to dilute the central laws • Encouraging internal resolution to conform to the ideology of 'building a harmonious society' • Forcing enterprises to resolve labour disputes internally
Labour inspection authorities	• Greater power/responsibility • Dramatic increase of workload	
Employment agency entities	• More restrictions on business operation • Increased demand for agency workers • Conflict of dual role of labour market monitoring (gatekeeper) and business operator (player)	• Profiting from the new laws as a result of employers' reaction • Innovative ways to maximize business opportunities through intricate relationships with local governments • Higher level of monitoring activities through site visits • More support functions to workers
Foreign client firms and NGOs	• More scope for monitoring labour standards	
HR consultancy firms	• New markets for employee benefits/social insurance administration • New markets for legal training and advice • New markets for outsourcing business on various aspects of HRM/employment practices	• Developing new businesses to create and meet market demands (from employers) • Alliance with employers to bypass legal constraints • Facilitating firms on legal compliance

Source: compiled by the author.

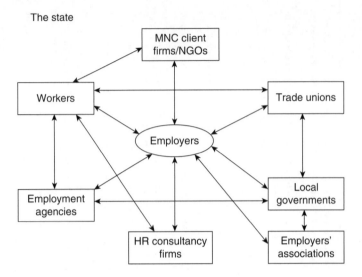

The state

Figure 8.2 Interrelations between institutional actors.
Source: compiled by the author.

specification on what types of fiscal policies and favourable conditions should be in place to promote entrepreneurship and self-employment (Han and Liu 2008), leading to a wide variety of local interpretations and implementation styles.

Labour Contract Law

The content of the Labour Contract Law has been highly controversial from the outset. Over 80,000 items of comments were received on its draft versions during the consultation period in 2006–7. Most of the feedback comments were submitted by employers and their pressure groups, both domestic and international. These include the European Union Chamber of Commerce and the American Chamber of Commerce. Foreign firms also threatened to withdraw their investment in China if the draft law were not amended. Numerous seminars and workshops were held with different interest groups, including government officials, international business lobby groups, trade unions/labour organizations, employers' associations and scholars, to discuss and refine the drafts. The enacted version of the Labour Contract Law 'represents a compromise between the competing demands of these many interest groups' (Cooney et al. 2007: 788).

A key point of unresolved tension in the Labour Contract Law is the clause on open-ended contracts. It was considered to be most inappropriate by many business owners and some economists. Critics held the view that this would mean the return to 'iron rice bowl' and 'job for life'. It would end the freedom of enterprises in labour deployment and ultimately lead to the destruction of China's economy (Xu and Luo 2008). A survey revealed that 70 per cent of enterprises had asked for amendment (Dong 2008). And the uncompromising attitude of the government on this clause led to a panic wave of retrenchment nationwide in the months prior to the enactment of the Labour Contract Law in order to pre-empt its impact (partially). Among those joining the redundancy rush were many multinational corporations and flagship Chinese firms, such as Huawei Technologies Ltd, which dismissed over 8,000 of its long-serving employees in November 2008 (with handsome redundancy packages) and rehired them under new contracts.

The common tactical response of employers to bypass legal constraints is to avoid entering formal employment relationships with workers. This typically takes two forms: one is hiring the workers through employment agency firms (see below for discussion); the other is not giving a formal contract other than a verbal agreement. Some employers also offer a small sum of money to the workers on top of their wage instead of the full amount of social security premium as a 'win-win' solution (see below for discussion on the problems of social insurance).

More broadly, it is believed that the enactment of the Labour Contract Law has a number of implications for employers in the management of their employees. First, labour costs are likely to increase significantly due to the costs associated with social insurance premiums, redundancy pay, reduction of flexible forms of employment, and compensation and penalty fines where employers are caught violating the law. Second, employers will face a higher level of employment risk as a consequence of stricter rules on probationary employment, greater freedom for employees to resign (abolition of unlawful private agreements that bind the employee to the employer) and the resultant risk of exposure of commercial confidences. Third, as noted above, the stable and long-term employment relationship promoted by the Labour Contract Law will lead to difficulties in labour deployment due to the lack of labour mobility and skill redundancy, particularly for long-serving employees. This renewed 'iron rice bowl' labour deployment system is likely to reduce the efficiency of the firm, a problem that has plagued the state-owned enterprises. Fourth, the Labour Contract Law presents a stricter requirement on firms' HRM policy in principle. Not only should the policy be lawful, but also the process of policy formulation needs to be democratic through consultation with workers' representatives and/or trade unions. Company policies formulated in the absence of democratic participation are deemed invalid (also see Qiao 2008).

In the long term, the Labour Contract Law will help employing organizations to improve their HRM capacity by encouraging them to be more careful in how they conduct recruitment and selection, and in managing other aspects of employment relations. However, a more immediate and negative effect of the Labour Contract Law is the reduction of recruitment by firms to avoid additional employment costs and the long-term business risk of being tied to unproductive workers. Increasingly, employers only hire job candidates who have at least two years of work experience. The costs of training and retention problems are the main reasons for employers' unwillingness to employ university graduates who have no work experience. The enactment of the Labour Contract Law further deters employers from hiring graduates to try them out, as the Labour Contract Law imposes a number of restrictions on employers in the probation period, and in regard to wage payments and termination of contracts. This problem has been exacerbated by the global financial crisis since late 2008. It has been reported that vacancies have either been filled internally or through agency firms (e.g. Fu 2008). In this sense, the enactment of the Labour Contract Law has had a negative knock-on effect on the objectives of the Employment Promotion Law. In fact, in under-developed regions of China, the return of higher education investment has been decreasing in recent years. For example, in 2006, the average monthly salary of new graduate employees was about 1,000 yuan, whereas rural migrant workers were earning over 1,100 yuan per month on average (Zang 2007).

Social security premiums are another major issue in the implementation of the Labour Contract Law; they have led to a range of creative initiatives on compliance by local government, employers and workers. In areas where economic development is slow, local governments issue favourable policy regulations and offer concessions to attract external investment. For example, in an inner city of Guangdong Province, businesses registered in Hong Kong enjoy an exemption period of five years during which social security contributions for their employees are voluntary instead of statutory. This has encouraged mainland Chinese entrepreneurs to register their business in Hong Kong and operate on the mainland to take advantage of the privileged policy conditions. Similarly, some local governments specify that participation in social insurance schemes is not compulsory for non-local firms. This has enabled firms with subsidiaries in adjacent cities to have their employees register with a subsidiary in one city but live and work in another to reduce employment costs. This was evident in the case of a French-owned multinational firm operating in Shanghai and Kunshan (Cooke 2010a).

Ironically, not all workers want to sign an employment contract with their employers. This is particularly the case for migrant workers. Contribution to social insurance is the crucial reason why workers avoid signing the contracts. According to the Labour Contract Law, both the employer and the employee need to pay social insurance premiums monthly. However, social insurance schemes are designed and launched locally. Many local governments also specify that workers can only enjoy insurance benefits (such as pensions) if they live in the same city where they pay contributions. The lack of coordination and transferability of social insurance schemes nationwide means that migrant workers only have the opportunity to pay into the scheme but not benefit from it, as they tend to roam around the country for work and return to their hometown when work is not available or when they are unable to work. While they are allowed to withdraw from the scheme if they leave the city, they can only get back what they have paid in without any interest. Nor can they benefit from what the employer has paid in for them. This is in fact a tactic deployed by some local governments to fill a hole in the social security fund, partly created by the compulsory early retirement programme implemented in the state sector during the mid-1990s and early 2000s.[1] Below is an experience shared by many private firms employing migrant workers.

> In fact, employees don't want to sign the contract because they don't want to pay into the social insurance, as the likelihood of them benefiting from the scheme is almost none. They prefer to keep the money with themselves instead of having it kept by the insurance company. When they quit and leave the city, they can only get back what they have paid in without any interest. They don't get the portion that the company has paid in for them, they used to but not any more according to the new local government policy. So what we pay in for the workers does not benefit the workers but the local government. It is a way for the government to increase their revenue to fill holes.... When the new workers joined the company, we asked them to sign the employment contract. But some of them refused to sign the contract by making all sorts of excuses in order to avoid paying in the social insurance. They may say, 'Oh, I am leaving the company next month anyway to go back home, so there is no point signing the contract'. And they say this every time we approach them to sign the contract. This is putting the company at risk because when the labour inspection authority comes, we will be fined for not signing the contracts. You just can't win, but what can you do?
>
> (Owner CEO of a private manufacturing firm, interviewed in April 2009)

At the same time, it is possible for individual workers to take advantage of the law to get the better of their employers. Here is an interesting example:

> One young man who is a troublesome worker was injured with a knife wound on his leg by a gang of people at midnight on his way back to his dormitory after a night out. He had caused the fight by provoking the gang – he had apparently teased the look of a girl, unaware that she was the girl friend of the gang leader. This was the biggest insult a gang leader could get in front of his girl friend and his gang mates. The incident happened just outside the factory compound in which the dormitory building's co-located. When the police interviewed the worker in the hospital, he claimed that he was injured in the process of defending the company's property which was being sabotaged by the gangsters. It would be difficult and costly for the company to provide evidence to prove his lies at court. So on balance, it was cheaper for the firm to pay for his hospital bill and two weeks' wages while he was on sick leave, which amounted to over 4,000 yuan [equivalent to two months' wages for this worker].
>
> (Owner CEO of a private manufacturing firm, interviewed in April 2009)

Labour Disputes Mediation and Arbitration Law

It was anticipated that the number of labour dispute cases would surge following the enactment of the Labour Contract Law and the Labour Disputes Mediation and Arbitration Law. This is largely to do with the abolition of arbitration fees. In some places, the surge of labour dispute cases has become a source of concern for social stability. Interviews with labour authorities, trade union officials and labour law scholars have highlighted a number of problems in the design and implementation of the Labour Disputes Mediation and Arbitration Law (also see Hou 2008; Wang and Zhang 2008).

First, there are insufficient guidelines on mediation – there are only seven articles in Chapter 2 for mediation compared to 35 articles in Chapter 3 for arbitration. This is a significant drawback given the fact that the overall mediation ability of grassroots mediators is extremely weak, with little training and professional background to facilitate them to carry out their tasks.

Second, the 'One Arbitration, Final Ruling' (Article 47) system does not work well because the low competence of arbitrators leads to unfair rulings and appeals. Even if the ruling is fair, employers who lost the case can still appeal to the people's court and cause delay in the implementation of the decision made by the arbitration commission.

Third, the new procedure of 'mediation – arbitration – first trial – second trial' that replaces the original 'one arbitration – two trials' procedure has in fact led to the lengthening of the dispute resolution period because the party who loses is entitled to appeal to the higher level. Employers may abuse this system as a tactic to delay payment to victim employees, as noted above.

Fourth, the abolition of fees for arbitration and a ten-yuan (less than two US dollars) fee for the law court for trial encourages abuse of the system and leads to a flood of cases, many without merits. While arbitration is more likely to be abused by employees, employers may use the law court stage to wear employees out. Interviews with informants by the author show that since there are no fees, employees are more likely to take their employers to the arbitration commission without careful consideration of whether the employer has acted unlawfully or not. Some of the complaints involve the workers' misinterpretation of their employment contracts and wage payment structure. Some employees who file complaints do so simply to seek revenge when they decide to leave their employing organization. An HR director (interviewed in July 2008) of a French-owned subsidiary revealed that:

> A good relationship between the line manager and the employees is very important to retain employees. And when they leave, they may sue you on labour regulation issues. I had to pay 2,000 yuan fine on the spot to one ex-employee who sued us for non-compliance of the overtime payment regulation. I only had 1,800 yuan with me after searching through all my pockets and handbag. The ex-employee then said to me quite cheerfully, 'Oh, just forget about the rest.' I was so surprised and asked her, 'Isn't the whole point of suing us to get some money from us?' She said triumphantly, 'Not really, I sued because I hated the supervisor. That's why I left the company. I sued in order to get my own back, to show her what I can do to the company to make her look bad.' Waiving the arbitration fees has definitely made it easier

for the employees to sue the company. Since the enactment of the Labour Contract Law, I have had two cases per month. This will increase when the employees become more knowledgeable about the law and find out how easy it is now to sue the company. We lose each time because we have not complied with the law in order to save cost. It is cheaper to pay the fines for a few workers who sue us than to pay overtime and social insurance for 1,500 workers who work for us.

Fifth, the abolition of fees, the sharp rises in the number of cases and the short-ened time for concluding the cases has resulted in serious resource constraints. The Labour Disputes Mediation and Arbitration Law specifies that the funding of arbitration bodies should be covered by the fiscal budget of local government. However, arbitration bodies cannot apply for the funding on their own. Many arbitrators are legal professionals who are brought in as part-time arbitrators. Without fee income, it is difficult to secure their services. As a result, labour authorities force the dispute cases back down to the enterprises and ask them to achieve settlement at the enterprise level. As a labour official admitted, 'there are too many cases for us to cope with and the rising number of dispute cases is causing bad publicity, which is not good for the harmonious society endeavour' (interviewed in April 2009). Interviews with enterprise managers also revealed the same experience, as an owner CEO of a private firm revealed (interviewed in April 2009):

> Sometimes even when we are on the right side, the labour authority will still force us to pay compensation to end the dispute, in their words: 'just swallow it'. We are given pressure to resolve dispute claims internally 'for the sake of building a harmonious society'. The authority does not like to see more cases being submitted and has no capacity or willingness to deal with them.

In addition, since the arbitration commission is set up within the labour authority department, it is prone to political intervention. Local governments may sacrifice labour inspection and protection for the sake of economic growth, as the saying goes: 'law and order enforcement needs to give way to economic development'. Certain enterprises are a 'no go area' for labour inspection, or indeed any inspec-tion, due to their (economic) bargaining power over local government. Some labour officials can be co-opted by employers and become negligent. Inevitably, the procedural standards governing the conduct of hearings and the quality of rulings vary considerably between arbitration commissions and across the regions.

Sixth, the coexistence of administrative (i.e. labour inspection and monitoring authority) and legal (i.e. arbitration and litigation) channels through which work-ers can seek to settle their disputes with the employers causes confusion and puts the labour authority in a very awkward position as their function straddles both. The labour inspection authority sometimes finds itself between a rock and a hard place, as aggrieved workers are seeking innovative ways to win their cases. For example, Article 9 of the Labour Disputes Mediation and Arbitration Law stipulates that workers can complain to the labour authority when their employer has violated state regulations through such actions as delayed wage payment, underpaid wages or delayed payment of medical expenses for work-related injury. The labour authority should deal with the complaint in accordance with the law. Instead of using the legal channels to resolve their disputes, workers opt to use the administrative channel, i.e. complain to the local labour inspection and monitoring authority directly and request the authority to deal with the disputes promptly. If their request is rejected or if they are dissatisfied with the recommendation, they will submit administrative litigation proceedings to the people's court suing the labour authority for their inaction or inappropriate action. Given the low capacity in handling the disputes, labour authorities lose in the majority of cases. Faced with a rising number of litigation proceedings, local authorities exert pressure on enterprises to settle the disputes internally and promptly. Therefore, workers and their legal representatives mobilize this method because they believe that it is an efficient and effective way to settle disputes (Zhai 2008).

Seventh, the Labour Disputes Mediation and Arbitration Law has strengthened the regulatory role of the trade unions, whose involvement in labour disputes resolution at all levels is legitimized and central. As enterprises are encouraged to resolve their disputes internally for ideological and practical reasons, this poses a serious challenge to the trade unions (see Chapter 7 for more detailed discussion of trade unions). The ineffectiveness of the Chinese trade unions in representing workers rights and interests has been widely observed (e.g. O'Leary 1998; Taylor et al. 2003; Clarke 2005). Given the limited legitimacy of unionism at the workplace level, and given the fact that consultation and mediation are the key mechanisms promoted by the government to prevent and resolve labour disputes, trade unions face a tough task ahead in gaining recognition and playing a mediator's role. Eager to play a key role in stemming the tides of labour disputes, the ACFTU sets the target that within two years, at least 80 per cent of the employing organizations 'which have the conditions to do so' (what this means precisely is not defined) should set up an internal labour disputes mediation committee. In addition, at least 10 per cent of the labour disputes arbitration cases should involve trade unions officials as arbitrators. The priority is to prevent labour disputes (ACFTU 2008).

The emergence of (new) institutional actors

As touched upon above, new institutional actors are emerging in the process as employers are grappling their way out of the new laws, particularly the Labour Contract Law. Notable 'new' actors include: employers' associations/pressure groups, employment agencies, foreign clients firms, international NGOs and HR consultancy firms (see Table 8.3). It should be noted that not all the actors are in fact new. Some of them, for example employment agencies and employers' associations, have existed for sometime but have gained power through 'episodic intervention' (Michelson 2008: 27) in the light of the promulgation of the labour laws. Others seize the opportunities created by the regulations to establish themselves (e.g. HR consultancy firms) or to form a more constant source of institutional influence (e.g. international NGOs). In this section, we examine the emergence and role of these (new) actors in the enforcement of the labour legislation.

The growing power of employers' pressure groups

As noted in Chapter 1, the state-controlled Chinese employers' associations have limited autonomy in organizing their employer members beyond state-sanctioned activities. Nevertheless, it is important to note that the lobbying power of Chinese employers is rising outside the official employers' association – the China Enterprise Confederation–China Enterprise Directors Association. Employers are able to form pressure groups rapidly to exert pressure on the government if forthcoming regulations and policies are likely to have a significant negative impact on their business environment. The approval process of the Labour Contract Law is an example of their episodic interventions – the final version was watered down from the draft version as a result of employers' lobbying (e.g. Cooney et al. 2007).

Employers' pressure groups continued to lobby for the amendment of the Labour Contract Law soon after its enactment. For example, individual entrepreneurs/business leaders used their opportunities as representatives on the National People's Congress and the National People's Political Consultative Conference to raise their requests for amendments during the plenary sessions of the congress/conference in March/April 2008. This is in spite of the fact that the National People's Congress and the Ministry of Labour and Social Security had repeatedly stressed that the discussion of the Labour Contract Law should focus on how to implement it effectively and not about making amendments (Ma 2008). In principle, the National People's Congress and the National People's Political Consultative Conference are the two highest forums for consultation and decision making in China's politics. As business owners/leaders make up a far higher proportion in these forums and are much better networked with other institutional actors than the ordinary workers, the voice of employers is more likely to be heard and their demands acted upon than that of the workers.

Regularization of employment agencies?

As noted in chapters 1 and 7, job centres and employment agencies represent a relatively new institutional actor in employment relations in China though their role in the labour market is not always positive. It was anticipated (by the state) that the enactment of the Labour Contract Law would see the reduction of those hired by employment agencies, promoting a more direct and stable employment relationship between the worker and the firm. The reality so far has been a stark contrast. As noted earlier, to pre-empt the negative impact of the new law on employment costs, many employers dismissed their long-serving workers and rehired them under new temporary contracts. Others dismissed their workers and rehired them as agency workers through employment agencies. As a result, employment agencies have prospered and the number of workers registered with employment agencies is growing. Agency workers often receive lower wages and much less social security protection than employees of the user firms. Managers interviewed by the author disclosed that employment agency firms have some sort of agreement with the local labour authority and the social security insurance company which allows them to provide only partial social security coverage to a certain number of workers. In other words, it is a partial (non-) compliance of the labour laws. This is how they drive down employment costs and make a profit.

Despite the central government's recent instruction that requests local governments to withdraw themselves from employment agency services in order to avoid compromising their monitoring role, many local governments continue to run employment agencies under the pretence of reducing involvement. In some cases, they do so through pseudo-privatization or sub-contracting to those who enjoy close personal ties with local government officials and profit from the business. In interviews with local labour officials by the author in 2008 and 2009 they suggested that a continuous link with the employment agencies is necessary for the local government to fulfil its responsibility set out in the Employment Promotion Law. With the protection, albeit somewhat hidden, of the local governments on the one hand, and the rising business demand from user organizations on the other, employment agencies are likely to become a more institutionalized actor in employment relations. And agency employment will be a thriving form of labour deployment, contrary to the objective of the Labour Contract Law.

In fact, the policy swing of the central government in 2008 suggests a partial retreat by the government in its attempt to regulate and shrink the employment agency sector. In early 2008, the 'Detailed Regulations on the Implementation of Labour Contract Law' (hereafter Detailed Regulations) was issued. It specified that an agency worker can be deployed for no more than a six-month period. This was a remedial regulation to prevent employers' abuse of the agency employment market as a result of the enactment of the Labour Contract Law. In September 2008, the 'Regulations on the Implementation of the Labour Contract Law' was promulgated, which removes the restrictions previously imposed on the agency employment sector by the Detailed Regulations (*Entrepreneurs* 2008).

Foreign client firms and international NGOs as monitors

Foreign client firms operating in the upper end of the product market and international NGOs have increasingly been a source of influence on labour standards in China, particularly in the export-oriented manufacturing sector.

As business competition intensifies globally, MNCs on the one hand are under increasing pressure to reduce their costs and on the other hand are under growing demand to review their sourcing strategy, the labour standards of their supplier firms, and their wider role in the economic and social development in developing countries (Frenkel 2001; Chan and Ross 2003; Kessler 2008). The corporate social responsibility of MNCs in the global economy is becoming an important aspect in the evaluation of corporate performance (e.g. ILO 1999; Cooke 2011a).

Interviews with owner CEOs/managers of private manufacturing firms that are export oriented revealed two scenarios. Those who operate at the lower end of the product market reported that they had not received any pressure from their foreign client firms on CSR issues, including labour standards. By contrast, those who operate at the upper end of the product market by producing brand-named products admitted that compliance to CSR requirements, including the labour laws and other business regulations of China, is paramount for securing business contracts with foreign clients. As revealed by informants:

> We abide by the labour laws. We sign contracts with all the employees in accordance to the requirement of the Labour Contract Law and pay all the social insurance premiums required. It is costing us a lot of money, but it has to be done. If we ever get sued by the employees, we will lose our reputation and will not get contracts from the foreign clients.
>
> (Owner CEO of a computer component manufacturing firm)

> Our client firms, mainly from USA and Europe, always come to visit the site before they give orders, they also come for annual site visit to check labour standard issues in accordance to the local standards and labour laws. They ask about human rights, Labour Contract Law, wage and social security issues. So we have to comply with all the regulations and avoid being sued by the workers or being seen as a bad employer. Otherwise we will lose our business. We don't operate at the lower end of the product market, there is no profit in it. You can't survive.
>
> (Owner CEO of a garment factory)

This evidence suggests that the Labour Contract Law does have regulatory impact on certain firms. It is effectively implemented where there are sufficient business incentives to do so. And foreign MNCs and international NGOs are playing an indispensible role in ensuring compliance. Nevertheless, the cost of compliance is largely borne by the Chinese manufacturers. As remarked by an owner CEO of a computer speakers manufacturing firm: 'The foreign client firms all come to inspect the factory when they negotiate new contracts. They demand top quality products and world-class labour standards from us but are only prepared to pay pedlars' price for it.'

Similarly, despite operating within immense political constraints and in limited locations and sectors, international NGOs and domestic NGOs under international patronage have been playing a role in monitoring labour standards and legislative compliance. The promulgation of the Labour Contract Law and related regulations undoubtedly provide them with more legal instruments to carry out their work, although gaining a wider political recognition from the state and operational legitimacy from the local governments remains a formidable challenge in the foreseeable future. According to government regulations, civil organizations are required to have a supervising body within the government which oversees their decision making and has the authority to close down the organization. This high level of government intervention makes it difficult for NGOs, some of whom criticized by the ACFTU officials as the representatives of foreign interests, to register as a non-profit organization. To overcome the legal and political constraints, many NGOs register as a commercial undertaking (K. Wang 2008).

The rise of consultancy firms and HR outsourcing providers as advisers

Another un-predicted change following the enactment of the Labour Contract Law and the Labour Disputes Mediation and Arbitration Law is the growth in HR outsourcing. This is in part due to the sharp increase in the number of labour disputes. Firms are increasingly looking to external experts to handle their labour disputes and employee benefits/social security administration and to design their staffing policy to bypass the constraints of labour laws. They do so with a similar rationale to that of deploying agency workers from employment agency firms – 'to save the hassles' and outsource risks.

The enactment of the labour legislation has undoubtedly brought new business opportunities to HR consultancy firms. These include legal training and advice, employee benefits/social insurance administration, and businesses on other aspects of the HRM/employment practices. It becomes clear that despite still being a small market and largely in an embryonic stage of growth, the HR consultancy industry is set to become a more established institutional actor, involved in and therefore influencing the design of organizational procedures and HR policies. Arguably these consultancy firms play an important role in raising the legal awareness of employers and the quality of employment relations through an educational effect, given the fact that a large number of employers may violate regulations as a result of ignorance of the legal requirements. Collectively, they also contribute to raising the professional standard and competence level of HRM in the country. However, it would be naive to think that the educational function is the primary *raison d'être* of consultancy firms. Profiting from the regulations, in the form of financial gains and/or social and political capital gains, remains the key motive for the emergence of these entities, as the HR consultants interviewed admitted.

Conclusion

This chapter critically analyses the legislative background and impacts of the enactment of the three labour laws in China in 2008. In particular, it shows that the working of the Labour Contract Law and the labour disputes system has implications for the broader employment relations system in China. According to Cooney et al. (2007: 802), the promulgation of the Labour Contract Law 'attests to the increased openness of the Chinese legislative process to a wide variety of external influences' and is a 'clear improvement on the legal position that prevailed prior to its enactment'. The efforts by the state in raising its legislative standards for the protection of workers need to be acknowledged. However, the conceptual, procedural and practical problems exhibited in the three laws suggest that the legislative capacity of China is still very weak, at least in the employment sphere. In particular, the new labour disputes resolution system appears rather ineffectual due to the conceptual ambiguity in the law, the structural problem in resolution routes and resource constraints in the resolution process. The enactment of the Labour Contract Law has had the unintended consequence of promoting non-compliance or creative compliance to the disadvantage of workers. The somewhat ironic and certainly unexpected outcomes of the Labour Contract Law and Labour Disputes Mediation and Arbitration Law further reveal that the efficacy of these laws has been compromised by the social, political and economic goals of lead actors (e.g. local government, trade unions, employers and employment agencies) at the local level. These actors operate across multiple sites and spaces, overlapping as well as supplementing each other's functions, and often interacting with each other in rather subtle and complex ways that can neither be seen nor officially endorsed. Collectively, they reconstruct and implement the laws at the local sites in the light of a range of dilemmas and constraints that have emerged and, in the process of doing so, reconfigure each other's responsibilities and boundaries in a pragmatic and mutually dependent manner.

For the workers as the least powerful institutional actor, whilst their access to justice may have been widened, the quality of justice is by no means guaranteed, being contingent upon the local jurisdiction and the attitudes of other actors. Some workers simply tolerate employers' blatant non-compliance of the labour laws in silence in exchange for employment opportunities. It must be noted, however, that workers are not entirely powerless or all innocent. Instead, a small number of them are able to navigate through, or even manipulate, the system effectively to their advantage. In the next chapter, we examine in more detail the extent to which workers are organized and represented officially and what alternative mechanisms they may have, if any, to protect and advance their rights and interests.

9 Leadership and management development

Introduction

Leadership skills and management competence are important for the effective management of people and organizations. Leadership management development in China remains a relatively under-explored topic in HRM. This chapter consists of three main sections. First, it highlights the nature of management and the key characteristics of leadership in China. We look at how the Chinese managerial outlook and leadership approach may differ from that of western societies. We also investigate how leadership styles and the mindset of the new generation of Chinese managers may have changed compared with the older generation of managers who were developed under the state-planned economy. The second section of the chapter focuses on management training and development as well as the management of managers in China. Here, we evaluate the role of the state in building up a national management education and development system through higher education institutes and the involvement of foreign educators in the last three decades. We also briefly review survey findings of how globally-oriented Chinese managers are and what perceived competence gaps have emerged. In the final section, we examine some of the management development practices in private firms and identify major challenges they face and how their practices may be a consequence as well as a cause of the current talent shortage problem in the Chinese management labour market.

Characteristics of leadership and nature of management in China

Existing studies on leadership and management in China have focused on three related aspects. The first investigates the unique characteristics of management in the state-owned sector, particularly during the state-planned economy period (1949–78) and the early stage of the ensuing marketization period. A second related strand of literature on Chinese leadership includes comparative studies of Chinese leaders/managers with those in other countries and regions. These studies not only reveal how behavioural characteristics of Chinese managers may have changed, but also how they differ from their counterparts in other economies as a result of societal cultural differences. A third aspect of the studies examines the perception of leadership of Chinese employees and how superiors and subordinates relate to each other at work. In this section, we are going to review these studies in order to highlight the implications for people management and leadership development in China.

Nature of Chinese management

According to Boisot and Guo (1991), managers in the state-planned economy era were mainly implementers of state-determined plans. They had few financial responsibilities and were not expected to respond strategically to the external environment. In a study of enterprise directors in Beijing in 1987, Boisot and Guo (1991: 45) observed that the 'enterprise manager is always on call and must do all he can to please his supervisors and other external stakeholders at a moment's notice, no matter how unreasonable or illegitimate the demands placed upon him'. Another characteristic of the Chinese management style observed by Boisot and Guo (1991: 46) is that 'the lack of delegation of managerial tasks and the *ad hoc* way they are handled' by the directors has caused work overload for themselves. One reason that explains this is that subordinates prefer to go to the top management directly for problems as lower level managers have no power to provide solutions. Boisot and Guo (1991: 50) argued that in the state sector, enterprise managers have four stakeholders:

> the state, the firm, the workforce, and other organizations that the firm deals with. These responsibilities are neither clearly defined nor ranked, and their interpretation is further obscured by the divergent and changeable construction that supervising bureaucracies place upon them.

It is important to note that two decades after Boisot and Guo's (1991) study, the way managers work and are expected to work has not changed significantly, but has perhaps become even more pragmatic and emergency driven at the lower level due to the advances in information communication technology and heightened competitive pressure. As we have noted in previous chapters, performance pressure and job insecurity have forced managers in both the private and public sectors to be highly responsive to instructions from a higher authority. Managers, including union officials as noted in Chapter 7, are contactable via mobile phones, emails or other electronic means anytime and are expected to be readily available for work duties outside their normal working hours. In fact, most managers interviewed by the author laughed at the expression 'normal working hours' as there is no such a concept in their work. Indeed, work intensification is a common phenomenon amongst Chinese workers and managers and there are few work–life balance initiatives to address the worsening problem (see also chapters 2 and 6).

Due to the shortage of managerial talent, many individuals have been promoted to managerial positions and are expected to deliver a high level of performance before they have developed their management skills and competence. A study of managers in four major cities (Beijing, Shanghai, Guangzhou and Shenzhen) by Li (2003) revealed 'six areas in which managers were most frustrated'. These include: 1) performance objective being set too high; 2) unclear directions of business development; 3) high staff turnover rate; 4) imbalance between workload and reward; 5) unfair competition in the labour market and 6) lack of recognition of contribution by their organization (cited in Wang and Wang 2006: 185).

The influence of cultural values in management style

In a comparative study of managerial values of managers in the USA, Hong Kong and China, Ralston et al. (1993: 249) found that 'culture and the business environment interact to create a unique set of managerial values in a country'. Indeed, studies on leadership and management have commonly identified societal culture as a key influence in the Chinese managerial behaviour, including the display of obedience to one's superiors (e.g. Branine 2005). Chen and Kao's (2009: 2534) study found that paternalistic leadership is 'a widespread people management phenomenon in Chinese organizations', which combines strong discipline, paternalistic authority and benevolent concern about the welfare and well-being of the employees and their families.

However, we should not assume that an authoritarian style of management is accepted by Chinese employees as a cultural given. Chen and Kao (2009) argued that an autocratic leadership style is positively related to job stress and negatively associated with job satisfaction and the physical and psychological well-being of Chinese employees in the Taiwanese context. As the younger generation of mainland Chinese employees have a somewhat different mindset than the previous generations in their cultural values and career expectations, they may experience psychological outcomes similar to their Taiwanese counterparts when subject to an autocratic management style.

In their study of reactions to psychological contract violation with over 400 Chinese managers, Si et al. (2008) observed that when a contractual violation has occurred, most Chinese managers would not display negative feelings in part because of their strong sense of self-discipline and in part because such behaviour conforms to the Chinese cultural norm. Instead, they would convey their disappointment in a positive way so that their message is heard while the smooth personal relationship is maintained. Furthermore, when a manager felt that his/her social relationship is unbalanced, he/she would work harder to improve the relationship in a positive way rather than using destructive mechanisms to obtain psychological balance.

Indeed, the significance of a positive relationship between superiors and subordinates and amongst colleagues cannot be emphasized enough. For example, Hui et al.'s (2008) study suggested that 'the values of harmony and face continue to influence Chinese management' and that open conflicts 'are often diffused to avoid face-to-face confrontation' (Hui et al. 2008: 147).

More importantly, Zhang et al.'s (2008) study of 545 middle managers showed that supervisory support is important in developing trust among middle managers. Similarly, Y. Wang (2008) and Cheung et al.'s (2009) studies both found that positive supervisor–subordinate relationships engender employees' job satisfaction and organizational engagement (e.g. participating in decision making and reduced job quit intent). This suggests that managers should endeavour to enhance employees' job satisfaction by matching the needs of the employees and that of the organization. Whilst the benefits of supervisory support in enhancing individual employees' psychological outcomes may be generic in many economies, this quality of the relationship is arguably more important in workplace relationships in Chinese societies. As Cheng et al. (2003) observed, a key role of the leader in China as a collectivist society is to develop and strengthen group identity. This task is crucial because organizational leaders are often regarded as the figure heads of their organizations and organizational loyalty is strongly associated with loyalty to the leader.

In an international business environment where employees from other ethnic and cultural backgrounds may have a different understanding of the moral underpinning of the Chinese paternalistic leadership style (Chen and Kao 2009) and the supreme importance of relationship maintenance, the strong influence of these Chinese cultural values in organizational management may cause problems. Wang and Wang (2006: 184) argued that the 'deeply embedded cultural norms are likely to have constrained Chinese managers from understanding and accepting business and social practices that differ from their own'. This problem could lead to further HRM problems including leadership, motivation, performance management, productivity improvement and organizational development, and ethical issues of managerial practices (Lau and Roffey 2002; Wang and Wang 2006). As an increasing number of Chinese firms are now expanding their business in different parts of the world, Chinese MNCs may need to develop their managers so that they are able to adapt to different cultural environments and accommodate local employees' cultural diversity and expectations.

It is interesting to note that cultural values and managerial behaviour are changing in the new generation of Chinese managers. Ralston et al.'s (1999) study on generational shift in work values amongst the older and younger generations of Chinese managers found that when compared with other studies that compared Chinese managers with western managers, the former are more collective oriented and Confucianist in their outlook and management style; but when comparing the older and younger generations of the Chinese managers, the latter are more independent, individualistic and risk taking in the pursuit of profits. Here, Ralston et al. (1999) argue that younger generations of Chinese managers may be seen as cross-verging their oriental and western influences on the road of modernization.

Ralston et al.'s (1999) study is supported by a more recent study by Howard et al. (2007) who revealed that Chinese managerial employees are less loyal to their company and had a stronger job quit intent (i.e. less likely to be working for the same firm in five years time) than professional and ordinary employees. They also have less positive feelings about their manager, company leader and the work environment than non-managerial employees. Given the significance of strong leadership in talent retention and the fact that many firms in China have difficulty in attracting and retaining well-qualified managers (see also Chapter 2), this finding raises strong implications for HR policies in leadership development and management.

Management education and development

The severe shortage of managerial and professional talent and skilled workers has been widely observed as the bottleneck in China's economic development (e.g. Child 1994; Ralston et al. 1997; Björkman and Lu 1999; Zhu et al. 2005; Wang et al. 2007; Dickel and Watkins 2008). This is in spite of the fact that considerable effort and resources have been invested in the training and development of managerial and professional workers in the last two decades (Wang and Wang 2006; Warner and Goodall 2010). Not only are state sector organizations short of managers with modern management knowledge and mindsets, but also entrepreneurs in private enterprises suffer from a relatively low level of education. For example, Zhejiang Province is well known for its strong private economy. However, nearly 80 per cent of the entrepreneurs come from a farming background and have low levels of educational attainment. Over 70 per cent of them had only junior secondary school education or below. Among the 1.52 million managerial employees, only 0.88 per cent had postgraduate degree qualifications and 11.4 per cent had bachelor degree qualifications (*Workers' Daily* 17 November 2005). In 2007, whilst heads of organizations made up 1.2 per cent of the total workforce, only 14 per cent of them held educational qualifications at university degree level (*China Labour Statistical Yearbook 2008*).

The shortage of well-trained and experienced managerial talent also has a significant impact on the capability of foreign MNCs to manage their subsidiaries effectively in China, posing a direct threat to China's ability to attract the foreign direct investment needed to sustain its high rate of economic development. A study conducted by Manpower in China found that 40 per cent of employers have difficulty in filling senior management positions. Whilst skill shortages in middle managers are slightly less pronounced, this has triggered a wage war (Arkless 2007). The widely cited McKinsey & Company study conducted in 2005 predicted that Chinese firms seeking global expansion would need 75,000 leaders who can work effectively in global environments in the next ten to fifteen years. However, the current stock was only 3,000 to 5,000 (cited in Farrell and Grant 2005). The same study by McKinsey & Company also reveals that fewer than 10 per cent of Chinese job candidates were deemed by foreign MNCs operating in China to be qualified for the nine professional occupations including engineers, accounting and finance workers, medical staff and life science researchers. This study highlights one of the main problems in the Chinese education system – the overemphasis on theory at the expense of application and practical solution and team working (cited in Farrell and Grant 2005). Similarly, Mercer's survey on attraction and retention revealed that 72 per cent of MNC respondents believed that the biggest challenge in recruitment was the lack of qualified candidates in the Chinese market (cited in Wilson 2008). To alleviate the managerial competence deficiency problem, the state has launched a number of initiatives. The most influential initiative measured by scale and financial commitment is funding management training and education through the development of management development institutes and business schools.

Management training and development through educational institutions

Broadly speaking, state intervention in management development can be divided into two stages.[1] The first was from the mid-1980s to the mid-1990s. It was the state's first serious attempt to professionalize state-owned enterprise managers and state cadres. The shift from the state-planned economy to a market-oriented economy accentuated the inadequacy of the old management style of direct administrative control. There was an increasing demand for professional managers with expertise in HRM, finance, marketing and strategic planning. As a result, training managers has become an urgent requirement for all enterprises. Thousands of SOE managers and government officials were sent to the state-funded and purpose-built management development institutes or schools of economics and management located in top-tier universities. This was typically full-time for two to three years, leading to a diploma or bachelor degree qualification in economics and management. In addition, part-time university/ college qualification education programmes were available for professionals and managerial candidates who sought career advancement, as educational qualification has became a prerequisite for promotion in the state sector.

According to Wang (1999: 312), by 1988, 'eight national management training courses were organized, involving more than 176,000 directors and managers from the large- and medium-sized enterprises'. During the 1980s and early 1990s, 23 national training centres and over 200 institutes of economics and management were established (Wang 1999). In addition, a number of international training programmes were developed by the Chinese State Economic Commission in collaboration with developed countries such as the USA, Britain, Germany, Canada and Japan. These domestic and overseas programmes have helped the country develop its organizational leaders from the state sector and equip them with management skills as well as market awareness. Nevertheless, by the early 1990s, this mode of management development became out of date and began to decline, as the practical relevance and career value of these programmes were increasingly questioned by those who had been through the training (Borgonjon and Vanhonacker 1994; Cooke 2005a). Two types of management education programmes characterized management development in this period. One is the formal programmes of two categories of academic degrees: economics and management. The other is on-the-job training programmes (Wang 1999).

The second stage of state intervention in management development started from the mid-1990s. It was characterized by the rapid development of business schools and MBA/EMBA and short-term executive management training programmes nation-wide. The globalization of China's economy exposed another significant gap in its human resources – managers who are competent in managing in an international business environment. The demand for up-to-date western management theories and applications surged, resulting in the rapid growth of business schools and MBA/EMBA programmes (see Wang 1999; Lau and Roffey 2002; Warner and Goodall 2010). According to Southworth (1999), when the China Europe International Business School (CEIBS), the top business school in China, was established in late 1994, there were only about 500 MBA graduates in China, half of them having been educated as management elites at the China Europe Management Institute in Beijing between 1984 and 1994.[2]

In contrast to the management development institutes established in the 1980s that were controlled by the state with little involvement from foreign educational bodies or individuals, the development of business schools and MBA programmes relied rather heavily on the input of western management scholars and business schools from the start. This has taken the form of imported MBA programmes and joint-venture programmes. Western management theories and case studies of MNCs feature heavily in the MBA/EMBA programmes and overseas trips form an integral part of the training. Management development in this period is no longer restricted to the state sector. An increasing proportion of students are self-funded or sponsored by private enterprise employers, as MBA qualifications become highly marketable.

According to Goodall and Warner (2010: 18–21), MBA education in China went through three phases. The first was the initial phase (1984–97) with only a few top universities having pilot MBA programmes. The second was the development phase (1998–2003) with 62 universities offering MBA education by 2000. The third phase began in 2004 when MBA education was in rapid growth. By 2004, some 90 institutes were offering MBA degree courses and 'the national importance of MBA education had become obvious' (Goodall and Warner 2010: 21).

Nevertheless, state involvement remains a defining feature in the second stage of management development, including the development of MBA education. As Wang and Wang (2006) noted, a range of management development related policies and regulations have been issued by the government, supported by a number of quality control and qualification management bodies as well as management research centres and institutes. A leadership assessment centre has been set up to provide an inventory of leadership qualities informed by western models and management disciplines. The MBA/EMBA training market is highly regulated, restricted to a number of top-tier business schools which receive fixed quotas of enrolment each year decided by the Ministry of Education.

Government funding remains the main source of financing these schools and all programmes have to be approved by the Ministry of Education.

In particular, the National MBA Coordination Group, set up in 1991 and under the leadership of the Academic Degree Commission of the Chinese State Council and the Graduate Education Office of the Chinese Ministry of Education, oversaw the whole process of MBA education. The National MBA Coordination Group was superseded by the National MBA Supervisory Committee in 1994 which consisted of academics, managers and graduate educational officials. Quality of the MBA programmes became a top priority of the committee (Wang 1999).

In addition, the government 'has played a key role in management development by actively seeking international collaborations', notably through MBA programmes and overseas executive training, to deliver formal planned training (Wang and Wang 2006: 187). A more recent phenomenon is that the government is taking advantage of foreign MNCs' corporate universities in China by sending senior managers from key SOEs there for training and development (Wang and Wang 2006). In short, management development activities in China are designed within the framework of state legislative and policy directions, and employers and individuals then carry out their management development activities within this system, as outlined in Figure 9.1.

The effect of leadership/management development through higher education institutions has not been fully evaluated, nor may it be possible to do so. The author's interviews with informants who were sent to the UK on government-sponsored training programmes (38 informants) and EMBA programmes (63 informants) in the late 2000s revealed that while all of them felt that the training was useful on the whole, the benefits of training had not been fully taken

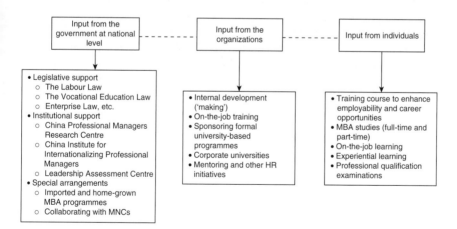

Figure 9.1 An overview of the Chinese management development system in the post-Mao era.

Source: adapted and expanded from Wang and Wang (2006: 190).

advantage of due to the lack of post-training evaluation and organizational mechanisms to provide opportunities for them to integrate what they had learned into the organizational system to improve organizational effectiveness. Elsewhere, the utility of imported MBA programmes to meet the urgent need for management development has been questioned due to the significant cultural and institutional differences between China and western societies in both teaching/learning styles and approaches to business management (e.g. Lau and Roffey 2002; Wang and Wang 2006). Moreover, since *guanxi* (personal connections) 'plays an important role in Chinese professional life', training alone is unlikely to lead to long-term behavioural changes without an organizational maintenance function (Wright et al. 2002: 173).

Nonetheless, MBA/EMBA programmes fill 'the management education gap at all levels and in all sectors' and contribute to the development of powerful management networks nationwide (Southworth 1999: 330). Indeed, informants who participated in the EMBA or executive development programmes reported that they were motivated by two main reasons to participate in the training: to learn new knowledge (known as 'to recharge one's batteries' in China) and to develop a wider business network to share ideas/information and provide mutual support. The latter is crucial in the Chinese business environment. This is because *guanxi* (relationships) are important substitutes for formal institutional support. They are often developed to compensate for the absence of the latter (Xin and Pearce 1996).

More broadly, a number of authors on management development in China have highlighted the tensions and challenges in the system and process. For example, Wang (1999) observed the need to deal with six sets of relationships when developing management education and training programmes. These include: 1) 'Relationship between quality control and size increase'; 2) 'Relationship between Chinese case materials and international textbooks'; 3) 'Relationship between theoretical principles and practical skills'; 4) 'Relationship between for m a l education and professional training'; 5) 'Relationship between technical training and management competencies'; and 6) 'Relationship between academic teachers and professional instructors' (Wang 1999: 315–16).

According to Branine (1996: 26), 'the Chinese approach to management training and development is rather cautious, yet also over-ambitious'. There is not only an emphasis on the quantity rather than quality of management training and development, but also a lack of appreciation of training priorities and post-training evaluation (Branine 1996; Sun 2008). For example, as Wang and Wang (2006: 186) observed:

[The] *Training Guidelines of National Enterprise Management Personnel for the Ninth Five-Year Plan* explicitly regulates that during the Ninth Five-Year Plan period, 1996–2000, all the SOE managers must attend a 3-month training on business administration that includes 12 subjects such as corporate finance, marketing, international business, economics, and human resource development. Meanwhile, they must also complete a minimum of

7 days training on newly formulated regulations, policies, and other pressing issues associated with enterprise reforms. However, no literature and documentation have been found to address whether and how well these policies have been implemented in reality.

Branine's (2005) study of 45 senior managers from 20 SOEs who went to the UK for training under the United Nations Development Programme for training Chinese managers found that these managers had a passive approach to learning and did not reap the real benefits of such a valuable training and development opportunity. Most of these managers 'saw management as a set of guidelines and techniques that can be learned and practised as given' (Branine 2005: 462). Branine (2005: 462) further observed that these Chinese managers tend to refer to western management as 'scientific management', which is different from Frederick Taylor's theory as understood in the West. Rather, they merely mean 'good management practice'. It must be noted that modern Chinese education and management systems value natural science and engineering disciplines far more than social sciences and arts. Hence the word 'scientific' often implies something positive such as being rational, objective and fair. As noted in Chapter 4, many managers interviewed by the author craved for a 'scientific' model of performance management.

Branine (2005) argued that western-developed management development programmes for Chinese managers need to take into consideration 'the culturally and politically bound learning habits of the Chinese'. It should be noted that Branine's observation was based on his study of managers from the SOEs who were primarily appointed by a higher authority. Whilst the overall level of competence of the Chinese management remains to be improved, there are considerable differences in the quality of the management stock across the traditional SOEs, privately-owned, prestigious privately-owned and foreign-funded firms. More specifically, the latter two categories of firms are more likely to be able to attract top talent in the country due to better employment packages and company reputations.

According to the author's observation of six cohorts (with nearly 30 delegates in each cohort) of EMBA delegates who visited the UK for a two-week overseas training course between 2007 and 2009, those from high-tech private firms and prestigious foreign-funded firms are in general far more strategic, academically able and well equipped with modern management theories than those self-made entrepreneurs of private firms who were brought up in villages and had received limited education in their formative years. While these self-made entrepreneurs possess acute business instincts and have been highly successful in developing their business, many of them seem to hold a short-term view with an emphasis on maximizing immediate profit levels rather than contemplating the strategic development of the firm in the long term. Some of them also lack awareness of what is socially acceptable behaviour in the western context and have attracted criticism from staff in the host institutes. What is interesting is that these EMBA trainees commonly emphasized the importance of developing one's political sensitivity as an organizational leader in order to navigate their business success-fully through the dynamic political environment due to the enduringly strong state intervention in the market and business at all levels. In addition, employer branding, corporate social responsibility, performance management and leadership development are amongst the most attractive topics to these Chinese EMBA trainees. In other words, they are keen to learn about the latest management theories and practices that will help enhance their organizational performance both financially and reputationally.

In a comparative study of Japanese, Chinese and Malaysian managers in their learning style and associated work satisfaction, Yamazaki and Kayes (2010: 2271) found that Chinese managers prefer 'learning through thinking and reflecting' and are 'more balanced as learners', and hence more able to adapt flexibly to various situations, compared with their Japanese and Malaysian counterparts. More interestingly, Yamazaki and Kayes's (2010) study revealed that despite China being a collectivist nation, Chinese managers make better decisions individually.

Towards global leadership? – Attitudes and perceived competence

As noted earlier, China as a major global economy is not only short of managers but also lacks managers who are capable of global operations. After mapping the attitudes and perceived competence (gaps) of senior Chinese managers in top-performing firms in China for three years, Baker's (2007, 2008, 2009) annual survey studies revealed insights into the global view of these Chinese managers. More specifically, Baker's (2007) survey of 1,580 senior organizational leaders revealed the gap between what they perceived to be the most important competences in global business leadership and the extent to which these respondents were seen to have possessed these competences against an international benchmark (see Table 9.1).

In addition, Baker's (2009: 2) survey of over 3,000 senior managers (two-thirds of whom were presidents/CEOs) showed that:

- Most companies are not preparing their executives for international postings;
- Some 92 per cent of respondents who have had overseas experience indicated that they had not received specific development beforehand;
- Only 15 per cent of the respondents have had non-Chinese (foreigners) as subordinates and only 7 per cent have any experience of working with non-Chinese overseas and
- 'Global knowledge' is only rated as the most important competence by 7 per cent of the respondents, including those who have had overseas experience, suggesting a China-centric viewpoint.

According to Baker (2009), there is a strong mentality of 'I am the boss' amongst executive managers which prevents Chinese leaders from effective learning and acquiring transformational leadership competence with a global vision. It may be

Table 9.1 Desired and actual competence gaps in global business leadership

Best-practice key characteristic for successful global business leadership	Respondents' rating of importance (%)	Assessment of respondents' competence (%)
Global perspective	83	22
Global knowledge	34	50
Effective in leading change	26	75
Open leadership style	39	34
Appreciating and managing cultural diversity	78	72
Comfortable with ambiguity	50	63
Optimism and a strong desire to achieve	27	72
Clear vision of the future	60	76

Source: adapted from Baker (2007, English version, p. 4).

argued that Baker's studies contain two limitations: one is the utility of the (adapted) western-designed instruments in benchmarking the Chinese managers; the other is the often superficial nature of survey findings. Without in-depth interviews with these managers to develop a more comprehensive understanding of what happens and why, it is difficult to establish more informatively what the aspirations of these managers are and what competence gaps may exist. Nonetheless, Baker's studies filled an important gap in the studies of senior leadership in China, which remain limited, and their findings have timely implications for Chinese firms in their leadership/management development.

Managing managers in the private sector

In the two previous sections, we have examined the evolving nature of management and leadership style. We have also reviewed the historical development and the role of institutional actors in management development in a broader context. Many of the studies in these topics in the 1980s and 1990s have drawn on examples from the state sector. In this section, we investigate management issues at the micro level, focusing on practices in private firms (also see Chapter 2 on the recruitment and retention of talent).

Management training and development

Studies on management training and development in the private sector in China, including foreign-funded firms, remain relatively limited. From what is known, it is clear that prestigious western-owned MNCs generally have a much more sophisticated management development programme than Chinese firms. It has been reported (Lane and Pollner 2008) that firms like P&G and Motorola have developed highly effective localized management development programmes to nurture Chinese talent. In addition, foreign MNCs tend to pay more attention to developing the soft skills, such as leadership skills, problem solving and communication. By contrast, Chinese MNCs, such as Huawei, put more emphasis on the grasp of technical skills, system knowledge and the internalization of corporate culture (Cooke 2011c).

Only a small number of firms in China have a formal graduate management trainee programme in place to develop their managers in-house. Some use this as an HR technique to attract talented candidates for recruitment. Others require their new recruits to go through a period of training and development before they can assume their position. These are primarily well-known MNCs, particularly those operating in the knowledge-intensive sector. The author's (Cooke 2009c) study of 65 well-performing private firms in a wide range of industries in 2007–8 showed that few firms had a graduate management trainee programme in place to raise the stock of managers. Nevertheless, managers reported that this is an increasingly popular method adopted by firms in China as an indication of the firms being more strategic and systematic in developing their talent. However, the quality of the candidates remains disappointing, according to the managers. For example, a CEO of a real estate firm interviewed by the author revealed that his firm had adopted a new management development method through a management graduate training programme. The firm set up a partnership with several good universities in the region to sponsor students and recruit some of them as management graduate trainees. Trainees receive three months' training by job shadowing in a given department of their choice, then another three months as follow-up training. In the first year the scheme was implemented, the firm recruited 18 management trainees after three rounds of selection. After one year, eight trainees had left the firm, the remaining ten found positions in the firm that they liked. But only four or five of them were deemed competent by the CEO who was responsible for the training programme.

In addition, the same study (Cooke 2009c) found that only six firms have some sort of succession planning or management development scheme to help identify talent and develop these employees as talent critical to the firm in the future. The majority of managers interviewed admitted that succession planning is very poor in the firm. While this may be a result of poor HRM for many, for some firms, this is a deliberate strategy. As one manager from a finance firm revealed:

> Some young employees are very superficial and restless. To avoid them being complacent, we don't tell them specifically when we are going to promote them. Instead, we have a few candidates for the post and select the best one to promote after a period of observation, let the employees compete amongst themselves.

Not surprisingly, when asked if their employees were happy with the career development opportunities provided by the company, 53 managers believed that their employees were only averagely happy, whereas nine managers admitted that their employees were not happy.

Promotions and the management of managers

Facing talent recruitment and retention problems as noted in Chapter 2, promotion is identified by managers in Cooke's (2009c) study as the second most effective mechanism for retaining key staff. And the inability to provide career progression opportunities for key talent has been a major reason for turnover. The remarks below reveal different tensions and solutions:

> Promotion is a big problem because supervisors don't leave. People at the bottom cannot be promoted, although there will be annual pay rise.
>
> (A manager of a law firm)

> In order to provide a career path/prospect to satisfy our employees' growth needs, we extended the company's organizational hierarchy by introducing 15 grades.
>
> (A manager of a wine manufacturing company)

> Some employees are over ambitious and eager to succeed. Employees grow faster than the company. We cannot grow the company fast enough to create new posts to satisfy their promotion needs. Even if we promise them that there will be vacancies in a couple of months' time, they don't seem to be able to wait for more than a week.
>
> (CEO of a real estate company)

> Fast tracking those being poached by other firms can sometimes back fire, as it tends to cause resentment from those who were not poached and therefore did not get the pay rise and promotion. They become jealous of the fast tracked individuals and make life difficult for them. As senior managers, we need to balance the relationship with all the key staff as the company needs them all to pull their weight. We cannot just keep certain individuals happy and antagonize others. So sometimes we have no choice but to let them go. We would obviously like them to stay and like to offer them more, but we can't.
>
> (A manager of a finance company)

> Early promotion of line managers can be a problem because they don't have managerial skills. They are good at doing their own job and their previous job, but no team leading and people management skills. The main problem is that the firm is developing too fast. People are promoted before they are ready. Another method is to hire external managers, but they may not be very good, no better than the ones we promoted internally. Also brought-in managers tend to dilute the company's culture because they tend to bring their ways of working and thinking which may not be what we want.
>
> (Technical director of a construction firm)

I have a key member who had worked for us for 2.5 years. He is an all round talent and would be ready for a senior management post in a few months time. As it happened, I had a post coming up in a few months time. I had planned to set up a new subsidiary and would have appointed him to lead it. But one day he told me he was resigning from the firm for a senior post elsewhere. I was disappointed and told him that, as a matter of fact, I already had a post in mind for him. I did not tell him earlier because my plan for the subsidiary was still being thought through and I wanted to observe him for a bit longer. He was surprised to hear that and said, 'I wish you had told me earlier.' It was of course too late then. I just let him go.

(CEO of a trading company)

The CEO did not persuade his subordinate to stay because he felt disappointed by his disloyalty without any prior discussion with him about his desire to move on. From the employee's point of view, the reason he left was because he could not envisage any promotion opportunity for him in the foreseeable future due to the lack of career development communication.

Where retention of managers is not an issue, companies may face another type of problem – motivating and managing existing managers. Several owner-managers pointed out their headaches in handling their business partners with whom they had built the business together some years back. A common issue is how to motivate or displace these complacent, outdated and under-performing veteran managers so that competent and motivated employees can be promoted as the new generation of managers to take the firm forward. Another issue is how to deal with managers who are competent but cannot get on with each other. As the CEO of a trading company revealed:

I have two middle managers who are both highly competent and doing a lot of good for the company. The only problem is that they have serious personality clash. They can't even sit in the same room together, let alone work together.

Perhaps the most significant challenge revealed in this study is how to manage managers and regenerate new blood at the senior management level without which the sustainability of many private businesses may be in jeopardy. Since the majority of private firms in China are small and medium-sized, with many operated by co-owner managers, leadership development becomes a crucial issue in maintaining business dynamics. As a manager of a media firm observed:

Some of the smaller private firms are owned and managed by a few share holders. They made a fortune by luck and became complacent. They lead by their intuition and practical experience, often guided by individual heroism rather than by any management knowledge or rational thinking.

This observation was confirmed by a CEO who was experiencing difficulty in managing his business partners. He remarked: 'Each share holding manager has his own idea of how to run the company and which direction it should go, making it very difficult for the company to move forward.'

Indeed, how to professionalize the management of family/privately owned business remains a key challenge that emerged in China's marketizing economy, as the case in Box 9.1 shows.

Box 9.1 Managing managers in a large family-owned business

AutopartCo is a large family-owned company that specializes in designing and manufacturing automotive parts. Initially set up by three family members in the 1980s as a small metal firm, the company grew rapidly into one of the largest privately-owned firms in the local area. By 2009, it had four subsidiaries in China, employing over 4,000 employees.

Like many family-owned businesses in China, the family members were the only managers of the firm at the start-up stage. As the business grew, non-family member (professional) managers were recruited, though the family members remained in charge of the key positions, with one of them being the CEO. Across the four subsidiaries, there are over 100 senior and mid-ranking managers. Some of them were recruited because they were friends of the family members and deemed more trustworthy in key managerial positions, even though they may not be the most competent managers. Others were recruited for their competence to fill a gap in in-house expertise. The CEO felt that in the current business environment, professional managers tend to have a low level of commitment to the firm, some even bordering on serious misconduct. Trustworthiness is therefore more important than competence. This preference of managerial quality reduces the perceived fairness in the promotion and staffing of managerial positions, although internal promotions are generally based on competence and performance in the firm.

In addition, the performance appraisal system is only implemented on non-family-member managers, as it is deemed difficult to evaluate family-member managers. The latter also enjoy a higher level of remuneration than the former. Management remuneration and bonuses are distributed in a non-transparent manner which reinforces perceptions of inequality between the family-member and non-family-member groups of managers. This differential treatment invokes a strong outsiders' feeling amongst the professional managers and further reduces their commitment and effort, leading to opportunistic behaviour (as noted in Chapter 5) and problems in managerial performance and retention. It is therefore not surprising that there is a strong resistance from the owner managers to professionalize the business management through the deployment of professional managers. Owner-managers continue to be involved in all strategic as well as operational decisions and process management. This not only makes their working life overburdened, but also puts professional managers in an awkward position as their plans and decisions may be overruled by owner managers.

It seems that, like many family-owned businesses, AutopartCo is caught in a vicious circle of management deployment and is trapped by problems in the labour market of management talent. On the one hand, rapid business development and expansion necessitates the firm to professionalize its management function. On the other hand, recruitment difficulties, the unethical conduct of some managers and kinship ties make the business owners favour family member managers, thus creating significant barriers to the professionalization of the management and the development of the business.

Source: case study conducted by the author in 2009.

Conclusion

Studies on leadership in the Chinese context have been conducted from cognitive, behavioural and emotional perspectives (Y. Wang 2008). Most of the studies have highlighted the cultural and political characteristics as key differentiating factors that mark the differences between Chinese management and that of other societies, including management competence and leadership style. These factors are also seen as potential barriers to the effective management of Chinese businesses in the global business context.

It is important to note that whilst the level of management competence is still relatively low, significant progress has been made under state intervention. For example, Wang (1999: 316) observed a number of trends in management education and training in China, including a transition from academic to professional orientation; from general knowledge learning to competence development; from technical orientation to managerial focus; from a common programme to an adaptive curriculum planning; and from one-off training to strategic distributive development. It is also important to point out that existing studies of management development in China suggest that while the level of state intervention is high, there is generally a lack of integration between policy and practice and between national strategy/aspiration and organizational implementational capacity.

It is interesting to note that studies on Chinese managers in the late 1980s and early 1990s focused primarily on the nature of managerial work and the management development system under the strong influence of the state, as most of these studies were conducted within the state sector (e.g. Boisot and Guo 1991; Borgonjon and Vanhonacker 1994; Bu 1994; Child 1994; Branine 1996). Whilst interest in management development continues, albeit often in the form of macro level and/or non-empirical based reviews (e.g. Wang and Wang 2006; Wang et al. 2009; Warner and Goodall 2010), studies on Chinese managers from the mid-1990s onward have broadened to the investigation of leadership style. These have often been conducted through a comparative lens to compare and contrast cross-country differences as a result of institutional and cultural variations (e.g. Ralston et al. 1993, 1995, 1999; Smith et al. 1997; Tsui et al. 2006). Managers in private firms, Sino-foreign joint ventures and foreign-owned subsidiaries in China have become the targets of analysis. This development not only reflects the changing political economy landscape in China, but also suggests that studies on management and leadership in China are becoming international and more closely in line with developments in the strategic HRM theories.

There are still many issues to study in this field. One of the most pressing areas for investigation is in the area of management development. Detailed studies should be conducted to understand what approaches organizations are taking to management development, the extent to which they are able to take advantage of institutional support to do so, and the values of EMBA programmes for individuals and their organizations. The understanding of these issues is important to make sense of the challenges China will continue to face in the development of its management capacity and ultimately national competitiveness. Another important area for future studies relates to group dynamics of owner managers and leadership development at the senior level in private businesses to identify what can be done to help sustain Chinese private firms and maintain healthy business growth, especially those co-owned by business partners. This is particularly important in view of the relatively short lifespan of the majority of Chinese private firms, despite their growing significance in the economy.

Finally, an important omission in this chapter is the gender issue in leadership and management development. Issues related to gender inequality as a result of institutional and cultural forces have been covered in a number of chapters (e.g. gender pay gap in Chapter 5 and gender discrimination in various stages of employment in Chapter 6). However, few studies have investigated gender differences in leadership and management from a psychological perspective in the Chinese context. Bu and Roy's (2008) study of 105 senior-and mid-level Chinese managers is one of these studies that fills an important gap. They found interesting differences as well as similarities between male and female managers in their attitudes and preferences (e.g. preferences of age and gender) in developing and maintaining career success network ties. It is important for future studies on leadership and management development in China to focus more on the gender dimension, as Chinese women, despite making up over 37 per cent of the total workforce, are still lagging behind their male colleagues by some distance on their career ladder.

10 Strategic human resource management – progress and prospects

Introduction

This concluding chapter recaps key changes in the institutional environment for HRM. It evaluates the extent to which Chinese firms have become more strategic in managing their employees. The chapter reviews existing studies on HRM and organizational performance in order to understand the extent to which western-originated HRM practices are applicable in the Chinese context, and how these practices may have different impacts across organizational forms and on employees with different demographic characteristics. In doing so, the chapter highlights a number of implications for HR professionals and their organizations if firms were to adopt a strategic approach to HRM to gain competitiveness. Finally, the chapter points out a number of research implications as a guide for researchers and students who wish to conduct studies in the area.

The new economic, political and social context and labour market environment

Following three decades of economic, political and social policy reform, the Chinese economy has been transformed from a state-planned economy to one that is market-driven, government-controlled and *guanxi*-based (Si et al. 2008). The radical changes in the nature of employment relations in the state-owned sector have led to fundamental changes in the psychological and social contracts of the state sector workers. The creation of the external labour market and the conditions under which it has been created and operated have not only attracted millions of surplus rural labour workers to urban areas to seek employment, but also enabled employers to take advantage of this readily available labour force in sub-quality jobs without penalty. After years of the single-minded pursuit of economic growth at the expense of environmental protection and workers' well-being, the Chinese government is now turning its attention to improving workers' employment rights and levels of income in the hope of reversing the trend of widening inequity and rising social unrest.

Meanwhile, the one-child policy enforced by the government since the early 1980s and improved living standards in rural areas have caused labour shortages in the eastern developed areas, particularly in the export-manufacturing zones. The increased level of awareness of their labour rights amongst the younger generation of Chinese workers has led to a string of self-organizing and spontaneous industrial actions in foreign-funded plants across the country. These actions present a direct challenge to the global production sector and force employers to readjust their employment practices at present and rethink their labour strategy for the longer term. More significantly, the series of high-profile strikes and protests in 2010 signalled an important power shift towards labour and marked the beginning of the end of the era of cheap manufacturing in China. More broadly, the labour market has been transformed from a once rigid internal labour market with restricted labour mobility to a more fluid external labour market that favours those who possess desirable skills and educational qualifications, leading to immense challenges to talent attraction and retention for many firms.

In short, the following related changes have taken place:

- The changing nature of employment relations as a result of the marketization of the economy and the introduction of new regulations;
- The changing structure of the economy (i.e. from a rural economy to industrial and service economy);
- The diversification of ownership forms (i.e. from state-owned to non-state-owned);
- The changing profile of workers and their employment prospects (i.e. the polarization of those who are at the top end of the labour market and those at the bottom who are largely unprotected);
- The emergence of a legalistic approach to employment relations (i.e. the introduction of the new labour laws) and
- The emergence of new institutional actors and the changing roles of existing actors in the development of new forms of collective representation.

Towards a strategic approach to HRM?

Given the significant changes in the labour market environment and challenges to talent management, are Chinese firms becoming more strategic in managing their human resources? Are we witnessing a level of convergence of HRM practices in Chinese firms towards western-originated HRM practices? Earlier studies of HRM in Chinese firms found that they tended to be less strategic than their western counterparts in their approach to HRM (e.g. Warner 1993; Child 1994). As the competition for talent has intensified, Chinese firms are reported to have become more strategic in linking their HRM practices to organizational performance (e.g. Law et al. 2003; Wei and Lau 2005; Zhu et al. 2005; Wang et al. 2007). They are now more market-oriented, with growing evidence of the adaptation of western HRM techniques (e.g. Ding and Akhtar 2001; Zhu and Dowling 2002; Cooke 2010a).

Studies by Wei and Lau (2005) and Wang et al. (2007) found that the differences in key HRM practices amongst firms of different ownership forms in China are diminishing, indicating a trend of convergence in the HRM practices adopted by foreign-invested and Chinese-owned firms. There is a continuing trend and increasing movement away from traditional Chinese HRM practices to westernized HRM practices, and the gaps in the HR competence between Chinese-owned private firms and MNCs are closing. In addition, Wang et al. (2007: 699) found that 'while foreign-invested companies emphasize humanistic goals the most, it was private-owned enterprises that linked these goals most tightly with the high-performance HR practices'. According to Wang et al. (2007: 699), '[t]he pattern of the organizational goals and HR practices linkage reflects that private-owned enterprises are more aggressively utilizing their HR functions to accomplish their organizational goals'. This is in spite of the fact that they have adopted fewer high-performance HRM practices than the foreign-invested companies.

From the empirical evidence revealed in the previous chapters (also see Warner 2010), we could argue that HRM practices in China are, in general, becoming more mature, systematic and relevant to organizational needs, and reflect labour market trends. These include, for example, the adoption of more sophisticated recruitment methods such as assessment centres and psychometric tests; the introduction of mentoring and coaching schemes; and the use of performance management systems and employee financial participation, as a high-performance, but not necessarily a high-commitment, model of HRM. In addition, there is evidence that well-performing domestic private firms are adopting commitment-oriented HRM practices (e.g. Ding et al. 2001; Ngo et al. 2008). Here, the ability of private firms to understand and align their HR strategy with employee expectation appears to be a crucial factor in managing talent effectively. This expectation is shaped by the need for personal growth. It is also informed by the deeply embedded traditional Chinese cultural values on the one hand, and the emerging (modern) values of materialism and social elitism on the other (see below for further discussion). It is worth noting that social elitism is a Confucian value that had been suppressed during the first four decades under socialism.

The increasing adoption of western-styled HRM practices and the development of HR competence in China are facilitated by a number of institutional actors at both the national and local levels. The new economic and labour market environment also brings in new actors and new roles to traditional actors. They play varying and at times overlapping roles as summarized in Table 10.1. However, it is important to note that state intervention remains crucial to the process. These new forms of interventions, both hard and soft, are designed to fulfil the state's continuing role. That is: to foster unity, to promote national economic and social development and stability, and to redistribute wealth.

As we can see from the discussions in previous chapters and in Table 10.1, the HRM practices promoted by the state and adopted by employers differ between

Table 10.1 New developments in HRM and the role of actors

HRM areas	New HR techniques/initiatives	Sources of influence and dissemination
Recruitment and selection	• Assessment centre • Outsourcing of recruitment function • Overseas recruitment fairs • Thousand Talents Plan to attract overseas Chinese scholars	• Promoted by foreign MNCs and foreign HR consultancy firms, increasingly popular in large private firms • Directed by central government policy, led by local government • Directed by central government policy, implemented by top universities and research institutions
Skill training	• On-the-job training, coaching, mentoring • Skill contest, apprenticeship training and occupational qualification certification initiatives • Skill training for rural migrant workers	• Promoted by foreign MNCs and foreign HR consultancy firms, increasingly popular in large private firms • Government policy driven, initiatives mainly adopted by state-owned and privately owned firms, skill training and occupational qualification certification training also conducted outside enterprises and funded by individuals • Government policy driven, reluctant adoption of initiative by employers
Organizational development	• Learning organization • *Chuangzheng* programme (2003)	• Central government-led initiatives, followed mainly by state-owned firms and some privately owned firms
Leadership/management development	• Management development programmes • MBA/EMBA programmes • Short-term executive training programmes • Corporate universities	• Initially targeted at SOE managers and government officials/cadres • Courses provided by business schools, sanctioned by the government, self-funded or funded by employers of all ownership forms • Extensive participation from western business schools and training bodies/individuals • Foreign-funded MNCs and flagship Chinese firms
Performance management	• Performance appraisal techniques (e.g. 360-degree appraisal)	• Promoted by foreign MNCs and foreign HR consultancy firms, increasingly popular in large private firms
Financial reward	• Market survey for benchmarking • Broad band payment system	• Promoted by foreign MNCs and foreign HR consultancy firms, emerging interest from private firms
Employee welfare	• Enterprise annual fund (superannuation fund)	• Policy regulation driven by central government, emerging adoption by leading firms of different ownership forms
Employee well-being	• Work–life balance initiatives • Employee assistance programmes	• Promoted by foreign MNCs and foreign HR consultancy firms, being piloted in large private firms
Employees representation	• Collective agreements • Labour standards • Training 'wage negotiators'	• Regulated by labour laws, enforced by local governments, reluctant adoption by MNCs and private firms • Promoted jointly by labour authority, trade union and employers' associations
HR competence	• HR professional qualification	• State-driven initiative, increasingly embraced by HR professionals

Source: adapted from Cooke (2011e).

groups of employees, with various employment outcomes. Whilst some common characteristics also exist across different groups of workers, it is clear that those well educated and with urban residential status fare much better in general than semi-skilled rural migrant workers. Table 10.2 provides a simplified summary on the two groups of workers. As competition intensifies, the polarization of employment conditions and outcomes between these groups of workers is likely to continue, with widening gaps, despite efforts by the state to reduce social inequality.

HRM practices and organizational performance in the Chinese context

Do western-derived HRM practices have any impact on organizational performance in the Chinese context? Do they have a uniform impact across different groups of employees in different types of firms and business sectors? As noted in Chapter 2, proponents of a high-performance/commitment model of

Table 10.2 Major similarities and differences in HRM practices and employment outcomes on different groups of workers

Group of workers	Differences in HRM practices and employment outcomes	Similarities in HRM practices and employment outcomes
Highly educated professionals	• Well paid • Selective training provisions • Good career prospects • Partial social security coverage • Changing work values • Relatively strong individual bargaining power	• Performance-related pay • Employment insecurity • Gendered employment practices and outcomes • Employment outcomes mainly determined by their labour market positions in the absence of an effective collective negotiation mechanism or legal protection due to weak enforcement of laws • Work intensification, deteriorating work–life balance and well-being
Semi-skilled rural migrant workers	• Poorly paid • Little training opportunities • Little career prospects • Little social security provision • Growing attempts of self-organizing to enhance their terms and conditions	

Source: compiled by the author.

HRM argued that recruiting competent employees, providing them with training and career development opportunities, extensive employee involvement in decision making and high levels of reward incentives are considered to be the key HRM practices in enhancing organizational performance. These western-developed theories and empirical studies have been applied and extended to the Asian context in the last decade (e.g. Lawler et al. 2000; Singh 2003). Since the mid-2000s, studies on HRM in China have diverged from focusing on the functional aspects of HRM to exploring and testing which types of western-developed strategic HRM practices would lead to positive individual HR outcomes which would in turn contribute to enhancing organizational performance (e.g. Wei et al. 2008; Gong et al. 2009). This is particularly notable in the number of studies published in one of the leading international HRM journals – the *International Journal of Human Resource Management* – since 2007.

Indeed, a growing number of studies have found a positive relationship between various types of HRM practices and enhanced HR outcomes, such as increased motivation, job satisfaction, commitment, organizational citizenship behaviour and reduced turnover intent in the Chinese context. For example, Lam et al.'s (2009) survey study of a Sino-Japanese joint venture in China found that retention-oriented compensation and formalized training were positively related to organizational citizenship behaviour which in turn discourages job quit intent. Similarly, Akhtar et al.'s (2008: 15) study of professional and managerial employees identified 'a valid set of strategic HRM practices (training, participation, results-oriented appraisals, and internal career opportunities)' which 'affect both product/service performance and financial performance'. In addition they found that employment security and job descriptions contribute uniquely to product/service performance but not financial performance, whereas profit sharing contributes uniquely to financial performance but not product/service performance or new product development (Akhtar et al. 2008). A possible explanation is that managers are more motivated by short-term financial gains and behave accordingly at the expense of the long-term development of the organization. This finding is supported by that of the author as discussed in chapters 4 and 5. Based on their research evidence, Akhtar et al. (2008: 15) regarded these practices as 'the "core" of strategic HRM in Chinese enterprises because they are common in explaining variance in the two performance indices'.

Akhtar et al.'s (2008) findings were supported by those of Zhang and Li (2009) who investigated the relationship between high-performance work practices and firm performance in a number of pharmaceutical companies in China. They found that high-performance HRM practices as prescribed in western HRM literature such as extensive training, employee participation, detailed job definition, result-oriented performance appraisal, career opportunities and profit sharing were significantly related to a firm's market performance. Equally, Qiao et al.'s (2009: 2326) survey study of 1,176 employees in six manufacturing firms in two cities showed that the perceived existence of a high-performance work system is positively correlated to organizational commitment. In their study of 241 firms in southern China in order to 'identify unique patterns of HR practices and business strategy that are posited to be maximally effective', Chow et al. (2008: 687) found that 'HR configurations are significantly related to effect in predicting overall outcome performance and turnover, but not significantly related to effect on sales growth and profit growth rates'. In addition, their study found that 'a commitment HR configuration (i.e. investment in training and development, opportunity for internal career progression), compared with other HR configurations, has a significantly positive effect' (Chow et al. 2008: 702).

The important role of organizational culture in facilitating the implementation of strategic HRM has been well argued (e.g. Barney 1986; Wright and Snell 2009). This is despite scepticism from critics of the notion of corporate culture (e.g. Legge 1994; Alvesson 1995). Similar findings have emerged in the Chinese context. For example, after examining 223 Chinese firms on the role of corporate culture in the strategic HRM adoption and implementation process, Wei et al. (2008) found that corporate culture has an impact on the adoption of strategic HRM and that different types of culture affect the strategic HRM process differently. More specifically, 'group and developmental cultures have positive effects on the adoption of [strategic] HRM, but the effect of hierarchical culture is not significant. Developmental culture is also found to have a direct effect on firm performance' (Wei et al. 2008: 777).

Together, the above studies demonstrate two important points. One is that high-performance oriented HRM practices do elicit employees' organizational citizenship behaviour which leads to enhanced firm performance. There is clear evidence that firms in China that adopt good HRM practices benefit from doing so. As Law et al. (2003: 263) argued, 'good HRM does matter to firm performance in a transitional economy'. The other point is that an increasing number of firms in China are becoming more systematic and strategic in their HRM. It is clear that they are aware of the labour market changes, particularly the erosion of organizational loyalty amongst the younger and well-educated workforce, and have started to adopt high-performance HRM practices to align the interests of the employees and those of the firm. However, empirical studies have also highlighted the significance of the Chinese societal context in the configuration and implementation of the western-prescribed high-performance HRM practices (e.g. Gamble and Huang 2008; Morris et al. 2008). In particular, ownership form, industrial sector, Chinese cultural values and the changing demographic profile of the workforce have been found to be influential. We turn to the discussion of these factors in the next section.

Context matters in HRM

The adoption of high-performance/commitment-oriented HRM practices by firms in China is undertaken in a vastly different social, economic and cultural context than that found in the USA, where the notion of the high-performance work system (HPWS) and many of the related HRM initiatives emerged. As Appelbaum and Batt (1994) observed, the HPWS emerged in the late 1980s as an alternative production system to the Tayloristic mass production system in the manufacturing sector in the capitalist United States against the backdrop of heightened global competition and the discovery of the perceived competitive advantage created by Japanese management techniques, such as quality management and lean production. Job security, empowerment, autonomous team-working and group-based rewards are seen as some of the most powerful practices for a HPWS. By contrast, state-owned and collectively owned Chinese firms were forced to move away, since the late 1980s, from the state socialist personnel system that was characterized by employment security and extensive welfare in order to compete in the market. Their company history and management styles are fundamentally different from those of the private firms that have primarily emerged since the 1980s following the opening up of the economy.

Influences of ownership forms and industrial sector in HRM practices

Organizations in different ownership forms therefore carry with them different legacies and characteristics. Compounded with the characteristics of the industrial sector and local institutional environment, firms' approach to HRM tends to differ and the same HRM practices may not yield similar effects across firms and regions. Research evidence shows that, compared with their counterparts operating in the labour-intensive sector, MNCs in the high-tech sector in China are far more proactive and developed in their HRM initiatives to manage their talent. However, these interventions are high-performance oriented that are often underpinned by financial rewards. The emphasis on financial incentive and performance-related pay reflects the high growth nature of these businesses on the one hand and the growing expectation of the employees to share organizational gains on the other.

More specific studies at the firm level revealed the interplay of ownership, industrial sector and local institutional factors in shaping HRM practices and outcomes. For example, Morris et al.'s (2009) study of foreign-owned garments and consumer electronics factories in China showed that the pursuit of a high-quality product strategy of these firms has not led to the adoption of HRM practices in line with those promoted to support the quality enhancement strategy (e.g. job security, extensive training, employee involvement, performance-based reward). This is because, as Morris et al. (2009) argued, the Chinese plants were only engaged in the labour-intensive part of the production chain which is prone to intensive global price competition. A different HRM strategy may well be pursued to support a quality enhancement and innovation strategy in other industries, such as automotive, in other parts of Asia, such as Hong Kong and Japan. Morris et al. (2009: 368) further revealed that in a number of cases in their study, the same firm 'was pursuing different HRM strategies at different points in the commodity chain and at different locations'. Based on their findings, Morris et al. (2009) concluded, in support of Taylor's (2001) argument, that strategy (e.g. cost reduction v. quality enhancement) and industrial sector (e.g.

mature industry with a low level of innovation v. new industry with rapid innovation) are more important than nationality in the adoption of HRM practices in foreign MNCs in China. In other words, MNCs may not be interested in adopting or transferring good HRM practices if they are pursuing a cost-reduction strategy in a mature industry such as garment and electronics.

Gong and Chang's (2008) study on employment security and internal career mobility of 478 firms in different ownership forms and the impact of such practices on employee and organizational outcomes found that there was a greater level of employment security in the state-owned than non-state-owned firms. By contrast, employees in the latter enjoyed more career advancement opportunities than those in the former. The study further revealed that the provision of career advancement opportunities was positively related to employees' organizational commitment, citizenship behaviour and firm performance. Similarly, employment security was positively related to employees' organizational commitment, but not to citizenship behaviour or firm performance. They concluded that 'employment security is not as effective as career advancement' as an HRM practice to enhance organizational performance (Gong and Chang, 2008: 45). This suggests that job insecurity in the non-state-owned firms may force employees to respond with a greater level of performance and citizenship behaviour in order to remain employed. By contrast, reduced job insecurity in the state-owned firms also reduces employees' motivation to excel.

Similarly, Ngo et al.'s (2008) study of Chinese firms from various industries and regions showed that the levels of adoption of strategic HRM and HRM practices were lower in SOEs than in foreign-invested enterprises and privately owned enterprises. They found that both strategic HRM and HRM practices have direct and positive effects on financial and operational performance and employee relations climate. However, 'the moderating effect of ownership type was significant for financial performance only' (Ngo et al. 2008: 73). Ngo et al. (2008) further argued that employee involvement and cooperation is crucial for Chinese firms to gain competitive advantage, as suggested in the literature on high-performance/commitment model of HRM. In short, research evidence points to the fact that state-owned firms are generally less advanced in their HRM practices than well-performing private firms and MNCs, although the gap is closing, and that there is much room for improvement if SOEs are to increase their competitiveness.

The continuing relevance of Chinese culture in HRM

Studies on international HRM and comparative employment systems (e.g. Rubery and Grimshaw 2003; Harzing and Pinnington 2011) have highlighted the enduring influence of societal culture in the configuration of national HRM and employment systems. Whilst a culturalist approach may run the risk of overplaying the significance of cultural factors and overlooking the crucial role of political, economic and institutional factors, it remains a valid perspective and is highly relevant to the study of HRM practices in the Chinese context (e.g. Frenkel and Peetz 1998; Westwood et al. 2004). This is because the 'socio-cultural context informs perceptions of, attitudes towards, and responses to the employment relationship, giving rise to cross-cultural differences' (Westwood et al. 2004: 366).

In addition, the political and social contexts of China differ significantly from those found in the USA and Britain where much of the debate on the HPWS has taken place. China as a political regime is state-centric and authoritarian and the Chinese people are collectivist in their socialization. The current emphasis on social harmony in the state political ideology is arguably a renewed acknowl-edgement of Confucianist egalitarianism and humanism under the disguise of socialism. By contrast, the contemporary political economy of the USA and Britain is informed by neo-liberalism in which the pursuit of individual rights and interests is a democratic given. According to Westwood et al. (2004: 365), employment relations in western economies 'are characterized by a model of impersonal rational economic exchange', whereas 'Chinese employment rela-tions remain more fully embedded in the wider socio-cultural system of which reciprocity is a vital and integral part'. However, there is evidence that the rational economic model of thinking is permeating the Chinese business system.

The high-commitment model of HRM promoted in the USA and Britain has been heavily criticized for being deceptive, unitarist and failing to recognize the pluralistic interests of labour and management/capitalists (e.g. Legge 1994; Ramsay et al. 2000; Godard 2004). Attempts to implement these unitarist HRM practices have therefore been found to encounter strong resistance from the unions and employees (e.g. Wood and Albanese 1995; Wood and de Menezes 1998; Delaney and Godard 2001; Godard 2004). It is arguable that the collectiv-ist and paternalist culture (e.g. employee care and obedience to authority as part of the paternalist expectations) and the weak institutional position of the trade unions vis-à-vis the employers may actually create a more conducive environment in China for the adoption of a unitarist approach to HRM than western societies that emphasize individual rights and interests.

Studies of organizational behaviour of Chinese employees and managers have revealed some interesting differences between them and their counterparts in other countries, indicating the influence of culture in moulding these behaviours. For example, in their comparative study of employees in Germany, Romania and China on the influence of cultural differences on employees' commitment and its impacts, Felfe et al. (2008: 230) observed that 'employees with a collectivistic orientation appreciate being part of a group and have a stronger striving to belong to a social entity'. This desire of social belonging fosters positive relationship-building behaviours in the organization and 'leads to a stronger affective commit-ment' (Felfe et al. 2008: 230). Felfe et al. (2008: 230) also found 'a clear relationship between collectivism and normative commitment' and argued that 'persons who generally tend to accept norms, obey rules, and value loyalty to the group also experience a stronger duty and obligation to fulfil organizational requirements'. Similarly, Y. Wang's (2008: 916) study that investigated 'the contribution of the emotional bond a Chinese worker has with his supervisor and with his co-workers in accounting for employees' organizational commitment in foreign-invested enterprises' highlighted the importance of 'personal relationships in shaping the linkage between employees and firms in China'. Similar findings were also yielded in other studies on the relationships between employees and their supervisors and their impacts on organizational commitment (e.g. Hui et al. 2004; Gamble and Huang 2008).

The strong desire of social belonging and its associated behaviours in positive relationship building of employees in a collectivist society like China is not confined to in-group employees. When examining the role of collectivist orientation, interpersonal affect, and *guanxi* in relation to the host-country nationals' (HCNs) willingness to support expatriates, Varma et al. (2009: 199) found that 'HCNs' perceived relationship quality with the expatriate has a significant impact on their willingness to provide assistance' and social support to expatriates. An implication of this finding for managing expatriates in foreign MNCs in China is to develop the cultural awareness of the expatriate employees in order for them to develop a quality relationship with local employees.

In many ways, Varma et al.'s (2009) finding is nothing new, nor is its management implication restricted to the Chinese context. Indeed, the need for cultural adaptation has been found crucial to expatriate management and successful international assignments in different societal contexts (e.g. Forster 2000; Sparrow et al. 2004; Selmer 2006). What is emphasized here is that cultural awareness is particularly important to positive relationship building in a society that highly values social relationships in all aspects of work and life. As Child (2009) observed, human resource management in China is essentially human relationship management (also see Warner and Goodall 2010).

Equally, whilst existing studies have highlighted the continuing effect of societal culture in shaping HRM practices and employees' perception of their effectiveness, it is important to note that the cultural distance between western society and China is somewhat shrinking in part due to globalization. As we have noted in previous chapters and earlier in this chapter, Chinese employees' cultural values and personal goals are evolving as the economic and social reform of the country deepens. A number of studies have also pointed to the fact that certain HRM practices may actually have a more general applicability than they have been given credit for. For example, Taormina and Gao's (2009: 102) study of acceptable performance appraisal (PA) criteria in Chinese firms concluded that 'it is possible to identify PA criteria that are generally acceptable to employees from a variety of industries, and that organizational socialization can influence the acceptance of PA criteria'.

Finally, the positive relationship between the collectivist culture and organizational outcomes found in the empirical studies discussed so far may not be widely generalizable in China, due to significant differences across firms, industrial sectors and regions on the one hand, and the need to be seen in relative terms against the national context on the other. For example, Hong and Snell's (2008) study of Chinese employees and Japanese expatriates in Japanese subsidiaries in China found that the former lack enthusiasm in problem solving and are less likely to adopt collaborative team-working behaviour than their Japanese counterparts. Chinese employees may adopt a compliance rather than commitment approach to organizational goals, value and culture. Brand reputation of the company (e.g. prestigious foreign MNCs) may be a reason for employees to stay with the firm instead of organizational loyalty elicited by high-commitment types of HRM practices. Similarly, Felfe and Yan's (2009: 448) study of absenteeism and turnover intent showed that compared to Germany, workgroup commitment is more powerful in the Chinese (collectivist) context and that employees 'in this cultural environment are more willing to behave on behalf of the group'. An implication for HRM is that firms in China may wish to focus on the development of the workgroup commitment of employees as this commitment is closely associated with organizational commitment.

The influence of demographics on HRM outcomes

As we have seen in the previous chapters, age and gender prove to be important factors in influencing career opportunities and labour market outcomes of individual workers. Here, we will further highlight how age and gender may influence individual employees' perceptions of HRM practices in the organization. For instance, W. Li et al.'s (2008) survey of 316 Chinese employees found that older workers, managers, better educated workers and male employees tend to hold higher work values than younger, less well-educated, non-managerial and female workers. This finding has important implications for employers because many of them tend to discriminate against older workers during recruitment and in the selection for redundancy without realizing the extra value they may get from older workers. W. Li et al.'s (2008) study further revealed that neither generation of the workers feel satisfied because the younger employees are often considered less experienced and the older employees are led to believe that they are of less value to the organization. In the same vein, Qiao et al.'s (2009: 2311) survey study of 1,176 workers in six manufacturing firms in two Chinese cities revealed that the perceived existence of HPWS is correlated with organizational commitment. In particular, 'age, marital status, and education, but not gender, correlated significantly with organizational commitment'; and interestingly, 'male and unmarried Chinese employees were significantly more affected by the existence of HR practices than female and married employees' (Qiao et al. 2009: 2311).

By contrast, Peng et al.'s (2009) study of 582 employees in Beijing showed significant gender differences in organizational commitment with women displaying a lower level of commitment than their male counterparts. Women informants in this study clearly felt a level of discrimination. They were assigned to less challenging tasks and were 'engaging in a low level of leader–member exchange' (Peng et al. 2009: 323). It is this perceived discrimination and lack of opportunities, rather than their marital status and family commitment, which contributed to female employees' lower level of organizational commitment relative to their male counterparts. It must be noted that organizational commitment and family commitment are linked and can affect each other in the Chinese context. The nature of work does have a strong impact on women's job and career choice in view of their family commitment and gender role informed by conventional ideology. Where job design proves to be not family friendly, women may quit their organization or even the profession, as was found in the case in Xiao and Cooke's (2010) study of auditing professionals and managers from five accountancy and consultancy firms in the private sector (see Chapter 6).

It is clear that organizations that wish to enhance their competitiveness through effective HRM need to develop HRM practices that are sensitive to demographic differences in their workforce. In the past, employers mainly targeted younger and male workers for recruitment; now they may need to look at recruiting older workers. These workers may have different work experiences, training needs and expectations of the firm than the younger generation, therefore requiring a different approach to HRM. Similarly, the dual work–family role of women workers should not lead to discrimination of women workers at work, but necessitates the adoption of a more family-friendly job design and work arrangements to engender commitment from female workers. Unfortunately, research evidence suggests that Chinese organizations are still a long way away from achieving true gender equality in different aspects of their HRM.

The role of the HR function

One important aspect of HRM has not been sufficiently discussed in this volume so far, that is the role of the HR function in Chinese firms. This is partly due to the limited studies available on the topic. However, from the data that exist, we can make preliminary conclusions that the HR function in China remains far from being strategic and effective. For example, Cooke's (2009c) interviews with senior managers from 65 private firms in 2007–8 found that at least 16 firms did not have a formal set of HR policies in place. Eight managers reported that there was a formal set of HR policies but it was not effective. Fewer than 20 managers believed that their firm had a strategic approach to HRM, but few could expand on what that meant. A number of managers saw the absence of a comprehensive set of HR policies as a barrier to effective HRM in their firm. In addition, there was a broad consensus amongst those interviewed that line managers lacked people management skills. Insufficient understanding of the importance of HRM by line managers and the deficit of HR professional skills were commonly reported as the major stumbling block to talent management. Some managers also reported that the HR department had little power and was too much influenced by the business departments. There was a consensus that the HR department merely played a supporting role 'to execute the top management thinking'. They became the scapegoat when HR plans failed. The remarks below summarize the inadequate role of the HR departments:

> The HR department has no voice and can't interfere by introducing HR initiatives because line managers have too much say and power, but no HR skills. They only focus on production needs. We need to train the line managers and let them know that the HR function is very important to retain talent.
>
> (CEO of a hotel)

> Before 2000, it was all called the personnel department. Now it is all called the HR department. Not many enterprises do their HR function well.
>
> (Marketing director of an electrical appliance manufacturing firm)

The lack of strategic importance and competence of the HR function has a direct impact on the resources allocated for HR activities. For example, a career development planning scheme was introduced in a wine making company. According to the manager interviewed, each employee was given opportunities to have private conversations with their line manager every month to review their performance and identify development needs. The effect was good but unfortunately the scheme was shelved after one year because there was no money for the second or third year.

Agenda for future research

A number of research implications have emerged from what has been discussed so far, some of which were raised in individual chapters. This section outlines a few more areas which deserve research attention.

First, it is clear that the growing autonomy of Chinese firms in managing their businesses, the maturing of these firms as the market economy is gradually taking shape and the growing confidence and experience of foreign firms operating in China have enabled these firms to formulate their business strategy more proactively. This is supported by a more informed HR strategy. In other words, firms are becoming relatively more free (from state control) in shaping their business strategy and HR strategy. In search of competitive advantages, aspirational Chinese managers are looking to business giants for recipes for success, often (mis)guided by popular literature on HRM and business management that prevails in the market. But few organizations are able to re-model these success stories without innovations of their own. There is a (mis)perception that 'big is beautiful' and that knowledge workers are the most creative and value-added to firms. But is being big essential to success? Do we have to employ the best and the brightest talent to create an innovative and high-performing workforce? Is it not the case that many innovations come from ordinary people with a need to solve basic problems of work and life? Future studies should investigate the role of ordinary employees in innovation, particularly in understanding the types of HRM practices needed to elicit these employees' creativeness. Here, an important research gap is the exploration of the role of HRM practices in contributing to corporate social responsibility. This includes not only ethical employment practices as a basic component of CSR, but also how to deploy employees' creativeness effectively to fulfil CSR through, for example, employees' engagement with local communities and good citizenship behaviour in energy consumption and environmental protection.

A second and related set of research on CSR in the HRM context concerns the issue of job quality and work–life balance. As we have seen in the previous chapters, job quality for the majority of Chinese workers is relatively low, measured by employment security, wage level, health and safety protection, provision of social security and working time. Job quality is important to both the well-being of individuals and national competitiveness. Research in this area should examine the likely consequences of poor job quality on employees' physical, mental and social well-being. Whilst attention has been given to the impact of poor job quality on the well-being of rural migrant workers, we need more systematic studies with convincing empirical evidence. We also need to study the job quality of those in professional and managerial positions, because work intensification is also affecting the well-being and retention of these workers.

As we have seen in Chapter 6, the Chinese context of work–life balance is significantly different from that in western societies. In China, the boundary of personal and work life is constantly redrawn in order to create space for work demands. Unable to change organizational practices, individuals, where financial conditions allow, may seek alternatives to protect their work–life boundary. In some ways, the retention problems with professionals and managers and recent self-organizing strikes from factory workers are emerging signs of the growing desire of Chinese workers for a better work–life balance and financial return for their work effort. Nevertheless, the boundary between work and personal sphere is often blurred in the collectivist nature of the Chinese social relationship, and research on work–life balance needs to take into account this unique nature of work and nature of workplace relations.

Third, poor HRM practices and work intensity are breeding grounds for grievances, a topic in contemporary Chinese workplaces that has been insufficiently studied. Here, grievances may be created amongst workers at the individual or group level. They may also be caused by management practices. In addition, how may the changing social values and work ethics of the younger generation of Chinese workers impact on the traditional values embedded in the workplace? For example, favouritism in resource allocation and reward distribution is quite common due to the subjectivity in performance appraisal, bonus distribution and the allocation of shifts/tasks and training opportunities. Favouritism creates a strong sense of unfairness and injustice amongst those who are not the recipients and may reduce their motivation to work and willingness to cooperate with management. What company procedures and preventative mechanisms may be in place to manage and prevent grievances? Are Chinese firms adopting innovative practices to handle workplace conflicts, especially in light of the government's intention to create a harmonious society? Given the widely reported low level of competence of Chinese managers, what training can be given to equip managers in effective grievance/conflict handling as part of their leadership development?

Fourth, not all workplace grievances and conflicts can be mediated smoothly, particularly in view of the divergent interests between labour and capital. This is evidenced in the rising level of labour disputes in the country as a whole and in export-oriented foreign-funded plants more specifically. Are Chinese (migrant) workers gaining increasing and sustainable bargaining power amidst signs of shifting dynamics in the labour–capital relationship since the mid-2000s? What is the role of the non-conventional institutional actors, such as NGOs and other types of civil societies, in employment relations and in organizing workers in China? How can their role in mediating employment relations be legitimized without undermining the institutional positions of the conventional actors? What may be the prospect of cooperation and alliances between the conventional and emerging institutional actors? These issues are only beginning to attract academic attention.

Fifth, studies on HRM and employment relations in China have so far focused mainly on formal organizations and formal employment. While a number of studies exist on rural migrant workers, the unit of analysis is primarily formal companies (e.g. sweatshops) or large workplaces (e.g. construction sites). There are few studies on informal working in the informal sector (e.g. home-working and freelancing as part of sub-contracting) in the production chain that is largely invisible in, and marginal to, the mainstream economy but nonetheless plays a vital role in the economy and the livelihood of a large proportion of the (rural) population. To what extent does the existence of these types of informal employment create opportunities for firms to adopt flexible labour strategies to gain a competitive advantage? In what ways can these types of employment create a better work–life balance environment for workers and their families? What may be the prospects for these workers to be integrated into the mainstream economy and employment?

Finally, as we have seen from the discussion so far, China is, institutionally and culturally, one of the most distanced societies in the world from the West. As such, many HR interventions that have been successfully adopted in other parts of the world may not be effective in China without adaptation. Future research should provide more detailed studies on the locally developed HRM practices that are found effective, and how western HRM practices may be adapted to suit the Chinese context, with an aim to disseminate good practices, share lessons to be learned and advance theories on HRM.

Notes

2 Recruitment, retention and staffing strategy

1 We define 'talent' here in a broad sense to include managerial, professional and skilled workers who are competent and are sought after by employers.

3 Human capital, training and development

1 This subsection and the next section 'Interpretation and configuration of "learning organization" in China' draw from Cooke (2005b).

4 Performance management

1 This chapter is an expanded and updated version of Cooke, F. L. (2008e) 'Performance management systems in China', in Varma, A. and Budhwar, P. (eds) *Performance Management Systems around the Globe*, London: Routledge, pp. 193–209.
2 Also see Zhu and Dowling (1998) for a summary of the history of performance appraisal in China.
3 The Civil Servant Law (2006) applies to the management of government officials and civil servants in other public-funded organizations. There were nearly 6.4 million civil servants and over 30 million personnel working in the public-funded organizations in China by the end of 2003 (*China Daily* 27 April 2005).

7 Workers' representation and voice

1 The word 'organizing' is used in broad terms here, although we are aware of the debates of 'organizing' and 'servicing' models in the western unionism literature.

8 Employment laws and regulations

1 The Social Security Law (SSL) of the People's Republic of China was enacted on 1st July 2011, which stipulates that social security is to be transferrable across the country, thus facilitating the mobility of human resources nation-wide and encouraging workers to contribute to the security fund. However, given the primary role of the local government in substantiating and implementing the law and the uneven nature in the enforcement of other major labour laws across the country, it is unclear what impact SSL may have on workers.

9 Leadership and management development

1 See Borgonjon and Vanhonacker (1994); Branine (1996); and Wang and Wang (2006) for overviews of management development; Warner and Goodall (2010) for the role of business schools in MBA education; also see Shambaugh (2008) and Pieke (2009) for an overview of the evolution of cadre/government official training.
2 See Warner and Goodall (2010) for detailed discussion of the development and role of CEIBS in MBA/EMBA education.

References

ACFTU (All-China Federation of Trade Unions) (2008) http://www.acftu.net, accessed on 12 May 2009.

Agocs, C. and Burr, C. (1996) 'Employment equity, affirmative action and managing diversity: assessing the differences', *International Journal of Manpower*, 17, 4/5: 30–45.

Akhtar, S., Ding, D. Z. and Ge, G. L. (2008) 'Strategic HRM practices and their impact on company performance in Chinese enterprises', *Human Resource Management*, 47, 1: 15–32.

Alvesson, M. (1995) *Cultural Perspectives on Organisations*, Cambridge: Cambridge University Press.

Appelbaum, E. and Batt, R. (1994) *The New American Workplace*, Ithaca, NY: ILR Press.

Appleton, S., Song, L. and Xia, Q. (2005) 'Has China crossed the river? The evolution of wage structure in urban China during reform and retrenchment', *Journal of Comparative Economics*, 33, 4: 644–63.

Appleton, S., Knight, J., Song, L. and Xia, Q. (2002) 'Labour retrenchment in China: determinants and consequences', *China Economic Review*, 13, 2/3: 275–99.

Argyris, C. and Schon, D. (1978) *Organisational Learning: A Theory of Action Perspective*, Reading, MA: Addison Wesley.

Argyris, C. and Schon, D. (1996) *Organizational Learning II: Theory, Method and Practice*, New York: Addison Wesley.

Arkless, D. (2007) 'The China talent paradox', *China-Britain Business Review*, June: 14–15.

Arthur, J. B. (1994) 'Effects of human resource systems on manufacturing performance and turnover', *Academy of Management Journal*, 37, 3: 670–87.

Au, A. K., Altman, Y. and Roussel, J. (2008) 'Employee training needs and perceived value of training in the Pearl River Delta of China: a human capital development approach', *Journal of European Industrial Training*, 32, 1: 19–31.

Aycan, Z. (2006) 'Paternalism: towards conceptual refinement and operationalization', in Yang, K. S., Hwang, K. K. and Kim, U. (eds) *Scientific Advances in Indigenous Psychologies: Empirical, Philosophical, and Cultural Contributions*, London: Cambridge University Press, pp. 445–66.

Bai, X. and Bennington, L. (2005) 'Performance appraisal in the Chinese state-owned coal industry', *International Journal of Business Performance Management*, 7, 3: 275–87.

Bailey, J., Chen, C. and Dou, S. (1997) 'Conceptions of self and performance-related feedback in the US, Japan and China', *Journal of International Business Studies*, 28, 3: 605–25.

Baker, L. (2007) 'How global are you?' *Fortune China*, April: 72–7 (in Chinese), English version, pp. 1–22.

Baker, L. (2008) 'How global are you?' *Fortune China*, June: 49–55 (in Chinese), English version, pp. 1–12.

Baker, L. (2009) 'How global are you?' *Fortune China*, June: 43–8 (in Chinese), English version, pp. 1–17.

Bamber, G., Lansbury, R. and Wailes, N. (eds) (2010) *International and Comparative Employment Relations*, 5th edn, London: Sage; New South Wales, Australia: Allen & Unwin.

Barney, J. (1986) 'Organizational culture: can it be a source of sustained competitive advantage?' *Academy of Management Review,* 11, 3: 791–800.

Baron, J. N. and Kreps, D. M. (1999) *Strategic Human Resource Management: Framework for General Managers*, New York: John Wiley.

Bauer, J., Wang, F., Riley, E. N. and Zhao, X. (1992) 'Gender inequality in urban China: education and employment', *Modern China*, 18, 3: 333–70.

Beggs, J. (1995) 'The institutional environment: implications for race and gender inequality in the U.S. labor market', *American Sociological Review*, 60, 4: 612–33.

Bellemare, G. (2000) 'End users: actors in the industrial relations system?' *British Journal of Industrial Relations*, 38, 3: 383–405.

Benson, J. and Zhu, Y. (eds) (2010) *The Dynamics of Asian Labour Markets: Balancing Control and Flexibility*, London and New York: Routledge.

Benson, J., Debroux, P., Yuasa, M. and Zhu, Y. (2000) 'Flexibility and labour management: Chinese manufacturing enterprises in the 1990s', *International Journal of Human Resource Management,* 11, 2: 183–96.

Bhattacharya, M. and Wright, P. (2005) 'Managing human assets in an uncertain world: applying real options theory to HRM', *International Journal of Human Resource Management*, 16, 6: 929–48.

Bian, Y. (1994) *Work and Inequality in Urban China*, New York: State University of New York Press.

Bian, Y. and Logan, J. (1996) 'Market transition and income inequality in urban China', *American Sociological Review*, 61, 5: 759–78.

Bian, Y., Shu, X. and Logan, J. (2001) 'Communist Party membership and regime dynamics in urban China', *Social Forces*, 79, 3: 805–41.

Bielby, T. W. and Baron, N. J. (1986) 'Men and women at work: sex segregation and statistical discrimination', *American Journal of Sociology*, 91, 4: 759–99.

Birdi, K., Wall, T. and Wood, S. (2005) 'What is an innovation culture?' http://www.esrccoi.group.shef.ac.uk/pdf/whatis/innovation_culture.pdf, accessed on 15 September 2005.

Bishop, A. J., Luo, F. and Wang, F. (2005) 'Economic transition, gender bias, and the distribution of earnings in China', *Economics of Transition*, 13, 2: 239–59.

Björkman, I. and Lu, Y. (1999) 'A corporate perspective on the management of human resources in China', *Journal of World Business*, 34, 1: 16–25.

Blau, F. and Kahn, L. (1997) 'Swimming upstream: trends in the gender wage differential in the 1980s', *Journal of Labour Economics*, 15, 1: 1–42.

Blecher, M. (2010) 'Globalization, structural reform, and labour politics in China', *Global Labour Journal*, 1, 1: 92–111.

Blossfeld, H. and Drobnic, S. (eds) (2001) *Careers of Couples in Contemporary Societies: From Male Breadwinner to Dual Earner Families*, Oxford: Oxford University Press.

Boisot, M. and Guo, L. (1991) 'The nature of managerial work in China', *Advances in Chinese Industries Studies*, 2, 1: 37–53.

Borgonjon, J. and Vanhonacker, W. (1994) 'Management training and education in the People's Republic of China', *International Journal of Human Resource Management*, 5, 2: 327–56.

Bosch, G., Lehndorff, S. and Rubery, J. (2009) *European Employment Models in Flux: A Comparison of Institutional Change in Nine European Countries*, Basingstoke: Palgrave Macmillan.

Boudreau, J. and Ramstad, P. (2005) 'Talentship, talent segmentation and sustainability: a new HR decision science paradigm for a new strategy definition', *Human Resource Management*, 44, 2: 129–36.

Boyle, P., Cooke, T., Halfacree, K. and Smith, D. (2001) 'A cross-national comparison of the impact of family migration on women's employment status', *Demography*, 38, 2: 201–13.

Bozionelos, N. and Wang, L. (2007) 'An investigation on the attitudes of Chinese workers towards individually based performance related reward systems', *International Journal of Human Resource Management*, 18, 2: 284–302.

Brainerd, E. (2000) 'Women in transition: changes in gender differentials in Eastern Europe and the former Soviet Union', *Industrial and Labor Relations Review*, 54, 1: 138–62.

Branine, M. (1996) 'Observations on training and management development in the People's Republic of China', *Personnel Review*, 25, 1: 25–39.

Branine, M (2005) 'Cross-cultural training of managers: an evaluation of a management development programme for Chinese managers', *Journal of Management Development*, 24, 5: 459–72.

Broadbent, K. and Ford, M. (eds) (2008) *Woman Organizing: Women and Union Activism in Asia*, London: Routledge, pp. 34–49.

Brown, R. (2006) 'China's collective contract provisions: can collective negotiations embody collective bargaining?' *Journal of Comparative and International Law*, 16, 35: 35–77.

Brown, R. (2009) *Understanding Labor and Employment Law in China*, New York and Cambridge: Cambridge University Press.

Bu, N. (1994) 'Red cadres and specialists as modern managers: an empirical assessment of managerial competencies in China', *International Journal of Human Resource Management*, 5, 2: 357–83.

Bu, N. and Roy, J. P. (2008) 'Chinese managers' career success networks: the impact of key tie characteristics on structure and interaction practices', *International Journal of Human Resource Management*, 19, 6: 1088–107.

Buchanan, J. and Callus, R. (1993) 'Efficiency and equity at work: the need for labour market regulation in Australia', *Journal of Industrial Relations*, 35, 5: 515–37.

Budhwar, P. S. and Debrah, Y. A. (eds) (2001) *Human Resource Management in Developing Countries*, London: Routledge.

Cai, W. (2009) 'China is opening its education door more widely', *China Scholars Abroad*, 5: 3 (in Chinese).

Campbell, I. (1996) 'Casual employment, labour regulation and Australian trade unions', *Journal of Industrial Relations*, 38, 4: 571–99.

Cappelli, P. (2000) 'A market-driven approach to retaining talent', *Harvard Business Review*, 78, 1: 103–11.

Carsten, J. M. and Spector, P. E. (1987) 'Unemployment, job satisfaction, and employee turnover: a meta-analytic test of the Muchinsky model', *Journal of Applied Psychology*, 72, 3: 374–81.

Casey, B., Metcalf, H. and Millward, N. (1997) *Employers' Use of Flexible Labour*, London: Policy Studies Institute.

Chan, A. (1998) 'Labour regulations in foreign-funded ventures, Chinese trade unions, and the prospects for collective bargaining', in O'Leary, G. (ed.) *Adjusting to Capitalism: Chinese Workers and the State*, New York: M. E. Sharpe, pp. 122–49.

Chan, A. (2001) *China's Workers under Assault: The Exploitation of Labour in a Globalising Economy*, New York: M. E. Sharpe.

Chan, A. and Ross, R. (2003) 'Racing to the bottom: international trade without a social clause', *Third World Quarterly*, 24, 6: 1011–28.

Chan, C. K. (2009) 'Strike and changing workplace relations in a Chinese global factory', *Industrial Relations Journal*, 40, 1: 60–77.

Chan, C. K. and Pun, N. (2009) 'The making of a new working class? A study of the collective actions of migrant workers in South China', *China Quarterly*, 198: 287–303.

Chan, D. and Goto, S. (2003) 'Conflict resolution in the culturally diverse workplace: some data from Hong Kong employees', *Applied Psychology: An International Review*, 52, 3: 441–60.

Chan, K. W. and Wyatt, T. (2007) 'Quality of work life: a study of employees in Shanghai, China', *Asia Pacific Business Review*, 13, 4: 501–17.

Chang, K. (2008) 'On the legislative basis and legal orientation of the Labour Contract Law', *Legal Forum*, 23, 2: 5–14.

Charles, M. and Grusky, B. D. (1995) 'Models for describing the underlying structure of sex segregation', *American Journal of Sociology*, 100, 4: 931–71.

Chen, C. C. (1995) 'New trends in rewards allocation preferences: a Sino-U.S. comparison', *Academy of Management Journal*, 38, 2: 408–28.

Chen, F. (2003a) 'Industrial restructuring and workers' resistance in China', *Modern China*, 29, 2: 237–62.

Chen, F. (2003b) 'Between the state and labour: the conflict of Chinese trade unions' double identity in market reform', *China Quarterly*, 176: 1006–28.

Chen, F. (2006) 'Privatization and its discontents in Chinese factories', *China Quarterly*, 185: 42–60.

Chen, F. (2007) 'Individual rights and collective rights: labor's predicament in China', *Communist and Post-Communist Studies*, 40, 1: 59–79.

Chen, H. (2000) 'Issues related to informal employment', *Employment in China*, 10: 4–7.

Chen, H. (2003) 'A survey on performance management in Chinese enterprises', *Development and Management of Human Resources*, 12: 28–31.

Chen, H. W., Gao, F., Chen, X. and Yang, S. (2009) *The Blue Book of China Corporation Training*, Beijing: Modern Education Publishing House.

Chen, H. Y. and Kao, H. S. (2009) 'Chinese paternalistic leadership and non-Chinese subordinates' psychological health', *International Journal of Human Resource Management*, 20, 12: 2533–46.

Chen, J. G., Lu, Z. and Wang, Y. Z. (2001) *China Social Security System Development Report*, Beijing: Social Science Document Publishing House.

Chen, M. Z., Wang, L. P. and Dai, H. R. (2004) 'Performance appraisal criteria and implementation in small IT enterprises in China', *Development and Management of Human Resources*, 3: 36–9 (in Chinese).

Cheng, B. S., Jiang, D. Y. and Riley, J. H. (2003) 'Organizational commitment, supervisory commitment, and employee outcomes in the Chinese context: proximal hypothesis or global hypothesis?' *Journal of Organizational Behavior*, 24, 3: 313–34.

Cheung, M. F., Wu, W. P., Chan, A. K. and Wong, M. L. (2009) 'Supervisor–subordinate *guanxi* and employee work outcomes: the mediating role of job satisfaction', *Journal of Business Ethics*, 88, 1: 77–89.

Chi, W. and Li, B. (2008) 'Glass ceiling or sticky floor? Examining the gender earnings differential across the earnings distribution in urban China, 1987–2004', *Journal of Comparative Economics*, 36, 2: 243–63.

Child, J. (1994) *Management in China during the Age of Reform*, Cambridge: Cambridge University Press.

Child, J. (2009) 'Context, comparison, and methodology in Chinese management research', *Management and Organization Review*, 5, 1: 57–73.

China Daily (2005) 'New law approved to improve China's civil servant system', 27 April, http://www.chinadaily.com.cn/english/doc/2005–04/27/content_438023.htm, accessed on 23 October 2006.

China Enterprise Confederation (CEC) (2009) Listed responsibilities, http://www.cec-ceda.org.cn/english_version/index.html, accessed on 6 May 1999.

China Labor News Translations (2008) 'Promising Wal-Mart trade union chair resigns over collective contract negotiations', http://news.ifeng.com/opeinion/200807/0729, accessed on 24 September 2008.

China Labour Bulletin (2009) '"Going it alone": the workers' movement in China (2007–8)', *China Labour Bulletin Research Reports*, http://www.clb.org.hk, accessed on 18 January 2010.

China Labour Statistical Yearbook [various years] (1995–2010) Beijing: China Statistics Press.

China Private Economy Yearbook (2003) Beijing: China Industrial and Commercial Association Publishing House (in Chinese).

China Statistical Yearbook [various years] (1995–2010) Beijing: China Statistics Press.

Chiu, R., Luk, W. and Tang, T. (2002) 'Retaining and motivating employees: compensation preferences in Hong Kong and China', *Personnel Review,* 31, 4: 402–31.

Choi, J. (2008) 'Work and family demands and life stress among Chinese employees: the mediating effect of work–family conflict', *International Journal of Human Resource Management*, 19, 5: 878–95.

Chou, B. (2005) 'Implementing the reform of performance appraisal in China's civil service', *China Information*, 19, 1: 39–65.

Chow, I. H. and Liu, S. S. (2009) 'The effect of aligning organizational culture and business strategy with HR systems on firm performance in Chinese enterprises', *International Journal of Human Resource Management*, 20, 11: 2292–310.

Chow, I. H., Huang, J. C. and Liu, S. (2008) 'Strategic HRM in China: configurations and competitive advantage', *Human Resource Management*, 47, 4: 687–706.

Chwee, W. (1999) 'Individual and organisational learning of Chinese executives at Compaq China', *Advances in Developing Human Resources*, 1, 4: 69–82.

CIPD (Chartered Institute of Personnel and Development) (2006) *Diversity: An Overview*, CIPD factsheet, Internet source: http://www.cipd.co.uk

CIPD (2007) *Diversity in Business: A Focus for Progress*, London: Chartered Institute of Personnel and Development.

Clarke, S. (2005) 'Post-socialist trade unions: China and Russia', *Industrial Relations Journal*, 36, 1: 2–18.

Clarke, S. and Pringle, T. (2009) 'Can party-led trade unions represent their members?' *Post-Communist Economics*, 21, 1: 85–101.

Clarke, S., Lee, C. and Li, Q. (2004) 'Collective consultation and industrial relations in China', *British Journal of Industrial Relations*, 42, 2: 235–54.

Coff, R.W. (1997) 'Human assets and management dilemmas: coping with hazards on the road to resource-based theory', *Academy of Management Review*, 22, 2: 374–402.

Cooke, F. L. (2003) 'Equal opportunity? Women's managerial careers in governmental organizations in China', *International Journal of Human Resource Management*, 14, 2: 317–33.

Cooke, F. L. (2004) 'Foreign firms in China: modelling HRM in a toy manufacturing corporation', *Human Resource Management Journal*, 14, 3: 31–52.

Cooke, F. L. (2005a) *HRM, Work and Employment in China*, London: Routledge.

Cooke, F. L. (2005b) 'Employee participation and innovations: the interpretation of "learning organization" in China', *The Human Factor*, November 2005–January 2006: 26–30.

Cooke, F. L. (2006) 'Informal employment and gender implications in China: the nature of work and employment relations in the community services sector', *International Journal of Human Resource Management*, 17, 8: 1471–87.

Cooke, F. L. (2007) 'Migrant labour and trade union's response and strategy in China', *Indian Journal of Industrial Relations*, 42, 4: 558–84.

Cooke, F. L. (2008a) *Competition, Strategy and Management in China*, Basingstoke: Palgrave Macmillan.

Cooke, F. L. (2008b) 'Enterprise culture management in China: an "insiders'" perspective', *Management and Organization Review*, 4, 2: 291–314.

Cooke, F. L. (2008c) 'China: labour organisations representing women', in Broadbent, K. and Ford, M. (eds) *Woman Organizing: Women and Union Activism in Asia*, London: Routledge, pp. 34–49.

Cooke, F. L. (2008d) 'Labour market regulations and informal employment in China: to what extent are workers protected?' Third Annual China Task Force Meeting, led by Joseph Stiglitz, Manchester, UK, 25–27 June.

Cooke, F. L. (2008e) 'Performance management systems in China', in Varma, A. and Budhwar, P. (eds) *Performance Management Systems around the Globe*, London: Routledge, pp. 193–209.

Cooke, F. L. (2008f) 'The dynamics of employment relations in China: an evaluation of the rising level of labour disputes', *Journal of Industrial Relations*, 50, 1: 111–38.

Cooke, F. L. (2009a) 'The changing face of women managers in China', in Rowley, C. and Yukondi, V. (eds) *The Changing Face of Women Management in Asia*, London: Routledge, pp. 19–42.

Cooke, F. L. (2009b) 'A decade of transformation of HRM in China: a review of literature and suggestions for future studies', *Asia Pacific Journal of Human Resources*, 47, 1: 6–40.

Cooke, F. L. (2009c) 'Performance and retention management in Chinese private firms: key challenges and emerging HR practices', AIRAANZ Annual Conference, Newcastle, Australia, 4–6 February.

Cooke, F. L. (2009d) 'The enactment of three new labour laws in China: unintended consequences and emergence of "new" actors in employment relations', Regulating for decent work: innovative regulation as a response to Globalization, Conference of the Regulating for Decent Work network, International Labour Office, Geneva, Switzerland, 8–10 July. Conference website: http://www.ilo.org/public/english/protection/condtrav/publ/rdw.htm

Cooke, F. L. (2009e) 'Globalization and the role of its HR strategy: case study of a leading Chinese telecom corporation – Huawei', International Industrial Relations Association World Congress, Sydney, Australia, 24–27 August.

Cooke, F. L. (2010a) 'The changing face of human resource management in China', in Rowley, C. and Cooke, F. L. (eds) *The Changing Face of Chinese Management*, Working in Asia Series, London: Routledge, pp. 28–51.

Cooke, F. L. (2010b) 'Women's participation in employment in Asia: a comparative analysis of China, India, Japan and South Korea', *International Journal of Human Resource Management*, 21, 10/12: 2249–70.

Cooke, F. L. (2010c) 'Employment relations in China', in Bamber, G., Lansbury, R. and Wailes, N. (eds) *International and Comparative Employment Relations*, 5th edn, London: Sage; New South Wales, Australia: Allen & Unwin, pp. 309–31.

Cooke, F. L. (2011a) 'Social responsibility, sustainability and diversity of human resources', in Harzing, A. and Pinnington, A. (eds) *International Human Resource Management*, 3rd edn, London: Sage, pp. 583–634.

Cooke, F. L. (forthcoming, 2011b) 'Gender organizing in China: a study of female workers' representation needs and their perceptions of union efficacy', *International Journal of Human Resource Management*.

Cooke, F. L. (2011c) 'Talent management in China', in Scullion, H. and Collings, D. (eds) *Global Talent Management*, Global Human Resource Management Series, London: Routledge.

Cooke, F. L. (2011d) 'Labour market disparities and inequalities', in Sheldon, P., Kim, S., Li, Y. and Warner, M. (eds) *China's Changing Workplace,* London: Routledge, pp. 259–276.

Cooke, F. L. (forthcoming, 2011e) 'The role of the state and human resource management in China', *International Journal of Human Resource Management*.

Cooke, F. L. and Jin, X. Y. (2009) 'Work–life balance in China: sources of conflicts and coping strategies', Special Issue on Work–Life Balance, *HRD Network,* August, 18–28.

Cooke, F. L. and Saini, D. (2007) 'Managing diversity in India and China: implications for western MNCs', APROS 12 Conference, Management Development Institute, Gurgaon, India, 9–12 December.

Cooke, F. L. and Saini, D. S. (2010) 'Diversity management in India: a study of organizations in different ownership forms and industrial sectors', *Human Resource Management*, 49, 3: 477–500.

Cooke, F. L., Prouska, R., Xu, T. and Wicks, N. (2007) 'Career Aspirations and Recruitment Skills of British and non-British Postgraduate Management Students in Manchester Business School: Identifying Career Skill Gaps and Enhancing Career Services Training', project report (project funded by the Faculty of Humanities, University of Manchester, UK.

Cooney, S. (2007) 'China's labour law, compliance and flaws in implementing institutions', *Journal of Industrial Relations*, 49, 5: 673–86.

Cooney, S., Biddulph, S., Li, K. G. and Zhu, Y. (2007) 'China's new Labour Contract Law: responding to the growing complexity of labour relations in the PRC', *University of New South Wales Law Journal*, 30, 3: 786–801.

Cox, T. (1993) *Cultural Diversity in Organizations: Theory, Research and Practice*, San Francisco: Barrett-Koehler Publishers.

Cox, T., Lobel, S. and McLeod, P. (1991) 'Effects of ethnic group cultural differences on cooperative and competitive behaviour on a group task', *Academy of Management Journal*, 34, 4: 827–47.

Crookes, D. and Thomas, I. (1998) 'Problem solving and culture – exploring some stereotypes', *Journal of Management*, 17, 8: 583–91.

Deckop, J., Konrad, A., Perlmutter, F. and Freely, J. (2006) 'The effect of human resource management practices on the job retention of former welfare clients', *Human Resource Management*, 45, 4: 539–59.

Delaney, J. and Godard, J. (2001) 'An IR perspective on the high-performance paradigm', *Human Resource Management Review*, 11, 2: 395–429.

DeNisi, A. S. and Griffin, R. W. (2001) *Human Resource Management*, Boston, MA: Houghton Mifflin.

Development and Management of Human Resources (2006a) 'Focus', *Development and Management of Human Resources*, 3: 8–9 (in Chinese).

Development and Management of Human Resources (2006b) 'Review', *Development and Management of Human Resources*, 10: 4.

Development and Management of Human Resources (2008) 'Review', *Development and Management of Human Resources*, 10: 4.

Dickel, T. and Watkins, C. (2008) 'To remain competitive in China's tight labour market, companies must prioritize talent management – and track compensation trends', *China Business Review*, July–August: 20–3.

Dickens, L. and Hall, M. J. (2003) 'Labour law and industrial relations: a new settlement?' in Edwards, P. (ed.) *Industrial Relations: Theory and Practice*, 2nd edn, Oxford: Blackwell, pp. 124–56.

Ding, D. Z. and Akhtar, S. (2001) 'The organizational choice of human resource management practices: a study of Chinese enterprises in three cities in the PRC', *International Journal of Human Resource Management*, 12, 6: 946–64.

Ding, D. Z., Akhtar, S. and Ge, G. L. (2009) 'Effects of inter-and intra-hierarchy wage dispersions on firm performance in Chinese enterprises', *International Journal of Human Resource Management*, 20, 11: 2370–81.

Ding, D. Z., Field, D. and Akhtar, S. (1997) 'An empirical study of human resource management policies and practices in foreign-invested enterprises in China: the case of Shenzhen Special Economic Zone', *International Journal of Human Resource Management*, 8, 5: 595–613.

Ding, D. Z., Ge, L. and Warner, M. (2001) 'A new form of Chinese human resource management? Personnel and labour-management relations in Chinese township and village enterprises: a case-study approach', *Industrial Relations Journal* 32, 4: 328–43.

Dong, B. H. (2008) 'From the Labour Law to the Labour Contract Law', paper presented at the International Conference 'Breaking Down Chinese Walls: The Changing Faces of Labor and Employment in China', Cornell University, 26–28 September, Ithaca, New York.

Easterby-Smith, M., Malina, D. and Lu, Y. (1995) 'How culture-sensitive is HRM?' *International Journal of Human Resource Management*, 6, 1: 31–59.

The Economist (2009) 'Chinese unemployment: where will all the students go?' 8 April, http://www.economist.com/world/asia/displaystory.cfm?story_id = 13446878, accessed on 12 May 2009.

Elsey, B. and Leung, J. (2004) 'Changing the work behaviour of Chinese employees using organisational learning', *Journal of Workplace Learning*, 16, 3: 167–78.

Entrekin, L. and Chung, Y. (2001) 'Attitudes towards different sources of executive appraisal: a comparison of Hong Kong Chinese and American managers in Hong Kong', *International Journal of Human Resource Management*, 12, 6: 965–87.

Entrepreneurs (2008) 'Halo and Reality', *Entrepreneurs*, 11: 85–6. (in Chinese).

Farh, J., Zhong, C. and Organ, D. (2004) 'Organizational citizenship behavior in the People's Republic of China', *Organization Science*, 15, 2: 241–53.

Farrell, D. and Grant, A. (2005) 'China's looming talent shortage', *McKinsey Quarterly*, No. 4, http://www.mckinseyquarterly.com/article_page.aspx?ar = 1685, accessed on 3 March 2007.

Felfe, J. and Yan, W. H. (2009) 'The impact of workgroup commitment on organizational citizenship behaviour, absenteeism and turnover intention: the case of Germany and China', *Asia Pacific Business Review*, 15, 3: 433–50.

Felfe, J., Yan, W. and Six, B. (2008) 'The impact of individual collectivism on commitment and its influence on organizational citizenship behaviour and turnover in three countries', *International Journal of Cross Cultural Management*, 8, 2: 211–37.

Felstead, A. and Jewson, N. (eds) (1999) *Global Trends in Flexible Labour*, London: Macmillan.

Feng, G. (2006) 'The "institutional weaknesses" of enterprise trade unions and their formative context', *Society*, 26, 3: 81–98 (in Chinese).

Ferner, A., Almond, P. and Colling, T. (2005) 'Institutional theory and the cross-national transfer of employment policy: the case of "workforce diversity" in US multinationals', *Journal of International Business Studies*, 36, 3: 304–21.

Forster, N. (2000) 'Expatriates and the impact of cross cultural training', *Human Resource Management Journal*, 10, 3: 63–78.

Frenkel, S. (2001) 'Globalization, athletic footwear commodity chains and employment relations in China', *Organization Studies*, 22, 4: 531–62.

Frenkel, S. and Peetz, D. (1998) 'Globalization and industrial relations in East Asia: a three-country comparison', *Industrial Relations*, 37, 3: 282–310.

Fu, Z. Y. (2008) 'The implementation of Labour Contract Law and employment of university graduates', *Journal of Qiongzhou University*, 15: 95–6 (in Chinese).

Fudge, J. and Vosko, L. (2001) 'By whose standards? Reregulating the Canadian labour market', *Economic and Industrial Democracy*, 22, 3: 327–56.

Gallagher, M. (2005) *Contagious Capitalism: Globalisation and the Politics of Labour in China*, Princeton, NJ: Princeton University Press.

Gamble, J. and Huang, Q. (2008) 'Organizational commitment of Chinese employees in foreign-invested firms', *International Journal of Human Resource Management*, 19, 5: 896–915.

Gamble, J. and Huang, Q. (2009) 'One store, two employment systems: core, periphery and flexibility in China's retail sector', *British Journal of Industrial Relations*, 47, 1: 1–26.

Gao, J., Xiao, Y. and Hu, T. Z. (2007) 'Employment barriers and strategy for those in flexible employment at the lower level of job ladder', *Statistics and Decision*, 6: 119–21 (in Chinese).

Gao, L. F. and Jia, L. N. (2005) 'On the definition and measurement of "informal employment"', *Statistical Research*, 3: 74–7 (in Chinese).

Gao, W. S. (2006) 'An analysis of factors influencing the employment situation and income of rural migrant workers', *China Village Economy*, 1: 28–34 and 80 (in Chinese).

Gardner, T. (2002) 'In the trenches at the talent wars: competitive interactions for scarce human resources', *Human Resource Management*, 41, 2: 225–37.

Gerhart, B. (1990) 'Voluntary turnover and alternative job opportunities', *Journal of Applied Psychology*, 75, 5: 467–76.

Gionfriddo, J. and Dhingra, L. (1999) 'Retaining high-tech talent: NIIT case study', *Compensation and Benefits Review*, 31, 5: 31–5.

Godard, J. (2002) 'Institutional environments, employer practices, and states in liberal market economies', *Industrial Relations*, 41: 249–86.

Godard, J. (2004) 'A critical assessment of the high performance paradigm', *British Journal of Industrial Relations*, 42, 2: 349–78.

Gong, Y. and Chang, S. (2008) 'Institutional antecedents and performance consequences of employment security and career advancement practices: evidence from the People's Republic of China', *Human Resource Management*, 47, 1: 33–48.

Gong, Y., Law, K. S., Chang, S. and Xin, K. R. (2009) 'Human resources management and firm performance: the differential role of managerial affective and continuance commitment', *Journal of Applied Psychology*, 94, 1: 263–75.

Goodall, K. and Warner, M. (1999) 'Enterprise reform, labor–management relations, and human resource management in a multinational context', *International Studies of Management and Organization*, 29, 3: 21–36.

Goodall, K. and Warner, M. (2010) 'Management training and development in China: laying the foundations', in Warner, M. and Goodall, K. (eds) *Management Training and Development in China*, London: Routledge, pp. 13–26.

Gospel, H. (2008) 'Trade unions in theory and practice: perspectives from advanced industrial countries', in Benson, J. and Zhu, Y. (eds) *Trade Unions in Asia: An Economic and Sociological Analysis*, London: Routledge, pp. 11–23.

Griffeth, R. W., Hom, P. W. and Gaertner, S. (2000) 'A meta-analysis of antecedents and correlates of employee turnover: Update, moderator tests, and research implications for the next millennium', *Journal of Management*, 26, 3: 463–88.

Gustafsson, B. and Li, S. (2000) 'Economic transformation and the gender earnings gap in urban China', *Journal of Population Economics*, 13, 2: 305–29.

Haesli, A. and Boxall, P. (2005) 'When knowledge management meets HR strategy: an exploration of personalization retention and codification-recruitment configurations', *International Journal of Human Resource Management*, 16, 11: 1955–75.

Hamel, G. and Prahalad, C. (1993) 'Strategy as stretch and leverage', *Harvard Business Review*, 71, 2: 75–84.

Han, G. J. and Liu, J. (2008) 'An examination of the Employment Promotion Law in the context of social harmony', *Legal Studies Analysis*, 5: 65–76 (in Chinese).

Han, J. and Han, J. (2009) 'Network-based recruiting and applicant attraction in China: insights from both organizational and individual perspectives', *International Journal of Human Resource Management*, 20, 11: 2228–49.

Harney, A. (2009) *The China Price: The True Cost of Chinese Competitive Advantage*, London: Penguin Books.

Harrison, R. (2002) *Learning and Development*, 3rd edn, London: Chartered Institute of Personnel and Development.

Harzing, A. and Pinnington, A. (eds) (2011) *International Human Resource Management*, 3rd edn, London: Sage.

Hassard, J., Sheehan, J., Zhou, M., Terpstra-Tong, J. and Morris, J. (2007) *China's State Enterprise Reform: From Marx to the Market*, London: Routledge.

He, P. (2003) 'A research report on the social insurance for workers in informal employment', in Zheng, G. C., Zeng, X. C., Zheng, Y. S. and Zhang, Q. H. (eds) *Employment Environment and Social Security in the Period of Reform*, Beijing: China Labour Social Security Press, pp. 495–513 (in Chinese).

Healy, G. and Oikelome, F. (2007) 'A global link between national diversity policies? The case of the migration of Nigerian physicians to the UK and USA', *International Journal of Human Resource Management*, 18, 11: 1917–33.

Healy, G., Heery, E., Taylor, P. and Brown, W. (2004) *The Future of Worker Representation*, Basingstoke: Palgrave Macmillan.

Heery, E. and Frege, C. (2006) 'New actors in industrial relations', *British Journal of Industrial Relations*, 44, 4: 601–4.

Heery, E. and Simms, M. (2010) 'Employer responses to union organising: patterns and effects', *Human Resource Management Journal*, 20, 1: 3–22.

Hempel, P. S. (2001) 'Differences between Chinese and western managerial views of performance', *Personnel Review*, 30, 2: 203–26.

Hempel, P. S. (2008) 'Chinese reactions to performance feedback: non-task attributions of feedback intentions', *Asia Pacific Journal of Human Resources*, 46, 2: 196–219.

Hishida, M., Kojima, K., Ishii, T. and Qiao, J. (2010) *China's Trade Unions: How Autonomous Are They?* London and New York: Routledge.

Hofstede, G. (1991) *Cultures and Organizations, Software of the Mind*, New York: McGraw-Hill.

Holtom, B. Mitchell, T., Lee, T. and Inderrieden, E. (2005) 'Shocks as causes of turnover: what they are and how organizations can manage them', *Human Resource Management*, 44, 3: 337–52.

Hong, J. F. L. and Snell, R. S. (2008) 'Power inequality in cross-cultural learning: the case of Japanese transplants in China', *Asia Pacific Business Review*, 14, 2: 253–73.

Horwitz, F., Chan, T., Qiiazi, H., Nonkwelo, C., Roditi, D. and Eck, P. (2006) 'Human resource strategies for managing knowledge workers: an Afro-Asian comparative analysis', *International Journal of Human Resource Management,* 17, 5: 775–811.

Hou, X. B. (2008) 'An analysis of the labour disputes treatment model and its weaknesses in the Labour Disputes Mediation and Arbitration Law', *Commercial Intelligence: Finance and Economic Study*, 8: 70 and 100 (in Chinese).

Howard, A., Liu, L., Wellins, R. and William, S. (2007) *"The Flight of Human Talent"*: *Employee Retention in China 2006–2007*, Bridgeville, PA: Development Dimensions International.

Howell, J. (2008) 'All-China Federation of Trades Unions beyond reform? The slow march of direct elections', *China Quarterly*, 196: 845–63.

HR *Manager* (2009) 'An analysis of the 2009 Chinese university graduates' employer of choice survey report', *HR Manager*, 8: 31–39. (HR经理人, '解读《2009中国大学生最佳雇主调查报告》' 《HR经理人》, 2009.08, 31–38页) (in Chinese).

Hu, A. G. and Yang, Y. X. (2001) 'Changing mode of employment: from formalization to informalization', *Management World,* 2: 69–78 (in Chinese).

Hu, X. J. (2004) 'On the legal system of China's labour market', *Journal of Anhui University of Technology* (Social Sciences Edition) 21, 5: 19–20 (in Chinese).

Huang, K. (2008) 'Developing HR systems in the acquired units after the acquisitions: case studies on acquisitions of Chinese firms by foreign-invested companies', unpublished PhD thesis, University of Manchester, UK.

Huang, Y. (2008) *Capitalism with Chinese Characteristics: Entrepreneurship and the State*, Cambridge: Cambridge University Press.

Hughes, J. and Maurer-Fazio, M. (2002) 'Effects of marriage, education and occupation on the female/male wage gap in China', *Pacific Economic Review*, 7, 1: 137–56.

Hui, C., Law, K. S., Chen, Y. F. and Tjosvold, D. (2008) 'The role of co-operation and competition on leader–member exchange and extra-role performance in China', *Asia Pacific Journal of Human Resources*, 46, 2: 133–52.

Hui, M. K., Au, K. and Fock, H. (2004) 'Empowerment effects across cultures', *Journal of International Business Studies*, 35, 1: 46–61.

Human Resources (2009) 'Outcomes of starting salary survey of 2009 university graduates', *Human Resources*, September: 40–2 (in Chinese).

Huselid, M. A. (1995) 'The impact of human resource management practices on turnover, productivity, and corporate financial performance', *Academy of Management Journal*, 38, 3: 635–72.

Huselid, M. A., Jackson, S. E. and Schuler, R. S. (1997) 'Technical and strategic human resource management effectiveness as determinants of firm performance', *Academy of Management Journal*, 40, 1: 171–88.

Hutchings, K., Zhu, C., Cooper, B., Zhang, Y. and Shao, S. (2009) 'Perceptions of the effectiveness of training and development of "grey-collar" workers in the People's Republic of China', *Human Resource Development International*, 12, 3: 279–96.

ILO (International Labour Organization) (1999) International Labour Conference, 87th Session, Report of the Director-General: *Decent Work*, Geneva: International Labour Organization, http://www.ilo.org/public/english/standards/relm/ilc/ilc87/rep-i.htm, accessed on 20 December 2008.

ILO (International Labour Organization) (2000) *World Labour Report, 2000: Income Security and Social Protection in a Changing World*, Geneva: International Labour Organization.

ILO (International Labour Organization) (2002) International Labour Conference, 90th Session, Report VI, *Decent Work and the Informal Economy*, Geneva: International Labour Organization.

Jayne, M. and Dipboye, R. (2004) 'Leveraging diversity to improve business performance: research findings and recommendations for organizations', *Human Resource Management*, 43, 4: 409–24.

Jia, L. P. (2007) 'A study of social security issues of workers in informal employment', *Population Journal*, 1: 41–6 (in Chinese).

Jiang, Y. P. (2003) 'Gender equality in the labour market: attention is needed', *Collection of Women's Studies*, 2: 51–8 (in Chinese).

Jiao, X. K. (2008) 'A study of health security for informal workers in urban areas', *Decision Exploration*, 1: 61–2 (in Chinese).

Jin, Y. H. (2006) 'Women in informal employment: current situation and strategy', *Journal of Hehai University*, 3: 18–21 (in Chinese).

Judd, E. (2002) *The Chinese Women's Movement between State and Market*, Palo Alto, CA: Stanford University Press.

Kelly, J. and Heery, E. (1989) 'Full-time officers and trade union recruitment', *British Journal of Industrial Relations*, 27, 2: 196–213.

Kessler, D. (2008) 'Business struggles with worker participation and its consequences for the role of NGOs', paper presented at the International Conference 'Breaking Down Chinese Walls: The Changing Faces of Labor and Employment in China', Cornell University, 26–28 September, Ithaca, New York.

Kidd, M. P. and Meng, X. (2001) 'The Chinese state enterprise sector: labor market reform and the impact on male–female wage structure', *Asian Economic Journal*, 15, 4: 405–23.

Kochan, T., Bezrukova, K., Ely, R., Jackson, S., Joshi, A., Jehn, K., Leonard, J., Levine, D. and Thomas, D. (2003) 'The effects of diversity on business performance: report of the diversity research network', *Human Resource Management*, 42, 1: 3–21.

Konrad, A., Prasad, P. and Pringle, J. (eds) (2006) *Handbook of Workplace Diversity*, Thousand Oaks, CA: Sage.

Korzec, M. (1992) *Labour and the Failure of Reform in China*, London: Macmillan.

Kreimer, M. (2004) 'Labour market segregation and the gender-based division of labour', *European Journal of Women's Studies*, 11, 2: 223–46.

Kuruvilla, S. (1996) 'Linkages between industrialization strategies and IR/HR policies in Singapore, Malaysia, Philippines and India', *Industrial and Labour Relations Review*, 49: 635–57.

Lam, N. and Graham, J. (2007) *China Now: Doing Business in the World's Most Dynamic Market*, New Delhi: Tata McGraw-Hill.

Lam, W., Chen, Z. and Takeuchi, N. (2009) 'Perceived human resource management practices and intention to leave of employees: the mediating role of organizational citizenship behaviour in a Sino-Japanese joint venture', *International Journal of Human Resource Management*, 20, 11: 2250–70.

Lane, K. and Pollner, F. (2008) 'How to address China's growing talent shortage', *McKinsey Quarterly*, 3: 33–40.

Lau, A. and Roffey, B. (2002) 'Management education and development in China: a research note', *Labour and Management in Development Journal*, 2, 10: 1–18.

Lau, D. and Murnighan, J. (1998) 'Demographic diversity and faultlines: the compositional dynamics of organizational groups', *Academy of Management Review*, 23, 2: 325–40.

Law, K., Tse, D. K. and Zhou, N. (2003) 'Does human resource management matter in a transitional economy? China as an example', *Journal of International Business Studies*, 34, 3: 255–65.

Lawler, J., Chen, S. and Bae, J. (2000) 'Scale of operations, human resource systems and firm performance in East and Southeast Asia', *Research and Practice in Human Resource Management*, 8, 1: 3–20.

Lee, C. K. (1995) 'Engendering the worlds of labor: women workers, labor markets, and production politics in the south China economic miracle', *American Sociological Review*, 60, 3: 378–97.

Lee, C. K. (2007) *Against the Law: Labor Protests in China's Rustbelt and Sunbelt*, Berkeley: University of California.

Lee, C. K. and Shen, Y. (2008) 'The anti-solidarity machine: labor NGOs in China', paper presented at the International Conference 'Breaking Down Chinese Walls: The Changing Faces of Labor and Employment in China', Cornell University, 26–28 September, Ithaca, New York.

Lee, C., Hsu, M. and Lien, N. (2006) 'The impacts of benefit plans on employee turnover: a firm-level analysis approach on Taiwanese manufacturing industry', *International Journal of Human Resource Management*, 17, 11: 1951–75.

Lee, S. and McCann, D. (eds) (2012) *Regulating for Decent Work: New Directions in Labour Market Regulation*, Basingstoke: Palgrave Macmillan.

Legge, K. (1994) 'Managing culture: fact or fiction?' in Sisson, K. (ed.) *Personnel Management: A Comprehensive Guide to Theory and Practice in Britain*, 2nd edn, London: Blackwell, pp. 397–433.

Leininger, J. (2007) 'Recent compensation and benefit trends in China', *China Business Review*, 34, 4: 28–30.

Lepak, D. P. and Snell, S. A. (1999) 'The human resource architecture: toward a theory of human capital allocation and development', *Academy of Management Review*, 24, 1: 31–48.

Levering, R. and Moskowitz, M. (2004) 'Fortune 100 best companies to work for', *Fortune*, 149, 1: 56–83.

Li, B. and Walder, A. (2001) 'Career advancement as party patronage: sponsor mobility into the Chinese administrative elite, 1949–96', *American Journal of Sociology*, 106, 5: 1371–408.

Li, B. A. and Xiang, S. Q. (2007) 'Harmonious labour relations: an important foundation of building a harmonious society', *Labor Economy and Labor Relations*, 6: 40–2 (in Chinese).

Li, H. (2000) 'An analysis of the situation of China's labour market', *Journal of Beijing College of Management of Planning and Labour*, 3: 14 and 57 (in Chinese).

Li, H. (2005) 'Weaknesses and remedial strategy in the Chinese labour market during transition period', *Economy Horizon*, 2: 30–3 (in Chinese).

Li, M. and Edwards, P. (2008) 'Work and pay in small Chinese clothing firms: a constrained negotiated order', *Industrial Relations Journal*, 39, 4: 296–313.

Li, S. and Gustafsson, B. (1999) 'An analysis of gender differences in urban workers' income', in Zhao, R. W. (ed.) *Further Research on the Distribution of Chinese Household Income: The Distribution of Income during Economic Reform and Development*, Beijing: China Finance and Economics Publishing House.

Li, T. Q. (2005) 'An investigation of enterprise training in China 2005, Part 1', (李滩奇, '2005中国企业培训现状调查（一）'), Internet source: http://www.chinahrd.net/zgi_sk/jt_page.asp?articleid = 78655, accessed on 20 December 2009 (in Chinese).

Li, W., Liu, X. and Wan, W. (2008) 'Demographic effects of work values and their management implications', *Journal of Business Ethics*, 81, 4: 875–85.

Li, X. J., Xu, Y. D. and Zhu, J. X. (2006) 'Employment relationship under the form of employment leasing', *Labor Economy and Labor Relations*, 1: 5–8 (in Chinese).

Li, Y. and Sheldon, P. (2010) 'HRM lives inside and outside the firm: employers' skill shortages and the local labour market in China', *International Journal of Human Resource Management*, 21, 10/12: 2173–93.

Li, Y. B. (2003) 'The progress and forecast of the Chinese labour market', *Contemporary Finance and Economics*, 3: 15–19 (in Chinese).

Liang, Y. L. (2008) 'New developments in the mediation and arbitration of labor disputes in China', King and Wood PRC Lawyers, http://www.kingandwood.com, accessed on 3 June 2009.

Lin, L. Y. (2008) 'A comparison of the labour dispute resolution system between Hong Kong and mainland China: from the angle of the new Labour Disputes Mediation and Arbitration Law', *Legal System and Society*, 11: 59–60.

Lindholm, N. (1999) 'Performance management in MNC subsidiaries in China: a study of host-country managers and professionals', *Asia Pacific Journal of Human Resources*, 37, 3: 18–35.

Lindholm, N., Tahvanainen, M. and Björkman, I. (1999) 'Performance appraisal of host country employees: western MNEs in China', in Brewster, C. and Harris, H. (eds) *International HRM: Contemporary Issues in Europe*, London: Routledge, pp.143–59.

Liu, H. X. (2005) 'Who should appraise the appraisers and who should monitor the monitors?', *Development and Management of Human Resources*, 11: 40–1 (in Chinese).

Liu, L. P., Wan, X. D. and Zhang, Y. H. (2006) 'Institutional shortage and labour shortage: a study of "Mingong huang"', *China Industrial Economy*, 8: 45–53 (in Chinese).

Liu, M. Li, C. and Kim, S. (2011) 'The changing Chinese trade unions: a three level analysis', in Sheldon, P., Kim, S., Li, Y. and Warner, M. (eds) *China's Changing Workplace,* London: Routledge.

Liu, P., Meng, X. and Zhang, J. (2000) 'Sectoral gender wage differentials and discrimination in the transitional Chinese economy', *Journal of Population Economics* 13, 2: 331–52.

Liu, Q. T. (2008) 'Interpreting the Employment Promotion Law', *Journal of Chongqing Institute of Technology* (Social Science Edition), 22, 2: 6–9 (in Chinese).

Liu, S. (2003) 'Cultures within culture: unity and diversity of two generations of employees in state-owned enterprises', *Human Relations*, 56, 4: 387–417.

Liu, Y. and Li, Y. Y. (2007) 'A study of the gender difference of rural migrant workers in informal employment in urban area', *China Village Economy*, 12: 20–7 (in Chinese).

Lockett, M. (1988) 'Culture and the problems of Chinese management', *Organisation Studies*, 9, 3: 475–96.

Lorbiecki, A. and Jack, G. (2000) 'Critical turns in the evolution of diversity management', *British Journal of Management*, 11, Special Issue, S17–S31.

Lu, Q. and Zhao, Y. M. (2002) 'Gender segregation in China since the economic reform', *Journal of Southern Yangtze University* (Humanities and Social Sciences), 1, 2: 22–48 (in Chinese).

Lu, Y. Z. (2008) 'Human resource development and management in the market economy', *Journal of Hubei University of Economics*, 5, 5: 57–8 (in Chinese).

Ma, J. J. (2008) 'A review of the labour laws legislation in 2007', *Lingnan Xuekan*, 4: 60–3 (in Chinese).

MacKenzie, R. and Martinez Lucio, M. (2005) 'The realities of regulatory change: beyond the fetish of deregulation', *Sociology*, 39, 3: 499–517.

Macky, K. and Boxall, P. (2007) 'The relationship between "high performance work practices" and employee attitudes: an investigation of additive and interaction effects', *International Journal of Human Resource Management*, 18, 4: 537–67.

Malila, J. (2007) 'The great look forward: China's HR evolution', *China Business Review*, 34, 4: 16–19.

Martin, R. (1989) *Trade Unionism: Purposes and Forms*, Oxford: Clarendon Press.

Martinez Lucio, M. and MacKenzie, R. (2004) '"Unstable boundaries?" Evaluating the "new regulation" within employment relations', *Economy and Society*, 33, 1: 77–97.

Martinez Lucio, M. and Stuart, M. (2004) 'Swimming against the tide: social partnership, mutual gains and the revival of "tired" HRM', *International Journal of Human Resource Management*, 15, 2: 410–24.

Maurer-Fazio, M., Rawski, G. T. and Zhang, W. (1999) 'Inequality in the rewards for holding up half the sky: gender wage gaps in China's urban labour market, 1988–94', *China Journal*, 41: 55–88.

Mellahi, K. (2007) 'The effect of regulations on HRM: private sector firms in Saudi Arabia', *International Journal of Human Resource Management*, 18, 1: 85–99.

Meng, X. (2000) *Labour Market Reform in China*, Cambridge: Cambridge University Press.

Meng, X. and Miller, P. (1995) 'Occupational segregation and its impacts on gender discrimination in China's rural industrial sector', *Oxford Economic Papers, New Series*, 47, 1: 136–55.

Michelson, G. (2008) 'New actors in Australian employment relations', in Michelson, G., Jamieson, S. and Burgess, J. (eds) *New Employment Actors: Developments from Australia*, Oxford: Peter Lang, pp. 1–31.

Milne, S. (2010) 'These strikes are good for China – and for the world', http://www.guardian.co.uk/commentisfree/2010/jun/30/china, accessed on 1 July 2010.

Mincer, J. and Polachek, S. (1974) 'Family investments in human capital: earnings of women', *Journal of Political Economy*, 82, 2: 76–108.

Moon, K. and Broadbent, K. (2008) 'Korea: women, labour activism and autonomous organizing', in Broadbent, K. andFord, M. (eds) *Woman Organizing: Women and Union Activism in Asia*, London: Routledge, pp. 136–55.

Mor Barak, M. (2005) *Managing Diversity: Towards a Globally Inclusive Workplace*, Thousand Oaks, CA: Sage.

Morrell, K., Loan-Clarke, J. and Wilkinson, A. (2001) 'Unweaving leaving: the use of models in the management of employee turnover', *International Journal of Management Reviews*, 3, 3: 219–44.

Morris, J., Wilkinson, B. and Gamble, J. (2009) 'Strategic international human resource management or the "bottom line"? The cases of electronics and garments commodity chains in China', *International Journal of Human Resource Management*, 20, 2: 348–70.

Morris, M. W., Podolny, J. and Sullivan, B. N. (2008) 'Culture and coworker relations: interpersonal patterns in American, Chinese, German, and Spanish divisions of a global retail bank', *Organization Science*, 19, 4: 517–32.

Mu,. J. (2003) 'Building a unified urban–rural labour market is an inevitable trend', *Journal of Kunming University*, 2: 11–14 (in Chinese).

Murdoch, H. and Gould, D. (2004) *Corporate Social Responsibility in China: Mapping the Environment*, Global Alliance for Workers and Communities Publication Series, Baltimore, MD: Global Alliance for Workers and Communities.

Nakata, Y. and Takehiro, R. (2002) 'Employment and wages of female Japanese workers: past, present, and future', *Industrial Relations*, 41, 4: 521–47.

Nathwani, A., Alves, F., Mahtani, S. and Vernon, K. (2007) 'Diversity and inclusion: a lever for solving talent pool dilemmas in India and China', a summary report presented to the Global Diversity Network, Schneider-Ross Limited and Community Business.

Nee, V. (1989) 'A theory of market transition: from redistribution to markets in state socialism', *American Sociological Review*, 54, 5: 663–81.

Nee, V. (1991) 'Social inequalities in reforming state socialism: between redistribution and markets in state socialism', *American Sociological Review*, 56, 3: 267–82.

Nee, V. and Cao, Y. (2004) 'Market transition and the firm: institutional change and income inequality in urban China', *Management and Organization Review*, 1, 1: 23–56.

Ng, E. and Burke, R. (2005) 'Person–organization fit and the war for talent: does diversity management make a difference?' *International Journal of Human Resource Management*, 16, 7: 1195–210.

Ngo, H. Y., Lau, C. M. and Foley, S. (2008) 'Strategic human resource management, firm performance, and employee relations climate in China', *Human Resource Management*, 47, 1: 73–90.

Nichols, T. and Zhao, W. (2010) 'Disaffection with trade unions in China: some evidence from SOEs in the auto industry', *Industrial Relations Journal*, 41, 1: 19–33.

Nie, W., Hopkins, E. W. and Hopkins, A. S. (2002) 'Gender-base perceptions of equity in China's state-owned enterprises', *Thunderbird International Business Review*, 44, 3: 353–77.

Niederman, F., Sumner, M. and Maertz, C. (2007) 'Testing and extending the unfolding model of voluntary turnover to IT professionals', *Human Resource Management*, 46, 3: 331–47.

Nishii, L. and Özbilgin, F. (2007) 'Global diversity management: towards a conceptual framework', *International Journal of Human Resource Management*, 18, 11: 1883–94.

Nishii, L., Lepak, D. and Schneider, B. (2008) 'Employee attributions of the "why" of HR practices: their effects on employee attitudes and behaviors, and customer satisfaction', *Personnel Psychology*, 61, 3: 503–45.

O'Leary, G. (1998) 'The making of the Chinese working class', in O'Leary, G. (ed.) *Adjusting to Capitalism: Chinese Workers and the State*, New York: M. E. Sharpe, pp. 48–74.

O'Reilly, J. and Fagan, C. (eds) (1998) *Part-Time Prospects: An International Comparison of Part-Time Work in Europe, North America and the Pacific Rim*, London: Routledge.

Oaxaca, R. (1973) 'Male–female wage differentials in urban labor markets', *International Economic Review*, 14, 3: 693–709.

Ortenblad, A. (2002) 'A typology of the idea of learning organisation', *Management Learning*, 33, 2: 213–30.

Osterman, P. (2006) 'Community organizing and employee representation', *British Journal of Industrial Relations*, 44, 4: 629–49.

Pan, C. G. and Lou, W. (2004) 'Study on situation and development environment for Chinese talents', in Pan, C. G. and Wang, L. (eds) *The Report on the Development of Chinese Talents, No.1*, Beijing: Social Sciences Academic Press, pp. 1–46 (in Chinese).

Paul, A. K. and Anantharaman, R. N. (2003) 'Impact of people management practices on organizational performance: analysis of a causal model', *International Journal of Human Resource Management*, 14, 7: 1246–66.

Pedler, M., Burgoyne, J. and Boydell, T. (1991) *The Learning Company: A Strategy for Sustainable Development*, Maidenhead: McGraw-Hill.

Peng, K. Z., Ngo, H. Y., Shi, J. and Wong, C. H. (2009) 'Gender differences in the work commitment of Chinese workers: an investigation of two alternative explanations', *Journal of World Business*, 44, 3: 323–35.

Peng, X. Z. and Yao, Y. (2004) 'Clarifying the concept of informal employment and promote the development of informal employment', *Social Science*, 7: 63–72 (in Chinese).

People's Daily Online (2007) 'Foreign firms turn to M&As for expansion', 27April, Internet source: http://english.peopledaily.com.cn/200704/27/eng20070427_370339.html, accessed on 21 February 2009.

People's Daily Online (2010) 'Chinese premier encourages university graduates to start own businesses', 27 February, Internet source: http://english.peopledaily.com.cn/90001/90776/90785/6904122.html, accessed on 2 October 2010.

People's Daily Overseas Edition, 13 February 2006.

People's Daily Overseas Edition (2009) 'Importing high level talent from overseas: China implements the "Thousand Talents Plan"', 21 March: 1.

Perry, E. and Selden, M. (2000) 'Introduction: reform and resistance in contemporary China', in Perry, E. and Selden, M. (eds) *Chinese Society: Change, Conflict and Resistance*, London: Routledge, pp. 1–19.

Petersen, T. and Morgan, A. L. (1995) 'Separate and unequal: occupational-establishment sex segregation and the gender wage gap', *American Journal of Sociology*, 101, 2: 329–65.

Pfeffer, J. (1998a) 'Six dangerous myths about pay', *Harvard Business Review*, May/June, 108–19.

Pfeffer, J. (1998b) *The Human Equation: Building Profits by Putting People First*, Boston, MA: Harvard Business School Press.

Pieke, F. N. (2009) 'Marketization, centralization and globalization of cadre training in contemporary China', *China Quarterly*, 200: 953–71.

Polachek, S. and Siebert, W. (1993) *The Economics of Earnings*, Cambridge: Cambridge University Press.

Poon, I., Wei, J. and Rowley, C. (2010) 'The changing face of performance management in China', in Rowley, C. and Cooke, F. L. (eds) *The Changing Face of Chinese Management*, Working in Asia Series, London: Routledge, pp. 149–74.

PricewaterhouseCoopers (2008) 'Work–Life Balance', PwC Careers, Internet source: http://www.pwccn.com/home/eng/graduate_worklife.html, accessed on 3 January 2008.

Pun, N. and Smith, C. (2007) 'Putting transnational labour process in its place: the dormitory labour regime in post-socialist China', *Work, Employment and Society*, 21, 1: 27–45.

Pun, N. and Yang, L. M. (2004) 'The Chinese working women's network', *Against the Current*, http://www.solidarity-us.org/atc/113luce.html, accessed on 13 November 2005.

Purcell, J. and Purcell, K. (1999) 'Insourcing, outsourcing and the growth of contingent labour as evidence of flexible employment strategies', *Bulletin of Comparative Labour Relations*, 35: 163–81.

Pye, L. (1986) 'The China trade: making the deal', *Harvard Business Review*, 64, 4: 74–80.

Qian, D. Z. and Zhang, Y. L. (2007) 'Adverse selection and counter measures for the training of rural migrant workers', *Journal of Nanjing Agricultural University* (Social Science Edition), 7, 1: 21–4 (in Chinese).

Qiao, J. (2008) 'Labor Contract Law in China: changes and implications', paper presented at the International Conference 'Breaking Down Chinese Walls: The Changing Faces of Labor and Employment in China', Cornell University, 26–28 September, Ithaca, New York.

Qiao, K., Khilji, S. and Wang, X. (2009) 'High-performance work systems, organizational commitment, and the role of demographic features in the People's Republic of China', *International Journal of Human Resource Management*, 20, 11: 2311–30.

Ralston, D., Gustafson, D., Cheung, F. and Terpstra, R. (1993) 'Differences in managerial values: a study of U.S., Hong Kong and PRC managers', *Journal of International Business Studies*, 24, 2: 249–75.

Ralston, D., Gustafson, D., Terpstra, R. and Holt, D. (1995) 'Pre-post Tiananmen Square: changing values of Chinese managers', *Asia Pacific Journal of Management,* 12, 1: 1–20.

Ralston, D., Holt, D., Terpstra, R. and Cheng, Y. K. (1997) 'The impact of national culture and economic ideology on managerial work values: a study of the United States, Russia, Japan and China', *Journal of International Business Studies*, 28, 1: 177–207.

Ralston, D., Egri, C., Stewart, S., Terpstra, R. and Yu, K. C. (1999) 'Doing business in the 21st century with the new generation of Chinese managers: a study of generational shifts in work values in China', *Journal of International Business Studies*, 30, 2: 415–28.

Ramsay, H., Scholarios, D. and Harley, B. (2000) 'Employees and high-performance work systems: testing inside the black box', *British Journal of Industrial Relations*, 38, 4: 501–31.

Rees, C., Mamman, A. and Braik, A. B. (2007) 'Emiratization as a strategic HRM change initiative: case study evidence from a UAE petroleum company', *International Journal of Human Resource Management*, 18, 1: 33–53.

Ren, Y. (2008) 'Some thoughts on how to improve the "Shanghai Model" of informal employment', *Social Science*, 1: 119–24.

Renmin Daily, 2 December 2004 (in Chinese).

Richard, O. C., Barnett, T., Dwyer, S. and Chadwick, K. (2004) 'Cultural diversity in management, firm performance, and the moderating role of entrepreneurial orientation dimensions', *Academy of Management Journal*, 47, 2: 255–66.

Rodgers, J. (2002) *Decent Work and the Informal Economy*, International Labour Conference, 90th Session, Geneva: International Labour Organization.

Rozelle, S., Dong, X., Zhang, L. and Mason, A. (2002) 'Gender wage gaps in post-reform rural China', *Pacific Economic Review*, 7, 1: 157–79.

Rubery, J. and Grimshaw, D. (2003) *The Organization of Employment: An International Perspective*, Basingstoke: Palgrave Macmillan.

Rubery, J., Smith, M. and Fagan, C. (1999) *Women's Employment in Europe: Trends and Prospects*, London: Routledge.

Rubery, R., Grimshaw, D. and Figueiredo, H. (2005) 'How to close the gender pay gap in Europe: towards the gender mainstreaming of pay policy', *Industrial Relations Journal*, 36, 3: 184–213.

Rynes, S., Gerhart, B. and Minette, K. (2004) 'The importance of pay in employee motivation: discrepancies between what people say and what they do', *Human Resource Management*, 43, 4: 381–94.

Scullion, H. and Collings, D. (eds) (2011) *Global Talent Management*, Global Human Resource Management Series, London: Routledge.

Selmer, J. (2006) 'Cultural novelty and adjustment: western business expatriates in China', *International Journal of Human Resource Management* 17, 7: 1209–22.

Senge, P. (1990) *The Fifth Discipline: The Art and Practice of the Learning Organisation*, New York: Doubleday.

Shambaugh, D. (2008) 'Training China's political elite: the party school system', *China Quarterly*, 196: 827–44.

Shao, S. M., Nielsen, I., Nyland, C., Smyth, R., Zhang, M. and Zhu, C. J. (2007) 'Migrants as Homo Economicus', *China Information*, 21, 1, 7–41.

Shaw, J. D., Delery, J. E., Jenkins, G. D. and Gupta, N. (1998) 'An organization-level analysis of voluntary and involuntary turnover', *Academy of Management Journal*, 41, 5: 511–25.

Sheehan, J. (1999) *Chinese Workers: A New History*, London: Routledge.

Shi, M. X. and Wang, B. Q. (2007) 'Modelling of labour relations in informal employment', *China Labour*, 11: 22–4 (in Chinese).

Shu, X. and Bian, Y. (2003) 'Market transition and gender gap in earnings in urban China', *Social Forces*, June, 81, 4: 1107–45.

Shue, V. and Wong, C. (2007) *Paying for Progress in China: Public Finance, Human Welfare and Changing Patterns of Inequality*, London: Routledge.

Si, L. (2009) 'Graduates appreciate brand value in career choice', *China Brand*, 4: 130–2. (司丽 (2009), '毕业生择业识品牌', 《中国品牌》: 130–2页) (in Chinese).

Si, S. X., Wei, F. and Li, Y. (2008) 'The effect of organizational psychological contract violation on managers' exit, voice, loyalty and neglect in the Chinese context', *International Journal of Human Resource Management*, 19, 5: 932–44.

Singh, K. (2003) 'Strategic HR orientation and firm performance in India', *International Journal of Human Resource Management*, 14, 4: 530–43.

Smith, C. (2003) 'Living at work: management control and the dormitory labour system in China', *Asia Pacific Journal of Management*, 20, 3: 333–58.

Smith, C., Daskalaki, M., Elger, T. and Brown, D. (2004) 'Labour turnover and management retention strategies in new manufacturing plants', *International Journal of Human Resource Management*, 15, 2: 371–96.

Smith, P., Wang, Z. M. and Leung, K. (1997) 'Leadership, decision-making and cultural context: event management within Chinese joint ventures', *Leadership Quarterly*, 8, 4: 413–31.

Snape, E., Thompson, D., Yan, F. and Redman, T. (1998) 'Performance appraisal and culture: practice and attitudes in Hong Kong and Great Britain', *International Journal of Human Resource Management*, 9, 5: 841–61.

Solinger, D. (1999) *Contesting Citizenship in Urban China: Peasant Migrants, the State, and the Logic of the Market*, Berkeley: University of California Press.

Solotaroff, J. (2003) 'Gender Inequalities in Urban China's Career Mobility Patterns', draft paper prepared for the SCR Graduate Student Retreat, Princeton University, NJ.

Soni, V. (2000) 'A twenty-first-century reception for diversity in public sector: a case study', *Public Administration Review*, 60, 5: 395–408.

Southworth, D. (1999) 'Building a business school in China: the case of the China Europe International Business School (CEIBS)', *Education and Training*, 41, 6/7: 325–30.

Sparrow, P., Brewster, C. and Harris, H. (2004) *Globalizing Human Resource Management*, London: Routledge.

Spitze, G. (1984) 'The effect of family migration on wives' employment: how long does it last?' *Social Science Quarterly*, 65, 1: 21–36.

Standing, G. (1997) 'Globalization, labour flexibility and insecurity: the era of market regulation', *European Journal of Industrial Relations*, 3, 1: 7–37.

The State Council (2006) *Report on Rural Migrant Workers in China*, Beijing: The State Council of China.

Stockman, N., Bonney, N. and Sheng, X. W. (1995) *Women's Work in East and West: The Dual Burden of Employment and Family Life*, London: UCL Press.

Storey, J. and Quintas, P. (2001) 'Knowledge management and HRM', in Storey, J. (ed.) *Human Resource Management: A Critical Text*, London: Thomson Learning, pp. 339–63.

Subeliani, D. and Tsogas, G. (2005) 'Managing diversity in the Netherlands: a case study of Rabobank', *International Journal of Human Resource Management*, 16, 5: 831–85.

Sun, X. (2008) 'The training of China's managers: an analysis and evaluation of using overseas training for management development', unpublished PhD thesis, University of Worcester, UK.

Takahara, A. (1992) *The Politics of Wage Policy in Post-Revolutionary China*, London: Macmillan.

Taormina, R. J. and Gao, J. H. (2009) 'Identifying acceptable performance appraisal criteria: an international perspective', *Asia Pacific Journal of Human Resources*, 47, 1: 102–25.

Tarique, I. and Schuler, R. (2010) 'Global talent management: literature review, integrative framework, and suggestions for further research', *Journal of World Business*, 45, 2: 122–33.

Taylor, B. (2001) 'The management of labour in Japanese manufacturing plants in China', *International Journal of Human Resource Management*, 12, 4: 601–20.

Taylor, B. and Li, Q. (2007) 'Is the ACFTU a union and does it matter?' *Journal of Industrial Relations*, 49, 5: 701–15.

Taylor, B., Chang, K. and Li, Q. (2003) *Industrial Relations in China*, Cheltenham: Edward Elgar.

Tong, W. D. (2008) 'Progress in the labour disputes system', *Law and Life*, 2: 22–3.

Tsui, A., Egan, T. and O'Reilly, C. (1992) 'Being different: relational demography and organizational attachment', *Administrative Science Quarterly*, 37, 4: 549–79.

Tsui, A., Zhang, Z., Wang, H., Xin, K. and Wu, J. (2006) 'Unpacking the relationship between CEO leadership behavior and organizational culture', *Leadership Quarterly*, 17, 2: 113–37.

Tung, R. L. (2007) 'The human resource challenge to outward foreign direct investment aspirations from emerging economies: the case of China', *International Journal of Human Resource Management*, 18, 5: 868–89.

Unger, J. (ed.) (2008) *Associations and the Chinese State: Contested Spaces*, Armonk, NY: M. E. Sharpe.

Unger, J. and Chan, A. (1995) 'China, corporatism, and the East Asian model', *Australian Journal of Chinese Affairs*, 33, 1: 29–53.

Varma, A., Pichler, S., Budhwar, P. and Biswas, S. (2009) 'Chinese host country nationals' willingness to support expatriates', *International Journal of Cross Cultural Management*, 9, 2: 199–216.

Walder, G. (1995) 'Career mobility and the communist political order', *American Sociological Review*, 60, 3: 309–28.

Walder, G., Li, B. and Treiman, D. (2000) 'Politics and life chances in a state socialist regime: dual career paths into the urban Chinese elite, 1949–96', *American Sociological Review*, 65, 2: 191–209.

Waley, A. (1995 [1938]) *The Analects of Confucius*, London: Routledge.

Wang, G. G., Rothwell, W. J. and Sun, J. Y. (2009) 'Management development in China: a policy analysis', *International Journal of Training and Development*, 13, 4: 205–20.

Wang, H. and Zhang, L. (2008) 'An analysis of the new problems in the implementation of the Labour Disputes Mediation and Arbitration Law', *Market Modernization*, October: 367–8 (in Chinese).

Wang, H. Y. (2006) 'Women rural migrant workers in informal employment and mobility of rural migrant workers families', *Literature and History Overview*, 4: 60–1.

Wang, J. (2005) *Gender Earnings Inequality in Urban China*, Department of Sociology of Yale University.

Wang, J. and Tan, J. B. (2003) 'Creating new opportunities for employment through developing informal employment', *Institutional System Reform*, 12: 545 (in Chinese).

Wang, J. and Wang, G. (2006) 'Exploring national human resource development: a case of China management development in a transitioning context', *Human Resource Development Review*, 5, 2: 176–201.

Wang, K. (2008) 'A changing arena of industrial relations in China: what is happening after 1978', *Employee Relations*, 30, 2: 190–216.

Wang, X., Bruning, N. and Peng, S. Q. (2007) 'Western high performance HR practices in China: a comparison among public-owned, private and foreign-invested enterprises', *International Journal of Human Resource Management*, 18, 4: 684–701.

Wang, Y. (2008) 'Emotional bonds with supervisor and co-workers: relationship to organizational commitment in China's foreign-invested companies', *International Journal of Human Resource Management*, 19, 5: 916–31.

Wang, Z. M. (1999) 'Current models and innovative strategies in management education in China', *Education + Training*, 41, 6/7: 312–18.

Wang, Z. M. and Wang, S. (2008) 'Modelling regional HRM strategies in China: an entrepreneurship perspective', *International Journal of Human Resource Management*, 19, 5: 945–63.

Warner, M. (1993) 'Human resource management "with Chinese characteristics"', *International Journal of Human Resource Management*, 4, 4: 45–65.

Warner, M. (1996) 'Human resources in the People's Republic of China: the "Three Systems" reforms', *Human Resource Management Journal*, 6, 2: 32–42.

Warner, M. (1997) 'Management–labour relations in the new Chinese economy', *Human Resource Management Journal*, 7, 4: 30–43.

Warner, M. (2008) 'Trade unions in China: in search of a new role in the "harmonious society"', in Benson, J. and Zhu, Y. (eds) *Trade Unions in Asia: An Economic and Sociological Analysis*, London: Routledge, pp. 140–56.

Warner, M. (ed.) (2009) *Human Resource Management 'with Chinese Characteristics'*, London: Routledge.

Warner, M. (2010) 'In search of Confucian HRM: theory and practice in Greater China and beyond', *International Journal of Human Resource Management*, 21, 12: 2053–78.

Warner, M. and Goodall, K. (eds) (2010) *Management Training and Development in China*, London: Routledge.

Warner, M. and Ng, S. H. (1999) 'Collective contracts in Chinese enterprises: a new brand of collective bargaining under "market socialism"?' *British Journal of Industrial Relations,* 37, 2: 295–314.

Warner, M. and Zhu, Y. (2010) 'Labour-management relations in the People's Republic of China: seeking the "harmonious society"' *Asia Pacific Business Review*, 16, 3: 285–98.

Wasserstrom, J. (2010) 'Strike out: what the foreign media misses in covering China's labor unrest', 18 June, Internet source: www.foreignpolicy.com/articles/2010/06/18/strike_out, accessed on 28 August 2010.

Watkins, K. and Marsick, V. (1993) *Sculpting the Learning Organisation: The Art and Science of Systematic Change*, San Francisco: Jossey-Bass.

Watts, J. (2010a) 'Chinese workers strike at Honda Lock parts supplier', 11 June, Internet source: www.guardian.co.uk/business/2010/jun/11/honda-china, accessed on 28 August 2010.

Watts, J. (2010b) 'Workers in China grasp the power of the strike', *The Observer*, 4 July, Internet source: http://www.guardian.co.uk/world/2010/jul/04/workers-china-power-strike-communist, accessed on 28 August 2010.

Wei, S. S. (2007) 'Female migrant workers in informal employment', *Journal of Xinyang Agricultural College*, 17, 3: 62–4 (in Chinese).

Wei, L. and Lau, C. M. (2005) 'Market orientation, HRM importance and competency: determinants of strategic HRM in Chinese firms', *International Journal of Human Resource Management*, 16, 10: 1901–18.

Wei, L., Liu, J., Zhang, Y. and Chiu, R. K. (2008) 'The role of corporate culture in the process of strategic human resource management: evidence from Chinese enterprises', *Human Resource Management*, 47, 4: 777–94.

Wei, Q. and Rowley, C. (2009) 'Changing patterns of rewards in Asia: a literature review', *Asia Pacific Business Review*, 15, 4: 489–506.

Wentling, R. (2000) 'Evaluation of diversity initiatives in multinational corporations', *Human Resource Development International*, 3, 4: 435–50.

Westwood, R., Chan, A. and Linstead, S. (2004) 'Theorizing Chinese employment relations comparatively: exchange, reciprocity and the moral economy', *Asia Pacific Journal of Management*, 21, 3: 365–89.

Wheeler, C. (2009) 'Journey to the east as scholars return home', *Times Higher Education*, 30 April: 18–19.

Wilkinson, B., Eberhardt, M., McLaren, J. and Millington, A. (2005) 'Human resource barriers to partnership sourcing in China', *International Journal of Human Resource Management*, 16, 10: 1886–1900.

Williams, K. and O'Reilly, C. (1998) 'Demography and diversity in organizations: a review of 40 years of research', in Staw, B. M. and Cummings, L. L. (eds) *Research in Organizational Behavior 20*, Greenwich, CT: JAI Press, pp. 77–140.

Williams, M. (2000) *The War for Talent: Getting the Best from the Best*, London: Chartered Institute of Personnel and Development.

Williams, R. (2002) *Managing Employee Performance: Design and Implementation in Organisations*, London: Thomson Learning.

Wilson, B. (2008) 'Hidden dragons', *People Management Magazine Online*, http://www.peoplemanagement.co.uk/pm/articles/2008/08/hidden-dragons.htm, accessed on 4 September 2008.

Wise, L. R. and Tsehirhart, M. (2000) 'Examining empirical evidence on diversity effects: how useful is diversity research for public sector managers?' *Public Administration Review*, 60, 5: 386–94.

Wood, S. and Albanese, M. (1995) 'Can you speak of a high commitment management on the shop floor?' *Journal of Management Studies*, 32, 2: 215–47.

Wood, S. and de Menezes, L. (1998) 'High commitment management in the UK: evidence from the Workplace Industrial Relations Survey, and Employers' Manpower and Skills Practices Survey', *Human Relations*, 51, 4: 485–515.

Woodham, C., Lupton, B. and Xian, H. (2009) 'The persistence of gender discrimination in China – evidence from recruitment advertisements', *International Journal of Human Resource Management*, 20, 10: 2084–109.

Workers' Daily, 12 October 2004 (in Chinese).

Workers' Daily, 18 October 2004 (in Chinese).

Workers' Daily, 19 October 2004 (in Chinese).

Workers' Daily, 28 October 2004 (in Chinese).

Workers' Daily, 2 November 2004 (in Chinese).

Workers' Daily, 3 November 2004 (in Chinese).

Workers' Daily, 9 November 2004 (in Chinese).

Workers' Daily, 30 November 2004 (in Chinese).

Workers' Daily, 7 December 2004 (in Chinese).

Workers' Daily, 22 February 2005 (in Chinese).

Workers' Daily, 25 February 2005 (in Chinese).

Workers' Daily, 8 March 2005 (in Chinese).

Workers' Daily, 15 April 2005 (in Chinese).

Workers' Daily, 29 October 2005 (in Chinese).

Workers' Daily, 17 November 2005 (in Chinese).

Workers' Daily, 27 December 2005 (in Chinese).

Wright, P. and Snell, S. (2009) 'Human resources, organizational resources, and capabilities', in Storey, J., Wright, P. and Ulrich, D. (eds) *The Routledge Companion to Strategic Human Resource Management*, London and New York: Routledge, pp. 345–56.

Wright, P., Szeto, W. and Cheng, L. (2002) '*Guanxi* and professional conduct in China: a management development perspective', *International Journal of Human Resource Management*, 13, 1: 156–82.

Wu, W. (2008) 'An estimation of the size of informal employment in the urban area in China', *Journal of Chongqing Technology Business University*, 1: 79–83 (in Chinese).

Wu, X., (2009) 'Income inequality and distributive justice: a comparative analysis of mainland China and Hong Kong', *China Quarterly*, 200: 1033–52.

Xiao, Y. C. and Cooke, F. L. (2010) 'Managerial career for women auditors in accountancy and consultancy firms in China: convention, aspiration and choice', unpublished working paper.

Xin, K. and Pearce, J. L. (1996) '*Guanxi*: connections as substitutes for formal institutional support', *Academy of Management Journal*, 39, 6: 1641–58.

Xu, F. (2009) 'The emergence of temporary staffing agencies in China', *Comparative Labor Law and Policy Journal*, 30, 2: 431–62.

Xu, K. (2000) 'Women in China', http://www.onlinewomeninpolitics.org/china/feschina.pdf, accessed on 13 November 2005.

Xu, K. and Luo, J. Q. (2008) 'Softening the Labour Contract Law', *Development and Management of Human Resources*, 12: 86–8 (in Chinese).

Xu, X. L. (2009) 'A study of factors influencing job quit intent amongst technicians in foreign-invested and privately owned electronics manufacturing plants', *Science and Technology Management Research*, 7: 349–51 (in Chinese).

Xue, F. and Wu, Z. H. (2009) 'Empirical study on difference of compensation incentive between family CEOs and non-family CEOs', *East China Economic Management*, 23, 9: 127–31 (in Chinese).

Yamazaki, Y. and Kayes, C. (2010) 'Learning and work satisfaction in Asia: a comparative study of Japanese, Chinese and Malaysian managers', *International Journal of Human Resource Management*, 21, 12: 2271–89.

Yang, B. and Wang, X. (2009) 'Successes and challenges of developing human capital in the People's Republic of China', *Human Resource Development International*, 12, 1: 3–14.

Yang, H. Q. and Li, J. (2008) 'An empirical study of the employment quality of university graduates', *Labor Economy and Labor Relations*, 2: 87–90 (in Chinese).

Yang, L. and Wu, X. L. (2006) 'An overview of enterprise superannuation fund', *Development and Management of Human Resources*, 6: 55–62 (in Chinese).

Yangcheng Evening News, 8 August 2003 (in Chinese).

Yangzi Evening News, 29 March 2001 (in Chinese).

Yi, Y. (2009) 'An analysis of some stock-listed firms' pay incentives in the machinery engineering sector between 2004 and 2008', *Construction Machinery Today*, 8: 100–3 (in Chinese).

Yu, H. (2006) 'Performance management of the Chinese style', *Development and Management of Human Resources*, 1: 34–5 (in Chinese).

Yu, K. C. (1998) 'Chinese employees' perceptions of distributive fairness', in Francesco, A. M. and Gold, B. A. (eds) *International Organisational Behavior*, Upper Saddle River, NJ: Prentice Hall, pp. 302–13.

Yuan, J., Yuan, C. and Deng, X. (2008) 'The effects of manager compensation and market competition on financial fraud in public companies: an empirical study in China', *International Journal of Management*, 25, 2: 322–35.

Zang, X. (2007) 'Interpreting the Employment Promotion Law: the government's responsibility in the employment of university graduates', *Legal System and Society*, 9: 534–5 (in Chinese).

Zhai, Y. J. (2008) 'The difficulty and challenge of labour inspection in China', *Administration and Law*, 8: 75–9 (in Chinese).

Zhang, A. Y., Tsui, A. S., Song, L. J., Li, C. and Jia, L. (2008) 'How do I trust thee? The employee–organization relationship, supervisory support, and middle manager trust in the organization', *Human Resource Management*, 47, 1: 111–32.

Zhang, D., Zhang, Z. and Yang, B. (2004) 'Learning organization in mainland China: empirical research on its applications to Chinese state-owned enterprises', *International Journal of Training and Development*, 8, 4: 258–73.

Zhang, J. S., Han, J., Liu, P. W. and Zhao, Y. H. (2008) 'Trends in the gender earnings differential in urban China, 1988–2004', *Industrial and Labor Relations Review*, 61, 2: 224–43.

Zhang, L. B. (2004) 'On the definition and policy of "informal employment"', *Economic Research Reference*, 81: 38–43 (in Chinese).

Zhang, L. B. (2007) 'Establishing informal social security for workers in informal employment', *Local Fiscal Studies*, 7, 39–42 (in Chinese).

Zhang, L. H. (2005) 'A case study analysis of the remuneration change strategy of a state-owned enterprise', *Development and Management of Human Resources*, 11: 47–9 (in Chinese).

Zhang, M. and Zhao, L. L. (1999) 'The situation of labour protection for female workers in Guangdong Province', *China National Conditions and Strength*, 12: 37 (in Chinese).

Zhang, Y. C. and Li, S. L. (2009) 'High performance work practices and firm performance: evidence from the pharmaceutical industry in China', *International Journal of Human Resource Management*, 20, 11: 2331–48.

Zhang, Y. H. (2008) 'On labour rights protection for workers in informal sector', *Journal of China Institute of Industrial Relations*, 1: 43–6 (in Chinese).

Zhao, P. and Ma, X. P. (2007) 'Raising the quality of human capital: a study of informal employment for unemployed women', *Hubei Social Science*, 8: 76–9 (in Chinese).

Zhao, S. (2008) 'Application of human capital theory in China in the context of the knowledge economy', *International Journal of Human Resource Management*, 19, 5: 802–17.

Zheng, W. (2000) 'Gender, employment and women's resistance', in Perry, E. and Selden, M. (eds) *Chinese Society: Change, Conflict and Resistance*, London: Routledge, pp. 62–82.

Zheng, X. C. (2007) 'Development, fairness and balance: a review of human resources in China in 2006 and prospect in the context of social harmony', *Development and Management of Human Resources*, 5: 38–43 (in Chinese).

Zheng, X. Y. (2001) 'Census and gender statistics', *Collection of Women's Studies*, 40, 3: 11–15 (in Chinese).

Zhou, F. (2002) 'What does it mean when foreign investors enter the talent market?' *Development and Management of Human Resources*, 2: 4–6 (in Chinese).

Zhou, X. (2000) 'Economic transformation an income inequality in urban China: evidence from panel data', *American Journal of Sociology*, 105, 4: 1135–74.

Zhou, X., Tuma, N. and Moen, P. (1997) 'Institutional change and job-shift patterns in urban China, 1949–94', *American Sociological Review*, 62, 3: 339–65.

Zhu, C. (2005) *Human Resource Management in China: Past, Current and Future HR Practices in the Industrial Sector*, London: Routledge.

Zhu, C. and Dowling, P. (1998) 'Performance appraisal in China', in Selmer, J. (ed.) *International Management in China: Cross-Cultural Issues*, London: Routledge, pp. 115–36.

Zhu, C. and Dowling, P. (2002) 'Staffing practices in transition: some empirical evidence from China', *International Journal of Human Resource Management*, 13, 4: 569–97.

Zhu, C., Cooper, B., De Cieri, H. and Dowling, P. (2005) 'A problematic transition to a strategic role: human resource management in industrial enterprises in China', *International Journal of Human Resource Management*, 16, 4: 513–31.

Zhu, L. (2001) 'Problems in the expansion of employment in the local communities and solutions', *Employment in China*, 9: 29–33 (in Chinese).

Zimmerman, A., Liu, X. and Buck, T. (2009) 'Employee tenure and the nationality of joint ventures in China', *International Journal of Human Resource Management*, 20, 11: 2271–91.

Zou, M. and Lansbury, R. (2009) 'Multinational corporations and employment relations in the People's Republic of China: the case of Beijing Hyundai Motor Company', *International Journal of Human Resource Management*, 20, 11: 2349–69.

Index

accountability, individual 76
age: discrimination on grounds of 16,
121–3; organizational commitment in
relation to 210; traditional respect
for 74–5
Akhtar, S. 204
All-China Federation of Trade Unions
(ACFTU) 10–11, 141, 151, 154–5;
administrative structure 137; and
Chinese Communist Party 10–11,
17, 135–6; *chuangzheng* initiative
48; collective consultation by 135;
functions of 10, 17, 136; funding of
10, 136; and informal employment
35; Labour Disputes Mediation and
Arbitration Law 174; membership
of 138–40, 142–3, 145; response to
economic transformation 143; role
in training and development 46–7;
workplace organization 143, 145, 150
All-China Women's Federation
(ACWF) 118, 146–8; role in training
and development 46
American Chamber of Commerce 168
Appelbaum, E. 205
Appleton, S. 92–3
Arkless, D. 24
Arredondo, P. 113
Aycan, Z. 128

Bai, X. 69, 76
Bailey, J. 75–6
Baker, L. 190–1
Bao Steel 49
bargaining power 76, 98, 153, 173; and
informal employment 37; weakness of
131, 133; *see also* collective bargaining
Batt, R. 205
Bauer, J. 99

Beijing Hyundai Motor Company
(BHMC) 38
Bellemere, G. 4, 6
benchmarking: of business operations 53;
of financial rewards 89, 104, 110, 153,
202; of leadership competences 190–1
Bennington, L. 69, 76
Bian, Y. 91, 93–4
Birdi, K. 53
Bishop, A.J. 92
Björkman, I. 68, 89, 102
Boisot, G. 181
bonuses 59, 88; equitable distribution
of 75; and performance management 72,
83, 101, 103, 195; in the state sector 89
Bosch, G. 4
Bozionelos, N. 81
'brain drain' 23
Branine, M. 188–9
Bu, N. 197
business ownership: growth in new
forms of 3–4; influence on HRM
policies 206–7
business schools 6, 45, 185–6, 202

career development opportunities 27, 207;
and employee turnover 23, 41; and
employer discrimination 98–9; in the
private sector 192–3; through working
abroad 26
career skills, development of 25–6
casual employment 33–4
Chan, C.K. 151
Chan, D. 121, 132
Chan, K.W. 25
Chang, K. 154
Chang, S. 207
Chartered Institute of Personnel and
Development (CIPD) 113–14, 128

Chen, F. 134, 136
Chen, H. 82
Chen, H.W. 59–60
Chen, H.Y. 182
Chen, M.Z. 72
Cheng, B.S. 183
Cheung, M.F. 183
Chi, W. 92, 95
Child, J. 89
childcare 129–30; affordability of 122;
    career breaks for 95;
    by family networks 124;
    government investment in 117
China Enterprise Confederation
    (CEC) 11, 47, 175
China Europe International Business
    School (CEIBS) 186
China Europe Management Institute 186
Chinese Communist Party (CCP) 143;
    and All-China Federation of Trade
    Unions 10–11, 17, 135–6; membership
    and political capital 93–4, 100;
    protection of women's employment
    rights 117
Chinese Household Income Projects (1988
    and 1995) 91
Chou, B. 83
Chow, I.H. 58, 205
chuangzheng initiative 47–9, 55, 64
Civil Servant Law of China (2006) 69, 136
civil service: corruption in 72;
    performance appraisal in 68–9, 72,
    80–1, 83; and trade unions 141
Clarke, S. 11, 153
co-habitation 124
collective bargaining 89, 134, 151
collectively-owned enterprises
    (COEs) 3; downsizing of 116, 121;
    gender discrimination in 95, 98, 118;
    and state socialist personnel system
    206; and trade unions 142, 145
collectivism 75–6, 208–9
commission-based wages 38, 103
competitive advantage: highly skilled
    labour as a source of 44; and human
    resource management 20
Confucian values 65, 110, 124, 183, 201
continuous learning 53, 59
contracts of employment 33, 36–7; and
    informal employment 33; and Labour
    Contract Law 161, 164, 170; and social
    security provision 170–1; unlawful
    clauses in 37

Cooke, F.L. 56, 71, 75, 108, 119, 129–30,
    151–2, 193, 202, 211; diversity
    management 112, 122, 160; employee
    participation and innovation 54;
    employee welfare 107; enterprise
    culture-building 41; enterprise training
    system 44; gender pay gap 96, 99–100;
    graduate management training 192;
    informal employment 33, 36; Labour
    Contract Law 161; life-long learning
    48; pay increases 58–9; pay systems
    88–9, 101; performance management
    69–70, 74, 81; 'post-80 generation' 23;
    post-graduate students 25; role of the
    state 8; rural migrant workers 120–1,
    123; skills shortage 57–8; succession
    planning 192; talent management
    29, 42; trade unions 139–42, 146;
    training and development 58, 61–2, 65;
    workforce discrimination 116–18, 123
Cooney, S. 133, 157, 179
corporate culture 27
corporate social responsibility 9–10, 150,
    177, 213
corruption 72, 103
Cox, T. 113
Cultural Revolution (1966–76) 68
cultural values *see* traditional cultural
    values

'decent work' 33
delegation of managerial tasks 181
Deloitte Human Capital
    Consulting 79, 82
demographics: influence on HRM
    outcomes 210–11; and talent
    management 20
Deng Xiaoping 8, 65
Development Dimensions
    International 24
Dickens, L. 16
Ding, D.Z. 68
dishonest employee behaviour 103
dispatch labour 37–8
diversity, definition of 113
diversity management 112–13; cultural
    characteristics of 124–5; and employee
    age structure 16, 121–3; and gender
    122–3; and HRM strategy 113–14,
    125; key organizational issues 125–31;
    monitoring of 128; objectives of 113;
    and residential status 119–21; and
    women workers 19

divorce 124
downsizing of organizations 1, 4, 33, 116, 121

Easterby-Smith, M. 75
Economic and Enterprise Reforms 4
Economic globalization 8
economic growth 9, 40, 45, 173, 199
economic policy 2, 76
economic transformation of China 1–4, 14, 76, 91–2, 118; ACFTU response to 143
education and development 23, 28; employer sponsorship of 27, 41, 102; and enhancement of career prospects 27; investment in 21, 65
educational attainment: gender gap in 91; and gender pay gap 94–5; and organizational commitment 210; and seniority 94
Edwards, P. 153
egalitarianism 2; in the pay system 89, 110, 124; traditional respect for 75
Eleventh Five-Year Plan (2001–05) 44–5
EMBA (Executive Master of Business Administration) qualification 18, 58, 186–90, 197
embedded systems 53
employee assistance programmes 31
employee bargaining power *see* bargaining power
employee empowerment *see* empowerment of employees
employee-manager relationships 24–5
employee turnover *see* turnover of employees
employee welfare 22, 32, 105–8
employer discrimination; and gender pay gap 98–9; on grounds of age 121–2; legal prevention of 160; and rural migrant workers 119–21; and women workers 116–19
employer staffing policies 38; flexible labour strategies 37–9; reduction of labour costs 38–9, 42; use of employment agencies 12, 37
employers' associations 11; growth in power of 175; training and development role of 62–4
employment: participation of women in 90–1; quality of 40; and type of business ownership 3–4

employment agencies 12–13, 37; characteristics of 12; and competitive advantage 12; growth of 12; and Labour Contract Law 175–6; regulation of 12, 149, 175–6; representation of workers 147–9
employment brokering 37–8
employment contracts *see* contracts of employment
employment laws and regulations 156–79; interconnection between 158; non-compliance with 37; *see also* Employment Promotion Law; Labour Contract Law; Labour Disputes Mediation and Arbitration Law; Labour Law of China
Employment Promotion Law (2007) 17, 156–7, 159–60, 166, 168, 170, 176
empowerment of employees 40, 53, 55, 102
Enterprise Minimum Wage Regulation (1993) 156
enterprise training system 45
equal opportunities management 112, 116; *see also* diversity management
European Union Chamber of Commerce 168
Executive Master of Business Administration qualification *see* EMBA
exploitation of workers 38, 140, 145, 155
export-manufacturing zones 17, 64, 200
export-oriented manufacturing plants: labour standards in 177; welfare benefits in 107
external labour markets 40, 199–200

'face', value of 75, 124, 182
family-friendly initiatives 128–9
family networks 124, 130
Fan, P.-L. 94
Farrell, D. 22
Felfe, J. 208, 210
Feng, G. 154
financial rewards: benchmarking of 89, 104, 110, 153, 202; andcorruption 103; and motivation 15, 24, 30–1, 40–1, 70, 101–3, 110; andretention of staff 24, 30, 101–2, 110, 204; *see also* bonuses; performance-related pay; stock options
500,000 Senior Technicians in Three Years' plan 45, 48
'flexi-working arrangements 41, 127–8

flexible employment *see* informal employment
flexible labour strategies 37–9
foreign client firms, labour standards of 176
foreign direct investment (FDI) 1, 184
foreign expatriate employees 125–6, 209
foreign-invested enterprises (FIEs): HRM practices in 207; married women employees 95; overseas returnee employees 23; performance appraisal in 68, 75; trade unions in 140; training and development in 60
Foxconn International Holdings Ltd 107, 152
Frege, C. 6, 8
Fudge, J. 156

Gamble, J. 37–8
Gao, J. 35
Gao, J.H. 69, 209
Gao, W.S. 123
gender discrimination 90, 92, 100, 116–19; and age 122–3; and residential status 123
gender pay gap 90–1, 118; causes of 93–101; patterns in 91–3
gender roles 99–101
gender segregation in the labour market 100; by industry 97; and the pay gap 96, 98
global financial crisis (2008) 27, 153, 170
globalization 8, 11, 20–1
Gong, Y. 207
Goodall, K. 186
Goto, S. 121, 132
government: development of talent 28–9; employment rights 199; human capital development 45; mobilization of institutional actors 57; promotion of informal employment 36; response to strike action 153; role in HRM and HRD 8; training policies and initiatives 45–52; *see also* local government
government organizations: downsizing of 1, 4, 33; performance appraisal in 68–9, 72, 80–1, 83; women employees in 94
graduate employment: 'brain drain' 23; career aspirations 25–8; career skills 25–6; choice of employer 25–8; Labour Contract Law 169–70; management training programmes 192;

starting salary levels 27; training and development in 57; *see also* overseas graduates
Grant, A. 22
guanxi concept 188, 199, 209
Guo, L. 181
Gustafsson, B. 91–2

haigui see overseas returnee employees
Hall, M.J. 16
Han, J. and J. 30, 42
harmonious working environments 31–2, 47, 75
harmony, traditional value of 74, 84, 124, 182, 208
He, P. 34
health and safety protection 119–20, 140, 213
Heery, E. 6, 8, 145
Hempel, P.S. 75, 83
hierarchy, respect for 74–5, 124
high performance/commitment model 19, 21, 40–1, 57, 101–2, 201, 205–6, 208, 210
higher education: expansion of 21–2, 28, 65; and gender pay gap 94; participation of women in 90
Holtom, B. 41–2
homosexuality 124
Honda Motor Company 145, 154
Hong, J.F.L. 210
Hong Kong: performance appraisal in 75; registration of Chinese businesses 170
Horwitz, F. 40, 102
Hotel Association Professional Management Committee 46
housing and housing benefits 27, 125–6
Howard, A. 24–5, 183
Howell, J. 155
Hu, A.G. 34–5
Hu Jintao 8
Huang, K. 76, 84–5
Huang, Q. 37–8
Huawei Technologies Ltd: corporate culture 70–1; performance management in 70; response to the Labour Contract Law 169; reward strategy 104–6; training and development in 60–1
Huawei University 60
Hughes, J. 95
Hui, C. 25, 182
hukou system 119

human capital, development of 28, 41; and future employment prospects 102; and gender pay gap 95, 100; role of the state in 45

human relations consultancy firms 13, 178

human relations professional qualifications 47

human resources development (HRD): funding of 65; institutional actors 44; role of the state in 8–10; in small and medium-sized enterprises 60; state-led initiatives on 44–5; systematic approach to 65;

human resources management (HRM) practices: Chinese context of 203–5; and Chinese cultural values 201, 207–10; competence in 47, 201–2, 212; and competitive advantage 20; demographic influences on 210–11; and diversity management 113–14, 125; empowerment initiatives 40; and financial rewards 40, 101; formal policies for 125, 127; high performance/ commitment model 19, 21, 40–1, 57, 101–2, 201, 205–6, 208, 210; function of 211–12; humanistic approaches to 41, 82, 102; hygiene factors 41; in industrial sectors 206–7; laws and regulations on 9, 169; mentoring schemes 61–2; new developments in 202; and performance management 67–8; practices of private firms 40; and retention of staff 20, 21–5; role of the state in 8–10, 201; strategic approach to 201–3; in the state socialist economy 3–4; and talent management 20, 29–33, 42, 192; and turnover 21–2; and types of ownership 206–7

Hutchings, K. 59

hygiene factors 40–1, 102

Hyman, R. 142

incentivization *see* motivation of employees

industrial relations competence 47

informal employment 33–7, 42; and competitive industries 35; and social security provision 33, 36, 108; terms and conditions of 36–7; of women 118

injuries, work-related 37

innovation *see* workplace innovation

insourcing 37

institutional actors 4, 6, 8–13; definition of 4, 6; emergence 174–5; and human resource development 44; impact of labour laws on 167; interrelations between 168

International Labour Organization (ILO) 33

international trade union organizations 11

interpersonal relationships,value of 25

'iron rice bowl' concept 168–9

Jiao, X.K. 108

jigong see technical workers, training of

Jin, X.Y. 129–30

job insecurity 38, 73, 117, 181, 207

job responsibility 89

job satisfaction and dissatisfaction 41, 182–3, 204

job security 18, 33, 74, 129, 147–8; and informal employment 36, 42; for state sector workers 206–7; *see also* job insecurity

jobs for life 2, 25, 124, 168

joint ventures *see* foreign-invested enterprises

Kao, H.S. 182

Kayes, C. 190

Kelly, J. 145

knowledge management 48, 53–4, 65

knowledge workers 40, 44, 47, 102. 212

Kochan, T. 114

Labour Contract Law (2007) 13, 17, 57, 108, 152, 157, 160–4, 168–71; and age discrimination 121; and contracts of employment 161, 170–1; and employee rights 134; and exploitation of workers 38; impact on institutional actors 167; influence of China Enterprise Confederation on 11; and informal employment 37; and labour disputes 149–50, 161, 163–4; and multinational corporations 177; non-compliance with 161, 179; and non-governmental organizations 176–8; and rural migrant workers 120; and trade unions 135; and wage arrears 161; and workers' rights 136

labour costs: and the Labour Contract Law 167, 169; reduction of 38–9, 42

labour disputes 107, 129, 151–4; mediation in 165–6; rising level of 133, 150, 161, 163–4, 172

Labour Disputes Mediation and
   Arbitration Law (2008) 13, 17–18, 57,
   152, 157, 164–6; abolition of arbitration
   fees 165, 172–3; funding of arbitration
   bodies 173; impact on institutional
   actors 167; and informal employment
   37; and labour disputes 150, 171–2; and
   rural migrant workers 120; and trade
   union regulation 174; and workers'
   rights 136
Labour Law of China (1995) 36, 121,
   135, 140
Labour Market Wage Rate Guideline
   (1999) 156
labour markets: demand and supply in 20;
   gender segregation in 96–8; prospects
   of employees 41; regulation of 8, 18;
   transformation of 199–200
labour mobility 20–1, 107, 123, 132, 140,
   164, 169, 200
labour rights 152; and informal
   employment 36–7; of rural migrant
   workers 119; workers' awareness of 200
labour shortages 120, 122, 200
labour standards 37, 157, 176–7
Lam, W. 204
Lansbury, R. 38
Lau, C.M. 201
Law, K. 205
leadership 180; autocratic styles of 182;
   and employee retention 25; of global
   businesses 190–1; and paternalism
   182–3; strategic 53; training for 42
learning organizations 47, 49, 64;
   central imperatives of 53; Chinese
   interpretation of 54–6, 65; as a western
   concept 52–4, 64
Lee, C.K. 122, 151, 153
legal centres for representation of workers
   147, 149–50
Li, B. 92, 95
Li, J. 40, 57
Li, M. 153
Li, S. 91–2
Li, S.L. 204
Li, W. 210
Li, Y. 64
Li, Y.B. 149, 182
Li, Y.Y. 123
life-long learning 48, 65; government
   promotion of 44
Lindholm, N. 69
Liu, P. 92

Liu, S. 124
Liu, S.S. 58
Liu, Y. 123
living standards 89, 105, 107, 130, 199
local government: and employment
   agencies 12, 176; funding of arbitration
   bodies 173; and representation
   of workers 146–8; training and
   development role of 46
local urban resident status 39
loyalty, reciprocal 41, 102
Lu, Y. 68, 89, 102

Mackenzie, R. 8
McKinsey & Company 184
management: Chinese style of 180–2;
   education and development of 45,
   184–92; gender differences in 197–8;
   influence of cultural values on 182–4; in
   the private sector 191–6
management by objectives 69
management competence 22, 180, 196;
   deficiencies in 9, 55, 58, 185; desired
   aspects of 191; and managerial
   frustration 182; and performance
   management 78–80; premature
   promotion 181–2
Manpower China 22, 24, 184
Marini, M. 94
marital status: and gender pay gap 95–6;
   and organizational commitment 210
marketization: of the economy 1, 21,
   65, 99, 133, 200; and employment
   services 12; and gender pay gap 92–3,
   100–1; and labour disputes 133–4; and
   materialism 24; and pay systems 87–8;
   and recruitment practices 42
Marsick, V. 53
Martin, R. 56
Martinez Lucio, M. 8
Maslow's hierarchy of needs 101
mass organizations 10
Master of Business Administration *see*
   MBA
materialism 24
Maurer-Fazio, M. 92, 95
MBA (Master of Business Administration)
   qualification 18, 186–8
medical insurance 108–9
Meng, X. 95
mentoring schemes 32, 61–2
Michelson, G. 6, 8
middle management 22, 183–4, 194

migration *see* labour mobility
Miller, P. 95
mingong huang see labour shortages
minimum wage levels 37
Ministry of Education 47, 186–7
Ministry of Enterprise Training 46
Ministry of Human Resources and Social
    Security 108
Ministry of Labour and Social Security 2,
    175; '500,000 Senior Technicians in
    Three Years' plan 45, 48; launch of HR
    professional qualification 47; Provisions
    on Collective Contracts (1994) 134
Ministry of Personnel 2, 72
money as a hygiene factor 40
monopoly service industries 35
Morris, J. 206
motivation of employees 42, 70, 110; by
    financial rewards 15, 24, 30–1, 40–1,
    70, 101–3, 110; and Maslow's hierarchy
    of needs 101; mechanisms for 14–15,
    31–2, 110; and performance appraisal
    72, 80–2; and personal recognition 80;
    and welfare benefits 107
Mu, J. 149
multinational corporations (MNCs): as
    employers of choice 26; HRM practices
    in 206–7; and Labour Contract Law
    177; migration of labour to 20–1;
    performance management in 69–70,
    75; recruitment of managers by 22;
    talent shortages in 184–5; training and
    development in 65, 191–2; western
    management theories about 186

Nathwani, A. 128
National Conference of *Chuangzheng*
    Promotion (2004) 48–9
National Employee Innovation Expert
    awards 49
National Employee Innovation Model unit
    awards 49
National MBA Supervisory Committee
    187
National Model of *Chuangzheng*
    Enterprises awards 49
National Model Learning Organization
    awards 49
National People's Congress 175
National People's Consultative
    Conference 175
National Training Plan for Rural Migrant
    Workers *see* Sunshine Project

National Training Programme for
    Advanced Technical Talents 48
Ngo, H.Y. 207
NGOs *see* non-governmental organizations
Nishii, L. 84
non-governmental organizations (NGOs)
    10; compliance with Labour Contract
    Law 177; and monitoring of labour
    standards 150, 176–8
non-standard employment *see* informal
    employment

older employees, benefits valued by 27
'one child' policy 23, 129, 199; and
    childcare 122, 129
'open door' policy 2; and participation in
    higher education 21, 29
Ortenblad, A. 53–4
overseas graduates 125–6
overseas returnee employees: government
    policy for attraction of 28–9;
    satisfaction with 23

part-time employment 33
paternalism 26, 41, 54, 102, 110, 128, 208
pay and benefits: composition of 88; and
    employee turnover 24, 41; andtotal
    rewards 22, 27; *see also* bonuses;
    financial rewards; performance-related
    pay; stock options
pay system 87; characteristics of 88–90;
    company-based welfare benefits 106–8;
    gender pay gaps and 90–101; private
    sector practices 101–8; social security
    provision 108–9
Pedler, M. 53
Peng, K.Z. 210
pension funds 9
performance management and appraisal
    67–71, 209; behaviour and outcome
    measurement 72; Chinese cultural
    influence on 72, 74–6, 80, 86; collective
    peer appraisal 83; cultural barriers to
    84–5; development of systems for 68–9;
    and financial rewards 68–70, 72, 79–80;
    key characteristics of 73; influence of
    organizational size and type 72–4; and
    managerial competence 78–80, 85;
    influence of; perceived as a formality
    80–1; self-appraisal 74–5, 83; and
    senior management 76–9; subjective
    nature of 81–3; 360-degree appraisal
    systems 79, 85

performance-related pay 30, 32, 69, 89, 101–2, 104, 110; and motivation 15; problems with 106
poaching of staff 15, 23, 57, 63–4
political capital 68; from membership of Chinese Communist Party 93–4, 100; and gender pay gap 93–4
'post-80 generation' 23
pressure groups 11, 63, 122, 168, 174–5
PricewaterhouseCoopers 129
Pringle, T. 153
private enterprises: growth of 4; HRM practices of 40; incentivization of employees in 42; performance appraisal in 69–70, 72; reward management in 110; training and development in 60, 65; transactional nature of employment relations in 41; welfare benefits provision in 107
private sector: management development in 191–6; pay system in 89; promotion and career development in 192–3
privatizationof state-owned enterprises 9, 91, 98, 133, 176
professionalization of occupations 46–7
profit-related pay 30, 32, 103
promotion and career development 55, 93–4, 102, 131, 192–3; age discrimination in 121; *chuangzheng* initiative 48–9; employee dissatisfaction with 24; gender discrimination in 96, 98–9, 123; of graduate employees 124, 126; and performance management 32, 68–9, 72–3, 75, 79; and staff turnover 29, 41
Provisions on Collective Contracts (1994) 134
public sector organizations: downsizing of 1, 4, 33; performance appraisal in 80; and trade unions 141

Qiao, J. 204, 210
Quintas, P. 53

Ralston, D. 182–3
recognition of achievements 31, 41
recruitment and staffing 20; cost of 169; employee's choice of employer 25–8; employee referral schemes 30; employer discrimination 98–9; financial rewards 102; and Labour Contract Law 169; managerial and professional 22; poaching of staff 15, 23, 57, 63–4; in

private firms 29–33; of ready-trained employees 29–30
Regulation on Enterprise Superannuation (2004) 9
Regulation on Enterprise Superannuation Fund Management (2005) 9
Regulation and Labour Market Management (2000) 156
Regulation on Talent Market Management (2002) 13
Regulations for State Civil Servants (1993) 69
Regulations on Employment Services and Management (2008) 156
repatriation of overseas talent 28–9
residential status of employees 39, 42; and discrimination 116, 119–21, 123
retention of staff 20, 21–5, 42; drivers of 23–5; employee's choice of employer 25–8; and employee-manager relationships 24–5; and financial rewards 24, 30, 101–2, 110, 204; and performance management 70–1; private firms' approaches to 29–33; in relation to training and development 60; wage premiums for 64
Rodgers, J. 108
Rowley, C. 87
Roy, J.P. 197
Rozelle, S. 93
rural migrant workers: ACFTU membership 140; discrimination against 119–21; labour rights of 119; and marketization of the economy 1; medical care insurance for 108–9; migration to urban areas 33; Sunshine Project 46; training and development of 46; unionization of 144; wage arrears of 37
Rynes, S. 101

Schuler, R. 20
seasonal employment 33
self-organization of workers 150–5
seniority: and authority 124; and education 94; and gender equality 118; and gender pay gap 93; as predictor of earnings 89; traditional respect for 74–5
Shambaugh, D.
Sheldon, P. 64
shock events, management of 41–2
Shu, X. 91, 93–4
Si, L. 27
Si, S.X. 182

sickness benefits 37
Simms, M. 145
Singapore 40, 102
skill shortages 9, 20, 64; and further
    education 27, 29; government measure
    on 28–9, 44–5; as an innovation
    bottleneck 44; in private firms 29;
    training programmes directed at 45;
    worsening of 21, 23, 45
Snell, R.S. 210
social exclusion 108
social harmony 8, 74, 124, 208; and
    ACFTU 143; traditional respect for 74
social security provision 9, 27, 108–9;
    employers not contributing to 37; and
    informal employment 33, 36, 108; and
    Labour Contract Law 170–1; in the
    private sector 89; regulation of 108; for
    rural migrant workers 119
social status: awareness of 124; and
    employee turnover 24; and informal
    employment 35–6; social value of
    gender roles 99–101
socialist ideology 2, 21; in the pay system
    89, 92; pursuit of universalism 116
Society for Human Resource
    Management 24
South Africa 40, 102
State Council 118–19
State Economic Commission 185
state-invested companies 23
state-monopolized industries 35
state-owned enterprises (SOEs): autonomy
    of 8, 44, 97; downsizing of 1, 4, 33,
    116; employee involvement in 56; as
    employers of choice 26–7; employment
    relations in 199; flexible employment
    strategies of 39; gender discrimination
    in 118; HRM practices in 207;
    international managerial recruitment
    to 29; 'learning organization' practices
    in 55; managerial competence in 27,
    185; married women employees of
    95; performance appraisal in 69, 72;
    privatization of 9, 91, 98, 133, 176;
    reform of employment practices in
    38; trade unions in 142; training and
    development in 60
state sector workers: job security for 1,
    207; pay system for 89; psychological
    and social contracts of 199; and
    transformation of state socialist
    economy 1–4; two-tier workforce of 39;
    workplace benefits of 1

stock options 30–2, 101–2, 104–5, 110
Storey, J. 53
strategic leadership 53
strike action 120, 133–4, 155; government
    response to 153; at *Honda* Motor
    Company 145; right to engage in 134;
    spontaneous 151–4
subsidies 88–9
succession planning 32, 192
Sunshine Project 46
superannuation schemes *see* pension funds
supervisory support 183
Suzhou Industrial Plant 64
sweatshop plants 38, 107
system connections 53

talent management 20, 29–33, 42, 192
talent shortages 21–5, 57, 184; government
    measure on 28–9; and limitations
    on growth 22, 184; in multinational
    corporations 184–5; premature
    managerial promotion 181–2
Taormina, R.J. 69, 209
Tarique, I. 20
Taylor, B. 206
Taylor, Frederick (and Taylorism) 55,
    189, 206
team learning 53
technical workers, training of 45–6
temporary employment 33
'Thousand Talents Plan' (2008) 28
Tiananmen Square event (1989) 135
tongxiang hui 151
Trade Union Law (2001) 56, 134–6
trade unions 10–11; collective negotiation
    by 89; efficacy of 145–6; and foreign-
    invested companies 140; and informal
    employment 36; regulation of 174;
    representation of women by 118,
    141; responsibilities of 135; role in
    development 56–7; three models of
    142–3; welfare function of 141–2;
    workers' perception of 145–6; and
    Workers' Representatives Congress
    140–1
traditional Chinese management style 52,
    54–5, 181–4
traditional cultural values 21, 25,
    41, 67; collectivism 75–6, 208–9;
    Confucianism 65, 110, 124, 183, 201;
    and harmony 74, 84, 124, 182, 208;
    and HRM practices 201, 207–10; and
    management 182–4; and paternalism
    26, 41, 54, 102, 110, 128, 208; and

patriarchy 100; and performance appraisal 72, 74–6; reciprocal loyalty 41, 102; and spiritual recognition 31, 41
training and development 65; employee-led programmes of 58–9; employer sponsorship of 27, 41, 102; and employers' associations 62–4; employers' unwillingness to invest in 29, 41, 57; '500,000 Senior Technicians in Three Years' plan 45, 48; formal plans for 60; and informal employment 36; internal delivery of 59–60; investment in 44, 59; of managerial and professional workers 184–91; provision by employers of 21, 29, 46, 57–64; and retention of staff 60; through skill-based programmes 45; state involvement in 45–52, 196–7; Sunshine Project 46; technical focus of 60; and turnover of employees 57–8; uneven distribution of 59; western-developed programmes of 189; *see also* education and development 23, 28
Trial Regulation on Enterprise Superannuation (2004) 9
turnover of employees 20–2; and economic status 24; reasons for 23–5, 41, 71; and shock events 42; traditional approaches to understanding 41; and training 29, 57–8
two-tier workforce 39

unemployment 110; age discrimination and 121; graduates and 94, 121, 159; higher educational enrolment and 28; rates of 20
unitarism 54
United Nations Development Programme 189
universalism 116
urbanization 119

Varma, A. 209
vendor representatives 38
vocational education 45–6
Vosko, L. 156

wage arrears 37; and Labour Contract Law 162
wage determination 89
wage premiums 64
wages *see* pay and benefits
Walder, G. 94

Wal-Mart 135
Wang, G. 58, 84, 183, 186–9
Wang, J. 58, 84. 92, 183, 186–9
Wang, L. 81
Wang, X. 60, 65, 201
Wang, Y. 183, 209
Wang, Z.M. 185, 188, 196
'war for talent' 20–1
Warner, M. 154, 186
Watkins, K. 53
Watts, J. 153
Wei, L. 201, 205
Wei, Q. 87
Wen Jiabao 8, 153
Wentling, R. 113
western HRM practices 19, 64, 203; adoption of 201; in a Chinese context 203–5; cultural barriers to adoption of 84–5; humanistic orientation of 41, 82, 102; and 'learning organizations' 52–4
Westwood, R. 208
Wilkinson, B. 103
Wilson, B. 22
Work China Employee Attitude Survey 24
work-life balance 31, 41, 128–31
worker exploitation *see* exploitation of workers
Worker's Daily newspaper 48
workers' representation 133, 141
Workers' Representatives Congress 140–1
workers' rights: and All-China Federation of Trade Unions 135–42; legal basis for 133–5; protection of 136
workforce diversity 112, 116; *see also* diversity management
workforce retention *see* retention of staff
working hours: and gender pay gap 96; and informal employment 36
workplace innovation 52–5
workplace organization 143
workplace welfare 41
Wu, X. 110–11
Wyatt, T. 25

Xiao, Y.C. 129, 211
Xu, F. 36, 42
Xu, X.L. 24

Yamazaki. Y. 190
Yan, W.H. 210
Yang, B. 60, 66
Yang, H.Q. 40, 57

Yang, Y. X. 34–5
Youth League 46

Zhang, A.Y. 183
Zhang, J.S. 92
Zhang, L.H. 79–80
Zhang, Y.C. 204
Zhao, S. 59

Zhou, X. 93–4, 99
Zhu, C. 85
Zimmerman, A. 27
Zou, M. 38
ZTE Corporation: corporate culture in 71; performance management in 70; training and development in 60–1
zuzhi bu 141